Editor
Janet Cain, M. Ed.

Editorial Project Manager
Ina Massler Levin, M.A.

Editor-in-Chief
Sharon Coan, M.S. Ed.

Illustrator
Ken Tunell

Art Coordinator
Cheri Macoubrie Wilson

Cover Artist
Denise Bauer

Art Director
Elayne Roberts

Imaging
Ralph Olmedo, Jr.

Product Manager
Phil Garcia

Publishers
Rachelle Cracchiolo, M.S. Ed.
Mary Dupuy Smith, M.S. Ed.

A Year Full of Themes

Early Childhood

• Skill-Based Lessons

• Developmentally-Appropriate Activities

• Reproducible Take-Home Books

W9-BZS-910

Author

Beverly Amaral Tavares, M. Ed.

Teacher Created Materials, Inc.
6421 Industry Way
Westminster, CA 92683
www.teachercreated.com

Materials, Inc.
)2, a
.A.
·311-7

PROPERTY
OF
RACHEL MARSHALL

Table of Contents

Introduction

Good teachers continually try to improve and perfect their skills and techniques. They frequently attend workshops designed to help them become more effective in the classroom and improve the quality of their teaching. They read books to learn new ways of teaching old skills. They purchase curriculum guides and resource materials that will enlighten, motivate, and direct them in their on-going quest to improve their craft. They do all this to get inspired, gain new knowledge, and find fresh ideas. These teachers end up with a variety of activities to use throughout the curriculum. They discover new ways of helping students learn important concepts. Some ideas are very innovative. The search for information is successful, and these teachers feel satisfied.

There's just one little problem. There never seems to be enough time to do all these wonderful activities during the instructional day. After teachers have done all the things they absolutely must accomplish, there just isn't enough time left for anything else. It may be tempting to skip a certain lesson in order to allow more time for a particular activity, but then guilt sets in. How can good teachers do it all? Wouldn't it be wonderful if different aspects of the curriculum could be tied up into one neat, interesting, educational package? *A Year Full of Themes* is a child-centered big book curriculum that was designed to meet this demand.

Let's examine the early childhood curriculum. What needs to be done? Which skills need to be developed? What are the areas that need to be taught? All of the following are basic to every early childhood classroom:

- Language
- Math
- Art
- Music
- Literature
- Science/Discovery
- Fine and Gross Motor Development
- Social Skills

The subject of art is an area filled with excitement as well as controversy. What is good art? Experts seem to agree that good art taps children's creative energies. In other words, it is developmentally appropriate art that the children create themselves. Activities that foster this type of art are terrific. However, what happens when you're studying farm animals and you want to use an adorable pig pattern? Since the pattern requires teacher direction, all the pigs will end up looking exactly the same. Unfortunately, this is not considered a creative art project.

Dictated art, which is sometimes referred to as crafts, occurs when all the students' art projects look like they've been cloned. They are about the same subject and have the same size, shape, and color. Experts say these activities should not be considered true art. As a result, you feel torn between what you want to do and what you've been told you should do.

Introduction *(cont.)*

The students add to your dilemma because many children enjoy crafts. They are anxious to make something they can take home and show to their families. Parents like dictated art because they know what it is. They generally feel more comfortable with it and aren't embarrassed to hang it on the refrigerator. They can give it a name. They can say, "This is a cute pig." Creative art is harder because parents must rely on their children to tell them what the creations are.

Research shows that developmentally appropriate, creative art expression is best. However, crafts do have a place in this child-centered big book curriculum. It is possible for teachers to merge the two methods while introducing and reinforcing necessary skills in the process. The purpose of this book is to help you see that with some minor revisions you can give old projects new life and make them cross-curricular and multifaceted.

Let's reconsider the pig pattern. It could become a springboard for all sorts of other activities. The body, head, and nose of this pig happen to be three different-sized circles. The pig's two feet that are visible and its two ears are made from two circles that are cut in half. Math lessons can be incorporated using the parts of the pig. The pigs can be any color the children choose. After the pigs are completed, students can sort them by color. Students can also make comparisons using the pigs. For example, a child could say that the pig is bigger than a glue stick but smaller than the table. The children could also take their finished pigs into the manipulative or block area and build a pen or farm for them.

If you point out that pigs love mud, the children could explore dirt and mud. What started with a dictated art project could turn into a science/discovery activity. The children could make chocolate pudding and pretend that it's mud. Then allow them to finger-paint with it for a creative art project. They could glue their pigs onto the "mud" paintings, integrating both art techniques. The children might enjoy making piggy noises as they finger-paint with the "mud." Imagine your students imitating pigs as they move around the art table in a pig-like fashion while squealing with delight. An activity like this could easily turn into a music/movement lesson.

Art/craft activities can serve yet another purpose and here is where *A Year Full of Themes* comes in to play. By adding literature to all the exciting activities that already incorporate so many language skills, the child-created big book curriculum is a complete package. It's a lifesaver for teachers because it contains guilt-free, time-condensed lessons, and it's a delight for students because it has a variety of fun-filled, child-oriented activities. This curriculum will provide you and your students with many learning adventures. Feel free to consider the ideas in this book as keys to unlock your own creative processes.

What It's All About

A Year Full of Themes takes various projects that span the entire early childhood curriculum and integrates them into book form. It uses subject matter with which the children are familiar and comfortable. In other words, the children create their own make-and-take books while learning necessary skills.

The process of making big books consists of using familiar songs, poems, or fingerplays. Sometimes favorite short stories may be used, incorporating the student's own ideas to create an adapted version that has personal meaning for each child.

Subjects and skills that are commonly covered in an early childhood classroom are incorporated into the big book package. There is an Additional Activities section to use in conjunction with each child-created big book. Many of the suggested activities can be used as motivational tools, as lesson introductions, or concurrently with activities for making the big books. Language, art, math, science, motor development, music, or social skills are built into every lesson.

Some books are completed in units, while others are not. Mostly, the projects are done in short periods of time with the children's understanding that they are publishing books. Students can see how the pages are interrelated. For example, a big book can be developed in the following manner: day one — page one, day two — page two, etc. Some books, however, are created over longer periods of time by saving unrelated art and paperplay. Paperplay consists of the interesting, creative activities students do using paper. This is not to be confused with paperwork that can be tedious and boring tasks. Pages that have been collected throughout the year are put together in book form to suit a certain theme. An example of this is the farm theme book (pages 199–214).

How can something that sounds this easy for teachers and like such fun for students teach so much? As you read through the lessons and units, you'll see how effortlessly it all works together. Each big book provides many opportunities for students to reinforce existing skills as well as acquire and develop new ones. A reference list has been included outlining subjects and corresponding skills that are covered within the framework of each child-created big book.

Themes

Thematic Units — All of the big book ideas utilize a cross-curricular, multidisciplinary approach that integrates all subjects into a theme. *A Year Full of Themes* concentrates on five broad themes that encompass various topics that are chosen as the subject matter for the child-created big books. The overall themes used for these big books are listed below.

- Me
- My Family and Me
- My Friends and Me
- My Community and Me
- My World and Me

What It's All About *(cont.)*

Themes *(cont.)*

At the end of this book, there is a blank Thematic Web (page 335) that you can use to map out topics and subtopics. The web is left blank for you to fill in the theme and topic on which you and your class would like to focus. This graphic organizer allows for creativity and gives you the opportunity to customize your child-created big book curriculum. Using this web will help you decide which additional activities will be most interesting to your class. If you have a good idea of the direction your students want to go, you will be better able to provide experiences that will encourage exploration according to their interests.

Styles

• *Type*

1. There are seven kinds of child-created big books—four of which evolve from:

   • Poems   • Songs   • Fingerplays   • Storybooks

   These can be copied word for word or adapted by making various changes in the story line and text.

2. Original, Student-Based Written Work—This could be any written work by an individual student or that the entire class joined together to create.

3. Personal—These books are formulated in such a way that the children become so familiar with the text, story line, and what the illustrations represent that they can enjoy them on an individual basis. The reader takes a passive role in the reading experience. Reactions to the book are cognitive and emotional.

4. Interactional—These books allow the reader to become actively involved through the use of sensory stimuli. Students are invited to actively explore their motor skills and sensory awareness as they react and respond to the content of a book. *Textured Bears* and *The Cloth Moth* are examples of this type of book.

• *Illustrations*

When publishing these child-created big books, the most important factors are:

   • Illustrations

   • Format and Assembly

There are many ways to visually complement the text in a child-created big book; below are explanations of different kinds of books and how to go about illustrating them.

1. Teacher-Directed Unit—These take a specific unit containing related lessons. Some illustrations may require teacher direction and teacher involvement, as well as dictated art and/or craft activities. Some illustrations may stem from a particular lesson in a subject area such as math or science. Others may evolve from a specific skill such as fine motor development, which is not necessarily designated as art.

2. Cut and Paste—This is when the children take existing pictures such as those found in magazines, catalogs, or store flyers and use them to illustrate their books.

What It's All About *(cont.)*

Styles *(cont.)*

• *Illustrations (cont.)*

3. Creative Art—This type of book is totally compiled from creative art experiences. Although the pictures match the text, each child's book will look different.

4. Photography—This is when actual photographs are used in conjunction with the big book text. Although using real photographs is not generally cost effective for big books, there are certain topics that lend themselves to this type of project. An example of this would be the creation of a big book for the theme entitled *My Family and Me*. Using photographs also works well for big books created solely for the classroom or lending library. A tote book such as the one depicting the school day (pages 269–287), is an example of this.

5. Combination Big Books—This involves combining two or more of the methods described above and on page 6.

• *Format and Assembly*

The amount of time spent on a particular big book is left to the teacher's discretion and may depend on student interest as well as the number of volunteers who are available to help with the project.

1. Long-Term Big Books—These particular books require teachers to save unrelated paperplay and art projects over a long period of time. Then all of the projects related to a specific topic, concept, or theme are brought together.

2. Short-Term Big Books—These are books that can be completely finished in one week or less.

3. Reproducibles—To save teachers time, each unit includes big book text pages that can be reproduced for students. The text can be photocopied and glued onto the page across from the corresponding illustration. Unit patterns that can be reproduced for students are at the end of each unit. All other reproducibles are located in the Management Tools section (pages 330–336).

Skills

The Additional Activities sections of this book categorize skills according to disciplines. Different schools and/or teachers have different criteria regarding skills, goals, and assessments. The skills list was designed to help with your planning and assessment tasks. Since these lessons integrate all subjects into a theme, the child-created big books often act as a springboard for activities that encompass more than one subject at a time. Language and literature are explored in the making of all the big books. Language development skills can be taught and reinforced in conjunction with all other subjects. Science/discovery and math include lessons on texture, color mixture, temperature, counting, less than/greater than, addition, and fractions.

Songs and fingerplays are often catalysts for creating books, thus blending music with fine and gross motor development. There are specific suggestions for these types of activities throughout each big book project. As you go through each unit, you may wish to use the list on page 9 to help you plan your lessons according to your specific teaching goals.

Assessment

The Skills List (page 9) was designed to help you with your planning, observation, and evaluation tasks. Since these units integrate all areas of the curriculum into a theme, the child-created big books often act as a springboard for activities that simultaneously encompass different subject areas. Language and literature are explored in the making of every big book, allowing language development skills to be taught and reinforced in conjunction with all other subjects. Multidisciplinary, cross-curricular activities are interwoven throughout the entire bookmaking process. For your convenience, the Additional Activities sections of this book categorize skills according to disciplines.

Different schools and/or teachers have varying criteria regarding skills, goals, and assessments. By defining what is important in content as well as teaching methods, assessment techniques play a fundamental role. It is apparent that student assessment, from the local to national level, is changing. Grades and standardized tests provide only a portion of the big picture regarding student progress. Teachers are investigating alternative methods of assessment. Regardless of the population of students, the primary purpose of any assessment is to improve student learning by evaluating whether the material was understood and determining whether the skills can be applied in new situations.

The content of what is taught and assessment should relate. As a result, the teaching methods described throughout these units can be used as tools for alternative assessment. By doing this, the assessment process becomes interactive and can be used in conjunction with traditional methods. Saving and dating paperplay on a long-term basis and then keeping this "date" in book form is only one of the alternative assessment techniques built into this big book program. Another method includes allowing the children to informally participate in brainstorming sessions in order to determine their previous knowledge. Using the student-made books for story retelling can also be an assessment device to determine comprehension skills, including an understanding of story structure. Educational games can be used to reinforce as well as test skills in an informal way. Throughout each big book unit, anecdotal records can be made by noting behaviors and progress during specific activities or at the end of the day. In addition, many activities suggested with the big book units allow students to use graphic organizers, such as the Venn diagram. Graphic organizers help students see the relationships between and among concepts. Different types of assessment can be used to gather information about styles of learning and what knowledge is acquired. This big book program provides teachers with the opportunity to incorporate various forms of assessment that can be used to collectively evaluate student performance and progress.

Innovative ways of tracking and evaluating student work and progress can be utilized in a teacher-friendly manner. As you go through each child-created big book unit, refer to the Skills List (page 9) in order to plan and assess according to your students' needs and your specific teaching goals.

Skills List

Art

- *Fine Motor*—finger-wrist dexterity, eye-hand coordination, arm-hand movement
- *Visual Perception*—color and shape recognition, location, matching, identification

Math

- *Conceptual Development*—many/few, counting, fractions (whole, half, quarter), sequencing, categorizing, classification, geometry, understanding the concepts of more and less, subtraction, addition, one-to-one correspondence, inclines, measurement, graphing

Science/Discovery

- *Sensory Perception*—gathering information using any or all of the five senses
- *Thinking Skills*—observing, problem solving, predicting outcomes, comparing and contrasting

Music/Movement

- *Motor Development*—arm-hand movement, balance, coordination, body awareness, left-right orientation
- *Auditory Perception*—recognition and discrimination of sounds, repetition, response, following directions

Social/Emotional

- *Personal*—creativity and imagination, role-playing, contributing ideas, seeking new experiences, taking pride in accomplishments, demonstrating self-reliance, participating in parallel and symbolic play, identification and acceptance of one's own feelings
- *Interactional*—co-active play, participating in small group activities, taking turns, participating in group decisions, making eye contact, acceptance of group decisions, sharing, awareness of the feelings and needs of others, recognition and acceptance of peer similarities and differences

Language

- *Expressive*—sentence structure, descriptions, relating words and pictures, giving information, articulation, imitation, identification, utilization, appropriate voice inflection and volume
- *Receptive*—response, recognition and discrimination, repetition, questioning

Ground Rules

Parental Involvement

There are parent letters (pages 19, 44, 45, 197, 241, 265–267, 313, 327, 330–332, 334) that can be reproduced and used throughout the year to keep parents informed and involved. It is important to explain to parents what the child-created big book curriculum entails (page 19). Some parents expect to see concrete evidence of what their children are doing in school. They like to see paperwork dotted with happy faces and stickers in their children's hands as they leave school every day. This gives them proof and reassurance that their children are working and doing well. Since the child-created big book curriculum is contingent on saving much of the children's paperwork, or paperplay as it is called in this book, it is important for parents to know their children may not be bringing something home every day. For this reason, the larger sheets of construction paper are better suited for art and craft projects. That way, if only part of their paperplay is used for the big books, the sheets can be cut into pieces that are sent home.

Many public schools schedule their Open House or Parent Night during the first few months of school. If this is true at your school, think of this get-together as a perfect opportunity to display the first big book project and inform parents about it. Parents and children can then take the books home at the end of the evening.

Size

All books should be the same size for easy storage. Using 12" x 18" (30 cm x 46 cm) pieces of construction paper is a good size for big books. It is the perfect size for almost all of the children's art and paperplay.

Dates

As the children complete each page, it is very helpful to date their work. It is interesting and enlightening to look back and see each child's progress. It gives parents an idea of how their children are doing and helps them understand why the children don't bring home a lot of daily work. The book pages may be saved in student portfolios. However, once the books are completed, most children will be anxious to take them home to share with family members.

Topics

The best child-created big books are those related to topics that have meaning for youngsters. Good choices for big books include fingerplays, poems, songs, and predictable short stories that children can personalize by making simple changes and adaptations. Choosing the right topic is an important motivational factor for children. Stories that are easily read and/or retold by children are ones that are fun to share with others. It gives the children a sense of accomplishment and pride and, in doing so, makes choosing the topic an activity that is worth repeating over and over again. The Thematic Web (page 335) can be used for this purpose.

Length

Most individually-made child-created big books should not be any longer than five or six pages so students can take them home as soon as possible.

Ground Rules *(cont.)*

Assembly

All children who participate should make their own copies of the big book. In addition, it is a good idea for the teacher to make one for the classroom library. It is important to point out that children should be given the choice of whether or not they make the books. There may be some children who decide they do not want to do the activities that are necessary to complete a book. However, chances are that once they see the others going home with their completed books, they will change their minds.

The child-created big book curriculum consists of fun-filled activities that are easy to complete in a reasonable time frame. The schedule for activities is very flexible so that anything that is started one day can easily be finished at a later date.

Storage

Compiling these books requires saving and storing large quantities of the children's paperplay and art expressions. It is helpful to have a designated area in which to keep these sheets. Any shelf or container, such as a cardboard box or plastic crate, will do as long as it is not used for anything else. It can get confusing if other papers are kept in the same area as the pages for these big books. Categorize the sheets by using page numbers and alphabetize the children's names to make final assembly of the book a snap.

Implementation

Flexibility is the key to making this curriculum work. This book provides suggested plans for making the big books. However, if certain art projects are not appealing to you or your students, feel free to change them. As long as the illustration matches the text and the essence of the book is not lost, you may wish to change and/or rearrange the activities. Use copies of the Planner Sheet (page 333) to create lesson plans.

Music Selections

Everyone's music center and album supply are different. If you take the time to review what you already have in your classroom, you may be surprised at the number of titles that will coincide with the activities proposed in this book. If you do not possess the suggested titles and cannot obtain them in ample time to proceed with a specific thematic unit, feel free to substitute something else.

Additional Activities

Subtopics can be covered throughout the big book process by setting up mini-learning centers, adding props to existing centers, or conducting additional small group and/or large group lessons. Choose from activities that are designed to encompass students' total learning experience, targeting the physical, academic, and emotional well-being of the children.

As you read through the following big book projects, try to think of them as a springboard for your own ideas.

Buddy Books

A buddy book is a big book worked on by a young student and an older partner. The following description explains how the buddy system works.

Upper-grade teachers who will be sending buddies need to be aware of what the child-created big books are. The older children will be using skills they have learned and act as role models and mentors for the younger students. Their task will be to help the younger children with the illustrations as well as the text. This will include any of the paperplay activities along with hand-printing the text or gluing the reproducible pages onto construction paper.

The teachers will need to get their classes together to form partnerships between the older students and the younger ones. The older children need to know that the reason the two grades are working together is so they can help with the making of these big books. The teachers should schedule meeting times to determine how they want to organize the buddy books and activity times for the two classes to work together. How you set up this type of program depends on the schedules and needs of the teachers involved.

Depending on curricular demands and special area instruction, the upper-grade teachers may decide only a couple of students can be spared at any one time. Teachers will have to get together to decide what's best for their students. Once this is accomplished, it is just a matter of implementation and publication.

As a culminating activity, it is great fun to have an Authors' Tea to celebrate the completion of the books. You may wish to consider inviting parents to this event. Use the invitation (page 334) to ask guests to attend. Having an Authors' Tea, or a similar type of presentation, is a great way to celebrate this joint venture between the classes.

Preparation for this social event may be as simple or elaborate as you wish. Consider asking parents to donate snack foods and drinks or to bring some freshly cut flowers for decorating the tables.

12

Options, Hints, and Timesavers

In order to make the necessary preparations to get your child-created big book program ready for implementation, you may wish to review the options presented on pages 13–18. Contained in this section are ideas for creating flannelboard kits (pages 13–15), customized bingo games (page 16), and a year-round voting/graphing board (page 17). These are referred to in the Additional Activities section of each big book. Also included is an introductory letter to parents (page 19) informing them of what the child-created big book program is.

Flannelboard Activities

- Throughout the Additional Activities sections of this book, there are ideas for lessons using flannelboard patterns that are cut out from felt. Producing custom-made felt kits is not as difficult as you may imagine, and the time and effort are well worth it since the end product is something that will be used for years to come. Following are some suggestions for making felt cutouts.

- In this book, specific patterns are included for each flannelboard activity. However, feel free to use other sources to expand your collection of cutouts. Coloring books are wonderful resources for patterns. There are some coloring books that have simple designs with few details that are designed for very young children. These are the easiest to use for making cutouts.

- You will need to have access to a variety of colored felt. Using many colors allows the activities to be extended into lessons about colors. It is not necessary to limit yourself to one color unless a song, poem, or fingerplay requires a specific color. For example, the song "Five Green and Speckled Frogs" needs to have green frogs, but the song "Five Little Ducks" gives you the freedom to make each duck a different color.

- When applicable, numbers can be written directly onto the felt cutouts to reinforce math skills. For instance, if you are doing a counting activity using five cutouts, you may want to write one numeral (1, 2, 3, 4, 5) on each of the cutouts. Simply providing students with these added visuals will do much to improve their number identification skills.

- Fabric paints can be used to outline and add details, such as eyes, nose, and mouth, to the cutouts. Some paint and craft companies will donate these paints if you explain why you need them. They may ask you to provide proof of employment with a school or district.

Options, Hints, and Timesavers *(cont.)*

Flannelboard Activities *(cont.)*

Felt-work accessories can include wiggle eyes, plastic craft gems, lace, yarn, fabric, feathers, silk flowers, pompoms, and large sequins. Keep in mind that if you add too many of these items, your felt pieces will become so heavy they will not stick to the flannelboard.

Warning: The small attachments described above are choking hazards and should never be applied to cutouts that are intended for use by children who are three years old or younger. Use only the fabric paint to add details.

Making Velcro® Mat Kits

If it is difficult for you to obtain felt or if you do not have a flannelboard in your classroom, you can make Velcro® Mat Kits. You may wish to enlist the help of older students or parent volunteers to make these.

Construction paper and tagboard can be substituted for the felt. Simply reproduce the picture on white paper and color it. You may want to limit the use of crayons for this task because some laminators will melt the wax, causing the colors to blend. Markers, colored pencils, and watercolor paint crayons work best. Once the picture is colored, mount it on construction paper or tagboard, laminate it, and cut it out. Attach the plastic looped side of a piece of self-adhesive Velcro® to the back of the cutout. Now the cutout will stick to commercially piled carpeting, which can be used instead of a flannelboard. Carpet mats are inexpensive and can be purchased at most discount or department stores. Some carpet dealers will be happy to donate their discontinued samples. You may want to pick up an extra mat to use for the Carpet Graph (page 15). Be sure to take a piece of Velcro® with you to the store to be sure it will stick to the carpet mat.

Storing Flannelboard or Velcro® Mat Kits

If you have mobile shelves in your room with pegboard backing or any pegboards mounted on your walls, the following are some inexpensive ideas for storing your kits.

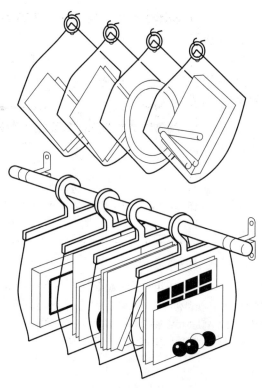

- Place them in resealable plastic bags and push a binder ring through the left-hand corner of each bag. Then you can hang the bags on peg hooks.

- Use two wooden curtain brackets and a wooden rod placed across the brackets. Then the kits can be hung on a wall, which allows you to free up floor and shelf space.

- Simply place them into a hanger-type plastic bag and hook them onto the rod. These bags can be found in library or school supply catalogs.

Options, Hints, and Timesavers *(cont.)*

Organizing Flannelboard or Velcro® Mat Kits

- For easy access, label each bag according to its contents and color-code it by theme or topic. You can use white folder labels to write the titles, themes, or topics and colored sticky dots for color-coding. To combine these two steps, simply use colored labels.

- Reproduce the song, poem, or activity directions that go with each lesson to make executing the activities a snap. Keep a copy of this information inside the bag along with the set of cutouts. You may wish to glue the information onto a large index card and laminate it for added durability.

- It is an incredible timesaver if you have access to a letter machine, which is a hand-operated press that allows you to cut out letters and shapes from a variety of materials with different textures such as paper, sponge, and felt.

Carpet Graph

A carpet graph can be used with any theme. To make this type of graph, you will need to obtain an 18" x 24" (46 cm x 61 cm) piece of commercially piled carpet and masking or electrical tape that is a contrasting color to the carpet. Use the tape to divide the carpet into 3" (8 cm) or 6" (15 cm) squares. Since temperature and humidity can cause tape to peel off, you may prefer to paint on the graph lines, using acrylic or fabric paint.

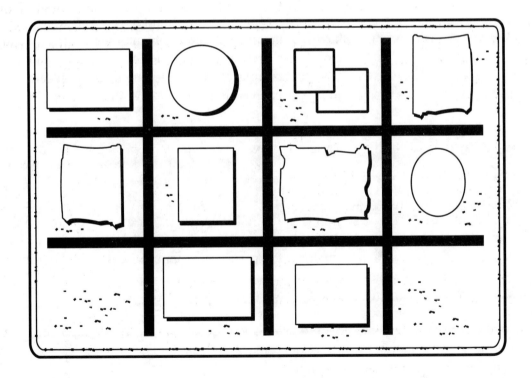

You can use this graph with pictures, paper cutouts, and other lightweight items. To make paper items more durable, mount the pictures on tagboard and laminate them. Then all you need to do is attach the plastic looped side of self-adhesive Velcro® to the items being graphed, and they will stick to the carpet. Items used for the graph can be stored the same way as the flannelboard or Velcro® mat kits (page 14).

Options, Hints, and Timesavers *(cont.)*

Theme Bingo

You can easily customize bingo games to fit any thematic unit. Following are some suggestions for creating your own playing cards.

Reproduce the Bingo Card (page 336), making enough copies for a small group. If you have a large class, make five or six cards. However, if you only have nine children, you may want one card for each child. Make sure you copy one or two extra cards to use as calling cards.

The next step is to obtain a variety of stickers that reflect either the big book themes or a general corresponding theme. For example, if you cannot get a diverse variety of apple stickers for the Apple Tree book, you can simply go with an autumn, fruit, or community theme. For very young children, each sticker should be easily distinguished. Older children should be able to discriminate among similar visual images; therefore the differences can be less noticeable.

Choose stickers that take up most of the space within each square of the bingo card. If they are too small, they will not be easy for students to identify. If they are too large, they may overlap the grid lines. However, if you have tiny stickers with identical designs in a variety of colors, you may place more than one sticker per square to make a number bingo game. You may wish to purchase colored dot stickers in bulk since these are perfect for this purpose.

The self-adhesive stickers are the fastest and easiest to use. You should have a variety of at least twelve different sticker sets. Randomly place the different stickers onto the blank bingo cards, placing one of each different type of sticker in each box of the grid. You may wish to invite older students or parent volunteers to help with this. Once the stickers are in place, mount the bingo cards on cardstock and laminate them. Don't forget to create calling cards, making sure you have one of every type of sticker.

You can keep these games in folders that have been stapled on the sides, large manila envelopes, or resealable plastic bags. Local hosiery or lingerie stores sometimes have boxes that are the perfect size for these cards. Then the games can be labeled, stacked, and stored.

Bingo can always be played in the traditional manner. However, you may want to play versions in which there aren't any losers. For very young children, have them cover all the squares on their bingo cards. The game continues until all children cover their cards. For older students, play more complicated versions of bingo. Have them cover the perimeter squares or cover the appropriate squares to make an "X" on their cards. The game continues until everyone completes the required task. As the children finish the game, give them stickers just for playing.

Note: The Bingo Card (page 336) can be reproduced and used for lotto games, graph charts, or tic-tac-toe boards. For tic-tac-toe playing tokens, use a permanent black marker to write Xs and Os on clean milk or juice caps.

Options, Hints, and Timesavers *(cont.)*

Clothespin Voting/Graphing Board

Throughout the big book projects, there are many opportunities for voting and graphing as suggested in the Additional Activities sections. For this reason, directions are provided below for making a generic graphing board. Feel free to modify the graphing board to suit your specific class goals and needs.

Using this graphing board provides students with cross-curricular experiences, including math, science/discovery, language development, and social/emotional growth. This type of activity incorporates visual discrimination and decision-making skills as well as important cooperative learning skills such as taking turns, participating in an organized group activity, and respecting other people's opinions.

Materials:

- Clothespins, two different colors per child
- Poster board
- Markers

Directions:

Use the markers to make a two-column chart on the poster board. Make one row for every student in your class. For example, if you have twenty children in your classroom, you should have twenty rows. Make sure to leave an extra, wider row at the top of the poster board. This section will be used for picture headings to indicate the categories on which students vote. Laminate the board for durability so it can be reused throughout the school year. The pictures for the headings can be fastened to the board using double-sided tape or Velcro®.

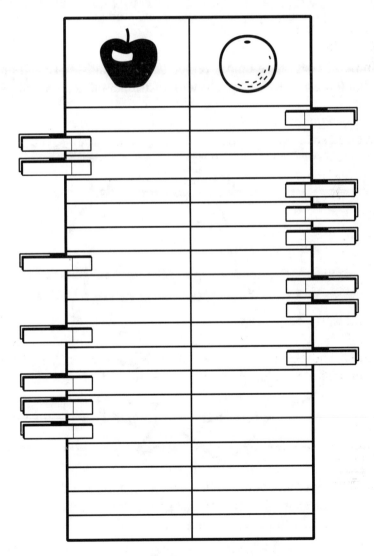

Options, Hints, and Timesavers *(cont.)*

Clothespin Voting/Graphing Board *(cont.)*

The clothespin voting board is an excellent way to introduce students to a voting/graphing procedure. Each child votes for one category or the other by attaching the designated color of clothespin under the appropriate heading. If possible, allow students to attach the clothespins themselves. Provide assistance as needed.

Follow up all voting/graphing activities with discussions. Point out concepts such as *more* and *less*. You may wish to call attention to the importance of each vote.

Books on Tape

To increase fluency and word recognition, consider recording each big book on tape. Young children love using battery-operated recorders with personal headsets. The lightweight headsets are preferable to the bulkier kind because they allow students the freedom to sprawl out on some soft furniture or curl up in a corner.

When taping these books, remember to speak slowly and emphasize each word. If it is a song, it should be recorded as such, with instrumental accompaniment if possible.

Record only one book on each tape. The children quickly learn how to start, stop, and rewind the recorders. If you wish, the story can be recorded several times on the same tape.

With very young children, use dots to color-code the buttons. This will help them recall the function of each. For example, you can use green for start, red for stop, and blue for rewind. In addition, teach students the following saying:

> *Press green to start, red to stop,*
> *and blue if you want to back it up.*

18

Parent Information

_____
(Date)

Dear Parent/Guardian,

This year our class will be traveling through the wonderful world of books. Throughout the following months, it is my goal to instill a love of literature in my students. As a result, we will not only be reading books, but we will also be writing and illustrating some big books of our own. We will be working on language arts, math, science, music, motor development, and social skills. Much of the children's schoolwork will be incorporated into the pages of these books. For this reason, I will be saving many of the products they create. However, I will be dating the pages of the books so when you get them you will be able to track your child's progress.

Every student will have the opportunity to make these child-created big books. These books can be used to begin a home library or expand an existing one. By the time your child brings home a big book, the story should be very familiar. Please give your child the opportunity to read the books to you. Then help your child find a special place to store the books. Pick a place that your child can reach for easy access. If you are reading the books together, it is beneficial to point to each word as it is said. This helps your child make the connection between the written and spoken word. Also, rereading these books is a great way to review what your child has learned.

Soon we will begin working on our first big book. Remember to ask your child to tell you all about it.

Thank you for your time and cooperation.

Sincerely,

_____
(Teacher)

_____
(School)

_____
(Phone)

Related Resources

Each unit contains a list of resources pertaining to its theme. These can be used anytime throughout the unit. You may decide to use them as introductory or motivational tools or to supplement the lessons. Many of the songs, books, and software listed can be acted out. In addition, they make a good springboard for future child-created big books.

Some of the suggested resources are in some way connected to the topic, although they may not be directly related to the specific theme. For example, every resource in the apple unit is not about apples. However, those that are not about apples are tied to activities that may be discussed or investigated during the making of the big book.

There is a variety of materials to choose from, depending on the ages and developmental level of your students. The targeted ages are approximately three to seven or early childhood through second grade. Below is a suggested list of books and software that can be used to introduce your students to the exciting world of books.

Books

Brown, Anthony. *I Like Books.* Random House Children's Publishers, 1997.

Hallinan, P. K. *Just Open a Book.* Ideal Publications Inc., 1995.

Kehoe, Michael. *A Book Takes Root: The Making of a Picture Book.* Carolrhoda/Lerner, 1993.

Langlois, Florence. *The Extraordinary Gift.* Abbeville Press, 1997.

Vivelo, Jackie. *Reading to Matthew.* Rinehart, 1993.

Software

Electro Dog's First Reader and Writer CD. MPC; National School Products, 101 East Broadway, Maryville, TN 37804; 1-800-251-9124.

Jo-Jo Joins the Reading Circus. PC; National School Products, 101 East Broadway, Maryville, TN 37804; 1-800-251-9124.

Reading Adventures in Oz. PC; National School Products, 101 East Broadway, Maryville, TN 37804; 1-800-251-9124.

Sunbuddy Writer. CD-ROM for WIN or MAC; Sunburst Communications, Inc., 101 Castleton Street, P.O. Box 100, Pleasantville, NY 10570-0100; 1-800-321-5711.

Sunbuddy Writer provides an alternate means of creating and writing stories. It is an easy-to-use word processor that is perfect for first and second graders. For younger children, this program could also be successfully utilized in combination with the buddy book program (page 12). In addition to writing stories, children can also illustrate and record them.

Apple Tree Big Book Materials

Unit Materials:

— apples: various types and colors
— construction paper: red, white, light brown, dark brown
— paint: various colors, including green, red, and skin tones
— containers such as old cake pans or clean, small milk cartons with the tops cut off
— 2–5 plastic scouring pads
— 2–3 magnifying glasses
— plastic or paper plates
— white butcher paper
— drawing tools: crayons, colored pencils, and/or markers
— glue
— items, such as sponge hair rollers, that can be used to make small, circular prints
— stapler
— safety scissors

Extra:

— red sticky dots
— collage items: shredded paper, yarn, buttons, spangles, felt scraps, craft straws, macramé cord, wooden bits, etc.

Optional Materials for Additional Activities:

— round kitchen sponges
— apple seeds
— paintbrushes
— felt
— fabric paint
— snack maker appliance
— empty 35 mm film canisters
— clean, empty milk cartons
— apple basket or laundry basket
— blender or food processor
— raisins
— apple juice
— honey
— cinnamon
— sliced bread
— canned apple pie filling
— bananas
— o-shaped apple-flavored cereal

Apple Tree Big Book

Theme: My Community and Me
Topics: Trees/Orchards/Apples
Duration: One Week
Approach: Familiar Song
　　　　　　　Teacher-Directed Activities
　　　　　　　Creative-Combination Activities

The first in this series of big books is part of an apple unit. Quite a few apples will be needed for the activities, especially if you have double sessions each day. If it is not against your school's policy, you may wish to send a note home asking that each child bring an apple to class. This cuts down the cost for you and usually provides a nice variety of apples. It is always interesting to compare and contrast the different types of apples. You can also inform parents that any extra fruit will be used for snacks.

Warning: Before serving anything to eat, ask parents if their children have any food allergies or dietary restrictions.

At the end of the unit, there are two parent letters (pages 44 and 45). One can be used to request apple donations and parent volunteers. If you promote parental involvement in your classroom, their help with these books will be a welcome addition. The other letter informs parents that you are having a Red Day as suggested in the Additional Activities (page 35). This letter has a space for you to write the date on which you plan to have that special day. The open-ended format allows you to use the letter for other units that target specific colors.

On the following pages you will find an explanation outlining the steps for setting up and implementing a child-created big book curriculum, beginning with the Apple Tree book. Other big books follow the same pattern and principles. Once you get the hang of making these child-created big books, you and your students may wish to personalize the topics.

Factored into the framework of this big book curriculum are some timesaving suggestions for how to make bulletin boards that require little or no effort.

Apple Tree

Way up high in the apple tree, *(Hold arms overhead.)*
Two red apples smiled at me. *(Hold out two fingers.)*
I shook that tree as hard as I could. *(Pantomime shaking.)*
Down came the apples. Mmm, very good. *(Rub stomach.)*

Making the Book

COVER PAGE

Activity: Make cover pages.

Setup: For the duration of this unit, set up easels for free painting. Take a stack of red construction paper (at least one piece per child) and cut a circle from the center of each sheet. The circle should be approximately a 6–7" (15–18 cm) in diameter. If you prefer and have the time, you can cut out an apple shape rather than circle. Be sure to save these cutouts since they will be used for page four of the Apple Tree book (page 28).

Directions: The children may paint on the red paper using any color. These sheets will be their cover pages.

PAGE 1 (PART 1)

Text: "Way up high in the apple tree,"

Activity: Make apple trees, using plastic scouring pads and green tempera paint.

Setup: Prepare a discovery table by setting out some magnifying glasses and plastic or paper plates. Set up two art tables. Cover one of these tables with several layers of white butcher paper. Place a stack of large white construction paper on the other table. Pour green paint into some containers. Cake pans, pie tins, or plastic containers work well for this. Set out several plastic scouring pads. The scouring pads give a great texture and print for this particular activity. Provide some brown crayons and/or large brown markers for students to draw their tree trunks. As an alternative, you can have the children use glue and tree trunks that you have already cut from brown construction paper.

Introduction: At circle time, sing or act out the "Apple Tree" song/fingerplay. Tell the children they will be creating a book based on this song/fingerplay.

Discuss apples. Compare/contrast different types of apples. Give each child some apple slices to taste.

Warning: Remember to ask parents if their children have any food allergies or dietary restrictions.

Discuss topics such as texture, taste, the sound of apples being eaten, and favorite ways of eating apples. Place some seeds, apple peels, and chunks of apple on the plates at the discovery table. Ask the children to guess what will happen to the pieces of apple if they are left out for a long time. Write down their predictions, and keep their hypotheses on or near the discovery table. While working on this unit, ask students to observe the changes exhibited by the pieces of apple. Take time to discuss the children's findings.

Making the Book *(cont.)*

PAGE 1 (PART 1, cont.)

Directions: Point out that you have prepared two art tables, one covered with butcher paper and the other set up with a stack of large white construction paper. Explain that the table with construction paper is for making books. Point out to students that they will be painting on the construction paper. Show them how to place the paper so it is laid out the long way. Tell them they are using the color green because this will become part of their apple trees. Explain that for children who wish to continue painting after doing their book pages or those who would like to paint but do not want to make a book, there is another table set up with large sheets of butcher paper. When the top sheet is completely covered with paint, simply lift that sheet off, and the next sheet is ready to be painted.

At the bookmaking table, the children can draw or color their own tree trunks or they can glue precut trunks onto the bottom part of their papers. Once this is done, they can make their scouring pad prints to put leaves on their trees.

Very little explanation or direction is needed for the painting activity. There is no right or wrong way to make this artwork, and the children will enjoy experimenting with the scouring pads.

Timesavers:

1. Save at least one of these painted pieces of butcher paper for a child-created bulletin board.

2. The other sheets, once dry, can be cut up. Use some of these scraps to precut 2" (5 cm) leaves. One leaf per child is sufficient. Save the leaves for page four of the Apple Tree book (page 28).

3. Send home some of the remaining scraps and place the rest at an art table. The children will love using their imaginations to make different creations out of these scraps.

PAGE 1 (PART 2)

Activity: Paint red dots to make apples.

Setup: Pour some red tempera paint into several small containers. Place by these containers any item(s), such as sponge hair rollers, that will leave small round apple prints. If you prefer, the children can make the prints using the tips of their index fingers or thumbs.

Directions: After the treetop scouring pad prints described above are dry, the children can begin printing the red apples on the green paint. As they are printing, take advantage of the opportunity to review colors, shapes, sizes, spatial relationships, and concepts such as few and many.

Alternative: Instead of painting, stickers that are red dots can be used to make the apples.

Making the Book *(cont.)*

PAGE 2 (PART 1)

Text: Two red apples smiled at me.

Activity: Make apple prints with real apples.

Setup: Bring out the large piece of butcher paper covered with green scouring pad prints. Place it on an art table. On another table, set out large green sheets of construction paper. On both tables, place some shallow containers with red tempera paint.

Introduction: Review the "Apple Tree" song/fingerplay. Ask the children if they remember painting their apple trees. Bring out a few samples of the tree pages completed for page one of their books (pages 23–24). Remind children that when their books are finished, this page will read, "Way up high in the apple tree." Tell children that today they will be creating the next page. Ask them if they can guess what the next page will read. Help them to conclude that the next page states "Two red apples smiled at me." Show them an apple that has been cut in half from the top, where the stem is, to the bottom. Explain to students that they will be making apple prints. A fraction lesson can follow as you slice an apple in half. Additional apples will be needed for this activity, depending on how many children will be printing at one time.

Directions: On both tables, place the apple halves facedown in the containers of red paint. The children can make red apple prints on the butcher paper in an undirected activity. You may wish to save this sheet to cover a bulletin board. The activity at the other table should be teacher directed with the lesson focusing on counting to two. Invite students to make two apple prints anywhere on the construction paper. As the children make their prints, reinforce positional words by describing where they are placing their apple prints. For example, you might point to one student's prints and say, "You made one apple print at the top of your paper and another at the bottom." Depending on the interest level and attention span of the children, you may wish to take this language exercise a step farther by stating, "The apple print at the top of the paper is on the right side, and the one at the bottom is on the left side."

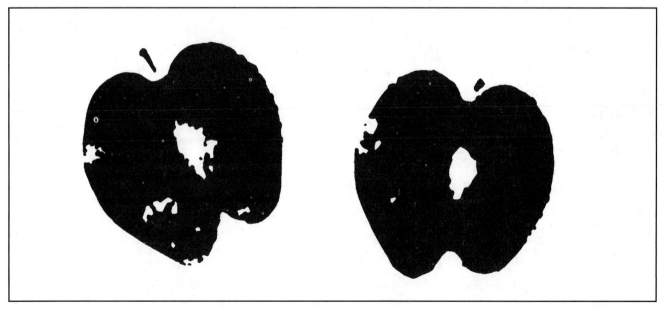

Making the Book (cont.)

Bulletin Board: Cut out a tree trunk from brown butcher paper and staple it onto the bulletin board. Cut out a treetop from the butcher paper with the green scouring pad prints with the red apple prints. Make a banner with a caption of your choice for the bulletin board.

PAGE 2 (PART 2)

Activity: Add facial features to the previously completed apple prints.

Setup: This activity can be done several different ways. It can be a teacher-created lesson during which specific facial features are targeted, and the children draw two eyes, a nose, and a happy smile. However, if you prefer, it can be a more creative activity during which various collage items are laid out and the children create their own faces on the existing apple prints. Since the text reads, "Two red apples smiled at me," stress to students that their apples should be smiling.

Skills: Math skills can be built by concentrating on counting the facial features. If collage items are used, point out any geometric shapes that the children utilize. Ask the following questions: *What shape are the eyes?* (circles or ovals) *What shape is the nose?* (triangle) Vocabulary and language skills can easily be reinforced by commenting on what the children are doing. Positional words, such as top, middle, and bottom, as well as opposites, such as right/left, top/bottom, and up/down, can easily be factored into the lesson through informal conversation. In addition, the children's understanding of math concepts, such as ordinal numbers (first, second, third, etc.), can be strengthened through this informal teaching method.

Introduction: Bring out a sample page with the apple prints. Begin by reviewing the "Apple Tree" song/fingerplay and asking the children to predict what they'll be doing next.

Making the Book *(cont.)*

PAGE 3

Text: I shook that tree as hard as I could.

Activity: Use paint to make hand prints that represent someone shaking the tree.

Setup: Prepare two art tables. One table will be for the children to make page three of their Apple Tree books. On this table, place different shades of brown construction paper and various skin-tone colored tempera paints in shallow containers. If a light color of paint is used, students should print on the darker colored construction paper. If a dark color of paint is used, students should print on the lighter colored construction paper. The other table should be covered with several layers of large sheets of butcher paper. Place shallow containers of various paint colors on the table. These colors do not have to be skin tones. Allow the children to use the different colors to make prints of their hands on the butcher paper. *Note:* If you have a large number of bulletin boards in your classroom, the butcher paper with hand prints can be used to cover one or more of these.

Introduction: Review the "Apple Tree" song/fingerplay. Ask the children to recite the line that comes after "Two red apples smiled at me." Help them recall the next line is "I shook that tree as hard as I could." Ask them how they would shake the tree. Let them stand up and act it out. Then ask them what they would use to shake an apple tree. Lead them to conclude that they would use their hands. Explain that today they will be making page three of their Apple Tree books.

Directions: Show students how to position the construction paper the long way on the table. Then have them choose the paints that most closely resemble their skin tones. Ask them to extend their right hands. Squirt small blobs of paint onto their hands, and direct the children to rub both hands together until they are completely covered with paint. Discuss how the paint feels. Once that is accomplished, the children can place their hands on the paper and leave hand prints by pressing down.

Bulletin Board: Use the butcher paper with hand prints to cover a bulletin board. Some possible captions include "Helping Hands," "Busy Hands," or for a health board "Let's Keep Our Hands Clean."

Making the Book *(cont.)*

PAGE 4

Text: Down came the apples. Mmm, very good.

Activity: Tear a "bite" out of an apple cutout and glue it onto construction paper.

Setup: On an art table, set out some glue, markers, and crayons. Bring out the red cutout circles from the easel painting sheets (page 23). Also retrieve the precut leaves saved from the butcher paper scraps (page 24).

Introduction: Review the "Apple Tree" song/fingerplay. Show the children samples of the book pages that have been completed so far as each verse is sung. This helps them understand how all their work is coming together to make a book. Ask if they know what line has not yet been put into their books. Explain that today they will complete the last page.

Directions: Ask the children how they know whether a food is "Mmm, very good," or not. Lead them to conclude that the only way to really tell is to taste it. Show them a red paper apple. Demonstrate how to tear a "bite" out of the paper apple. Explain to students that you will give them red paper apples, and each of them will tear out a bite. Point out that it does not matter if these torn pieces look like real bite shapes.

Once the children have torn off their bites, have them glue the apples onto white or manila construction paper. Then tell them to draw a stem on top and glue a precut leaf on the right or left side of the stem.

Hint: When cutting the apple shapes from the construction paper, the scissors may leave an uneven edge where they were inserted. This is where the bite should be.

Note: This page should not take very long to do, allowing more time and greater opportunity for additional activities that are theme related.

Making the Book *(cont.)*

PUTTING IT ALL TOGETHER

During circle time, review the "Apple Tree" song/fingerplay, as you show sample art for each page. Tell the children their books need a title. Ask students to brainstorm a list of titles as you write them on the chalkboard. Invite the children to vote for the title they like best.

Take out the printed red papers done on the easel (page 23). On a piece of white copier paper, neatly print or use a computer to print out the title that the class has chosen. Make sure the letters of the title fit into the hole in the red construction paper. Reproduce this title page, making enough copies for every book. Glue each copy onto the backside of the cover page with the words showing through the hole. If you prefer, you can reproduce the title page (page 38) that has been provided in this book. Assemble the books by placing the pages in order and stapling along the left side of each.

Reproduce the text for the "Apple Tree" song/fingerplay (pages 39–42) for students. For each book, glue the text onto the page that is opposite the illustration. For page one, glue the text right on top of the existing title sheet.

Although the children will need help with placing the pages in the correct order, this is an activity where the children can probably do the gluing by themselves. Initially it may take some time to teach them proper gluing techniques, but they will soon get the hang of it. Glue sticks or glue bottles with roll-on-balls or sponges work well for little hands. Teach the children to glide the glue around the perimeter of the paper. After each page is glued on, you may want to point to each word as you read it aloud. This will help to visually reinforce the words they already know by heart.

Additional Activities

Art/Language

Sponge Painting

Using two circular sponges, leave one sponge whole and cut out two leaves and a separate stem from the other sponge. Place the whole sponge in a shallow container of red, green, and/or yellow paint. Put the leaf shaped sponges in a shallow container of green paint and the stem in a shallow container of brown paint. Invite the children to make apples by printing with the circle sponge and then adding the leaves and stems to their apples with the other sponges.

Star Prints

For an additional printing activity, cut an apple horizontally. A star shape can be seen in the center. These make interesting prints.

Apple Seed Color Collage

Cut out large apple shapes from red, yellow, and green construction paper. Allow each student to pick his/her favorite color apple. Have the children glue some clean, dry apple seeds in the center of their apple shapes. Provide some magazines, catalogs, and store flyers along with scissors and glue. Have them cut out pieces of paper and sections of print or pictures containing the color of their apples. Tell them to glue these scraps onto their apples, surrounding the seeds. For example, the children with red apple cutouts will cut out shades of red from various magazine pages to glue around their seeds. After the glue dries, students may draw stems and leaves on their apples.

Additional Activities *(cont.)*

Art/Language *(cont.)*

Hand Print Fruit Trees

Step 1: Provide green watercolor pencils or watercolor crayons and white construction paper. Have the children use the pencils or crayons to make treetops by scribbling some lines and circles on the construction paper, covering an area approximately the size of a saucer. Once they have done this, give them cups of clean water and paintbrushes. Tell them to paint with water over the scribbled section. This will make the scribbling spread to fill in the white spaces so it looks like the leaves on trees. Allow the pictures to dry.

Step 2: Using brown paint and a stubby paintbrush, invite one child at a time to come to the art table. Spread some paint onto the child's hand and wrist. Ask the child to hold his/her fingers apart. Guide his/her hand to make a print halfway on and halfway below the painted tree top. The print from the fingers should look like the branches of the tree, and the print made by the wrist should look like the tree's trunk.

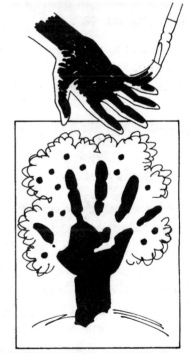

Note: With very young children, make sure you mention which hand you are painting and count out each finger as you brush on the paint. Finger names can also be reinforced with this activity. For example, as you hold the child's hand and paint each finger, you can say, "I'm painting your thumb. I'm painting your pointer. I'm painting your middle man. I'm painting your ring finger. I'm painting your pinkie."

Step 3: Set out a variety of paints that are fruit colors, such as red, green, yellow, orange, and purple, in small shallow containers. Ask the children to select the type of fruit that will grow on their trees. If children have difficulty with this, brainstorm a list of fruit. Ask what colors their chosen fruits are. Provide the appropriate color of paint to each child. Then show the class how to dip the pointer finger into the paint and make a print with it. Ask the children to follow your example to add their plums, oranges, bananas, pears, etc. This activity can be combined with a math lesson by giving the children a designated amount of fruit to place on the tree.

Note: If you have a wide variety of fruit pages, you may consider saving these sheets for a tote book (pages 262–329).

Apple Necklaces

Have the children make necklaces by stringing together apple flavored, o-shaped cereal.

Note: In place of plastic darning needles, masking tape tightly wound around a piece of yarn makes the perfect safety needle. It provides a firm tip for threading without the danger of getting stuck by the point of a real needle.

Additional Activities *(cont.)*

Math/Language

Graphing

Do the crunchy/chewy activity as suggested on page 34. Ask the children which fruit they enjoyed eating the most. Graph results on the Clothespin Voting/Graphing Board (page 17). Discuss the results of the graph.

With older children, this activity can be done cooperatively in small groups of three. The groups can graph their results separately using copies of the Bingo Card (page 336) as their grid sheets. Once this task is accomplished, the groups can then compare/contrast the results during a discussion.

Sorting

Use a variety of apples you provide or ones that your students bring for the Apple Tree big book. Invite students to sort the apples by size, color, or type.

Theme Bingo

See page 16.

Fruit Roll

Make an inclined plane by placing one end of some wooden boards on blocks in the Block Center. Encourage the children to experiment with rolling different types of fruit down the incline. Plastic fruit will work well for this activity.

Felt Apple Pie

Cut out three identical circles from tan colored felt. Each of these should be about the size of a dinner plate. Use fabric paint or markers to decorate one side of the circles to look like apple pies. Keep one circle intact. Cut the second into halves. Then cut the third into fourths.

Read the following poem as you place the corresponding felt pieces on a flannelboard.

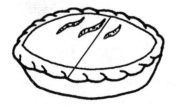

Apple Pie

A whole pie counts as one.
In half, there's two—no more.
But if it's cut in quarters,
That means it will serve four.

Alternative: This poem can be sung to the tune of "Row, Row, Row Your Boat."

Additional Activities *(cont.)*

Science/Discovery/Language

Food Safety

This unit provides a good opportunity to talk about food handling. Discuss how farmers often spray chemicals on the trees in their orchards in order to keep insects away from the fruit. Talk about the importance of thoroughly washing fruit, such as apples, before eating. Point out that fruit that is always eaten after the peel is removed, such as bananas, does not have to be washed.

Apple Mushy

Warning: Before serving anything to eat, ask parents if their children have any food allergies or dietary restrictions.

Materials: blender or food processor, apples that are peeled and cut into wedges, apple juice, honey and/or cinnamon (optional)

Directions: Place a few apple wedges in the blender or food processor. Add a little juice to lubricate the apples and keep them from getting stuck in the appliance. If honey is used in the blender, less juice will be needed. Blend until mushy. You may wish to sprinkle some cinnamon on top.

Alternative: If you don't want to try this recipe, there are plenty of traditional applesauce recipes. However, they usually require cooking.

Mini Apple Pies

If you have a snack maker appliance that makes triangular shaped pockets out of sliced bread, students can enjoy some small apple pies.

Step 1: Place one slice of bread in the snack maker.

Step 2: Scoop some canned apple pie filling onto the piece of bread.

Step 3: Top this with another slice of bread. Then close the lid until the snack maker is done.

Parts of an Apple

Use felt and the patterns on page 46 to cut out an apple and apple core. Place the pieces on the flannelboard as you recite the following poem.

Apple Parts

This is an apple. It grows on a tree.
It's the best tasting fruit if you ask me.
The seeds are inside. The stem is on top.
Once I start eating, I can't seem to stop.
This is an apple—the peel to the core.
I ate it all. Now I'm ready for more.

Alternative: This poem can also be sung to "Twinkle, Twinkle Little Star."

Additional Activities *(cont.)*

Science/Discovery/Language *(cont.)*

Crunchy/Chewy

Warning: Remember to ask if children have any food allergies or dietary restrictions.

Give the children apple wedges and some raisins. Have them take a bite from the apple wedges. Discuss the apple's texture, flavor, smell, the sound made when eating it, etc. Then do the same with the raisins. Ask the following questions: *Which type of fruit was noisy to eat? Which type was quiet?* Discuss the difference between crunchy and chewy. Encourage the children to name other crunchy and/or chewy foods.

Apple Bobs

At the water table, ask the children what will happen if you drop an apple into the water. Allow them to find out for themselves. This may trigger impromptu sinking/floating experiments.

Hide and Seek the Apple

Invite the children to play a game called Hide and Seek the Apple. Have one child hide an apple in the sand table. The child who looks for the apple can play with or without a blindfold.

Field Trip

If possible, take your class to visit an apple orchard, a local grocery store, or a fruit/vegetable stand. Compare and contrast different types of apples.

Music/Movement/Language

Seed Music

Version I (described below) and Version II (described on page 35) require saving, washing, and drying all the seeds from the apple projects and snacks throughout this unit. Use the version that best fits your schedule and the amount of time you have available.

• Shakers—Version I: Limited Time/Limited Help

Materials: empty 35 mm film canisters, one per child

Directions: Begin by placing a few seeds in one film canister and a large number of seeds in another. Compare the sounds these make when they are shaken. Mix up the containers and ask the children to guess which has only a few seeds and which has many seeds. Place some seeds in each child's canister. Play some music, and allow them to shake their canisters along with the tempo. This is fun to do with both fast and slow songs. The children can play and march along to the music. As an alternative, they can do a start/stop activity. Examples: (1) When the music stops, the shakers stop. (2) When the children hear a specific sound, such as a bell, they stop playing the shakers. When they hear another specified sound, such as a tambourine, they resume playing the shakers.

Additional Activities *(cont.)*

Music/Movement/Language *(cont.)*

Seed Music *(cont.)*

• **Shakers—Version II: Extra Time/Extra Help**

Materials: empty small milk cartons that have been cleaned, glue, decorating materials, apple seeds, stapler

Directions: Have the children put some seeds into their empty milk cartons. *Note:* You can easily turn this into a math lesson by having them count out a certain number of seeds that you designate according to their level of ability.

After the seeds are in the cartons, staple the tops closed. Then ask the children to decorate their containers. Once the containers are dry, students can play them during any musical activities such as a parade.

Basket Toss

Gather some plastic apples. Have the children take turns tossing one apple at a time into a basket. If you cannot get a real apple basket, an inexpensive laundry basket or even a milk crate will do.

Apples and Bananas

Play the song "Apples and Bananas" (such as the version by Raffi). *Warning:* Remember to ask parents if their children have any food allergies or dietary restrictions. Serve apples and bananas for a snack. Follow up with a discussion about crunchy vs. chewy, loud vs. soft, etc. Take a vote to determine which fruit the children like best.

Social/Emotional/Language

Red Day

Send copies of the letter (page 45) to parents, requesting that the children wear red-colored clothing on a certain day. As the children enter the room on Red Day, greet them at the door by placing a red stamp or sticker on one of their hands. You may wish to use apple stickers (TCM 1252).

During circle time on Red Day, ask students to name their red articles of clothing. If some children are not wearing anything that is red, remind them about the red stamps or stickers on their hands.

Apple, Apple, Orange

Play a variation of the children's game "duck, duck, goose" by substituting the word *apple* for *duck* and the word *orange* for *goose*. The directions for "duck, duck, goose" are provided on page 205.

Additional Activities *(cont.)*

Social/Emotional/Language *(cont.)*

Fruit and Vegetable Stand

Set up a fruit and vegetable stand complete with a cash register and scale. Keeping in mind what is developmentally appropriate for your students, reinforce math skills by listing specific prices on the fruit and vegetable baskets. Encourage the children to make their own money at the art center. Then have them use this money to purchase the desired fruits and/or vegetables.

Pass the Apple

This game reinforces color recognition in a fun, friendly fashion. The children sit in a circle with a plastic red, yellow, or green apple. The object of the game is to pass the apple while singing "The Apple Game" song below. When the song ends, the child holding the apple must stand up and quickly pick up something in the room that is the same color as the apple. Once the child finds an object, she/he names it. For example, she/he could say, "I found a red block." Then she/he puts the item back and returns to the circle so the game can continue.

The Apple Game

Sing to the tune of "It's a Small World."

The_____(color name) apple goes round and round,

We pass it quickly without a sound,

If we're the one to hold it last,

We must find something (color name) real fast.

Apple Hunt

Hide plastic apples or paper apple cutouts around the room. Let the children hunt for them. This game can be extended into a math lesson by cutting the apples out of red, yellow, and green felt and using various amounts of the differently colored apples. As the children find the felt apples, have them make a pictograph on the flannelboard by lining up the apples according to color. When all the apples have been located, discuss the graph. Ask the following questions: *How many red apples were found? green? yellow? Which apple color has the most? Which apple color has the least? Do any of the colored apples have the same number?*

Apple Relay

For a fun, noncompetitive activity during your Apple Tree unit, plan a relay. Have the children roll apples across the floor, using plastic spoons or their noses. Give all the children some apple juice after they pass the finish line.

To add some science/discovery questions to the game, comment on how the apples are rolling. Ask the following questions: *Do the apples roll evenly? Why or why not?* Compare rolling a ball, using the same method as the relay. Ask: *Are the results the same? Why or why not?*

Where Do We Go From Here?

Throughout the bookmaking process, questions may arise, preparing the way for future lessons and discoveries. Using the Apple Tree unit as an example, some possible questions that may provide fuel for future child-created big books are listed below.

What are some other things that contain seeds?

What else grows from seeds?

How are seeds moved from one place to another?

What else grows on trees?

What is your favorite type or color of apple?

What is your favorite type of fruit?

What is your favorite food?

Is there a special food that your entire family enjoys?

Is there a particular food that your entire family dislikes?

What is the difference between an orchard and a farm?

What kinds of food are grown in orchards?

What kinds of food are grown on farms?

Do you know anyone who works at an orchard or on a farm?

Would you like to work at an orchard or on a farm? Why or why not?

Where would you like to work when you grow up? Why?

Where does your family get apples?

How do apples get to the grocery store?

What kinds of animals like eating apples?

What else is the color red? yellow? green?

What else rots like an apple when it gets old?

If any of these questions spark interest in your students, go in that direction. You may consider using the Thematic Web (page 335) to jot down some ideas during a particular unit. Then you can use that graphic organizer for future reference.

My
Apple Book

by_____

Way up
high
in
the
apple tree,

page 1

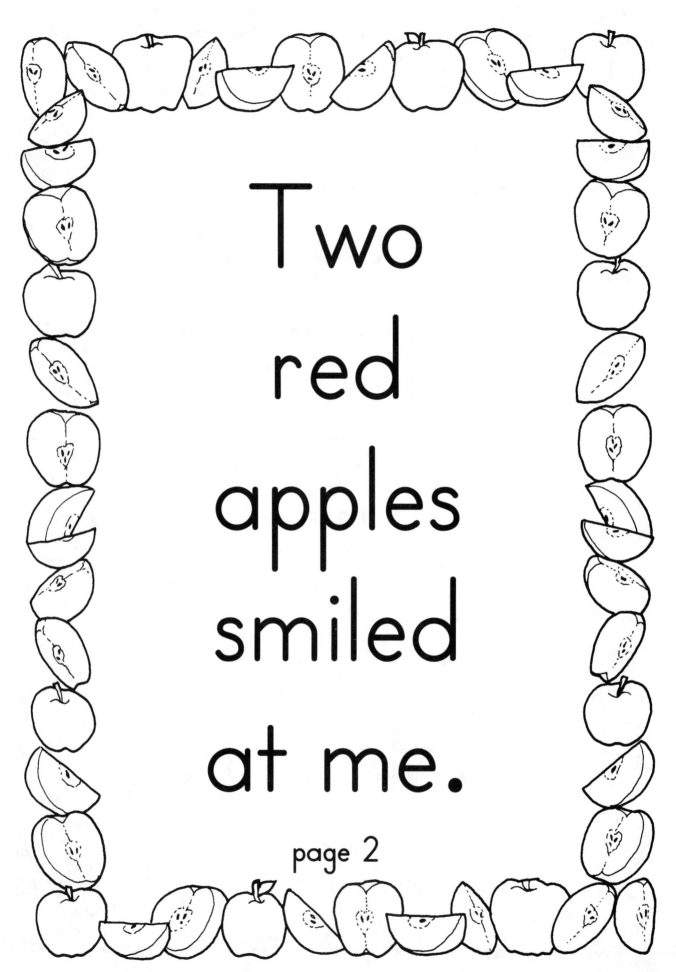

Two red apples smiled at me.

page 2

I shook that tree as hard as I could.

page 3

Down came the apples. Mmm, very good!

page 4

Related Resources

Books

Carle, Eric. *The Tiny Seed.* Scholastic Big Book, 1987.

Ehlert, Lois. *Eating the Alphabet: Fruits and Vegetables from A to Z.* HBJ Big Book, 1989.

Ehlert, Lois. *Red Leaf, Yellow Leaf.* HBJ, 1991.

Fowler, Allan. *How Do You Know It's Fall?* Children's Press, 1992.

Fowler, Allan. *It Could Still Be a Tree.* Children's Press, 1990.

Fox, Mem. *Wilfred Gordon McDonald Partridge.* Kane Miller, 1985.

Gibbons, Gail. *The Seasons of Arnold's Apple Tree.* Harcourt Brace Children's Books, 1988.

Goodall, John S. *Little Red Riding Hood.* McElderry, 1988.

Imershein, Betsy. *Finding Red Finding Yellow.* HBJ, 1989.

Kellogg, Steven. *Johnny Appleseed.* Scholastic, 1988.

Le Sieg, Theodore. *Ten Apples Up On Top.* Random House, 1961.

Leonard, Marcia. *Bear's Busy Year: A Book About Seasons.* Troll, 1990.

Maestro, Betsy. *How Do Apples Grow?* HarperCollins, 1992.

Micucci, Charles. *The Life and Times of the Apple.* Orchard Books, 1992.

Rockwell, Anne. *Apples and Pumpkins.* Scholastic, 1989.

Stinson, Kathy. *Red Is Best.* Firefly Books, 1988.

Zoe, Hall. *The Apple Pie Tree.* Scholastic, 1996.

Music

Raffi. *One Light, One Sun.* "Apples and Bananas." Troubadour Records Ltd., 1994.

Sharon, Lois and Bram. *One, Two, Three Four, Live.* "Apple Picker's Reel." Elephant Records, 1982.

Tickle Tune Typhoon. *Circle Around.* "Tree Dancin'." Tickle Tune Typhoon Records, 1983.

Software

Changes Around Us. (Software about seasons, plants, and families); CD-ROM for WIN or MAC; Sunburst/Edunetics, 101 Castleton Street, P.O. Box 100, Pleasantville, NY 10570-0100; 1-800-321-5711.

Sammy's Science House. (Software about plants, animals, seasons, weather); CD-ROM for MAC, WIN, or DOS; National School Products, 101 East Broadway, Maryville, TN 37804; 1-800-251-9124.

Parent Letter

_____
(Date)

Dear Parent/Guardian,

Next week our class will begin a fun-filled unit about apples. We will use apples to conduct experiments, play games, cook, and create books, just to name a few of the activities.

These activities will require the use of many apples. If possible, on _____ please have your child bring in one apple of any kind. All leftover apples will be used as snacks for the children. Please let me know if your child cannot eat apples or apple products because of food allergies or dietary restrictions

I have found that the children learn better when parents are actively involved. If you would like to be a volunteer in our classroom, please fill out the bottom portion of this page and send it back to school with your child by _____ .

Thank you in advance for your help.

Sincerely,

_____
(Teacher)

_____
(School)

_____
(Phone)

- **Volunteer Information** -

Please print the following information.

Your Name: _____

Your Child's Name: _____

Day and Time Available: _____

Daytime Phone Number: _____

Announcing Our Color Days

_____
(Date)

Dear Parent/Guardian,

Our class is learning about colors. Please encourage your child to wear something in the color of the day. A schedule of the day, date, and color is shown below.

Day	Date	Color Day
		Red Day
		Yellow Day
		Orange Day
		Blue Day
		Green Day
		Purple Day
		Black Day
		Brown Day
		Pink Day
		White Day
		_____ Day

Thanks for your help!

Sincerely,

_____
(Teacher)

_____
(School)

_____
(Phone)

Apple Patterns

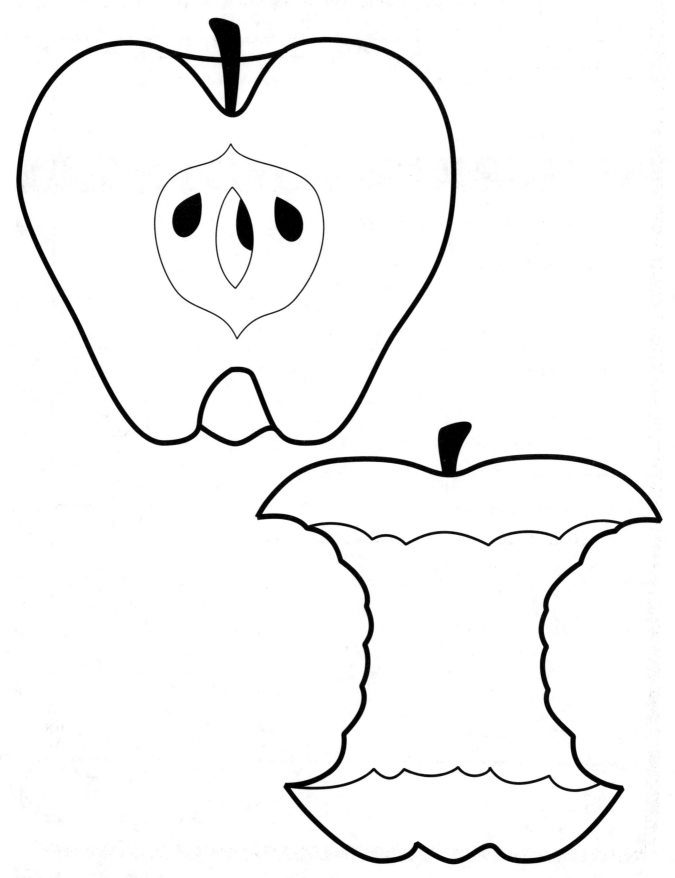

Traffic Light Big Book Materials

Unit Materials:

— paint: red, yellow, and green
— scissors
— glue
— stapler
— drawing tools: pencils, markers, crayons
— 3–4 large marbles or golf balls
— large box lid or cake pan, approximately 12" x 18" (30 cm x 46 cm)
— construction paper: all colors
— shallow containers
— items, such as circular sponges, grapefruit or orange halves, and circular pieces of foam rubber, that will leave large, circular prints
— items, such as hair roller sponges, carrots cut in half, corks, cups, spools, cardboard tubes, bottle caps, and round potato chip canisters, that will leave circular prints of different types and sizes

Extra:

— sticky dots
— bingo markers such as beans or tokens
— dish detergent
— bowl
— plastic straws

Optional Materials for Additional Activities:

— large cardboard box
— straws
— glitter
— flavor extracts
— o-shaped oat cereal
— felt
— fabric paint
— Velcro®
— food coloring
— sugar cookies
— white frosting
— cellophane: red, yellow, green
— tagboard
— craft sticks
— musical instruments
— blank index cards

Traffic Light Big Book

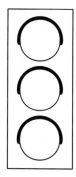

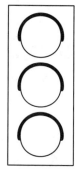

Theme: My Community and Me
Topics: Traffic Lights/Safety
Duration: One Week
Approach: Original Song
           Teacher-Directed Activities
           Creative-Combination Activities

The next child-created big book unit is based on the following question and visual clue, using leftover apples from the apple book or plastic apples from the Home Center. Using the apples makes this a nice transition from the apple unit to the next big book project on traffic safety.

Take three differently colored apples: red, yellow, green. Stack one on top of the other—with the red apple on top, yellow in the middle, and green at the bottom.

Pose this question to the children, "What does this remind you of?" Lead students to conclude that the apples look similar to a traffic light because of the order of the colors.

Teach the children the following "Traffic Safety Song." Each big book page is a song verse. Review the song each day before doing any traffic safety activities.

Traffic Safety Song

Sing to the tune of "Twinkle, Twinkle, Little Star."

Red says, "STOP!" It's up on top.

Green says, "GO!" It's down below.

"Hey diddle, diddle. I'm yellow in the middle.

Better SLOW down, 'cause red's coming 'round."

Now you know what the three colors mean,

Top, middle, bottom—red, yellow, green.

One of these colors shining bright

Is what we see on a traffic light.

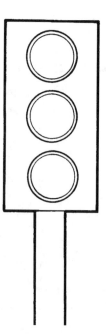

Note: The last verse of the poem repeats the same tune as the last verse in "Twinkle, Twinkle, Little Star."

Making the Book

COVER PAGE

Set up any creative art activity of your choice that allows students to utilize the colors red, yellow, and green. Activities such as painting with large marbles or golf balls, painting by blowing through a straw, or blot painting work nicely. To decorate this particular big book cover and illustrate the book-making procedure, use the following activity.

Activity: Paint using large marbles or golf balls.

Setup: You will need containers of red, yellow, and green tempera paint, three large marbles or golf balls, and a shallow container such as a box lid or a cake pan. The container must be large enough for a 12" x 18" (30 cm x 46 cm) sheet of white construction paper to fit in the bottom, and it needs to have sides that are taller than the marbles or golf balls.

Introduction: Sing the "Traffic Safety Song" with students. After discussing the colors that appear in traffic lights, tell the children they will be painting with those same colors.

Directions: Drop 1–3 large marbles or 1–2 golf balls into each paint container. Invite each child to place the construction paper in the box lid, spoon out the marbles or balls, and drop them onto the paper. Ask the child to tilt the lid from side to side so the marbles or balls will roll across the paper, creating an interesting design.

Cooperation is an important skill that can easily be built into this activity. Have each child work with a partner to manipulate the marbles or golf balls in the pan or box lid. Position one child on each side of the pan/lid and have them join forces to complete this activity.

Save this cover page for the final assembly. Tell the children their books need a title. Ask students to brainstorm a list of titles as you write them on the chalkboard. Invite the children to vote for the title they like best.

On a piece of white copier paper, neatly print or use a computer to print out the title that the class has chosen. Reproduce this title page, making enough copies for every book. If you prefer, you can reproduce the title page (page 56) that has been provided in this book. Glue the title pages onto the painted covers. Assemble the books by placing the pages in order and stapling along the left side of each.

Reproduce the text for the "Traffic Safety Song" (pages 57–61) for students. For each book, glue the text onto the page that is opposite the illustration.

Making the Book *(cont.)*

PAGES 1, 2, and 3

Text: Red says, "STOP!" It's up on top.

Green says, "GO!" It's down below.

"Hey diddle, diddle. I'm yellow in the middle.

Better SLOW down, 'cause red's coming 'round."

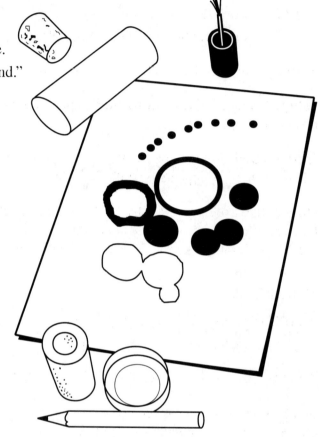

Activity: Make circle prints using a variety of circular objects.

Setup: Set up two tables, one for the teacher-directed big book pages and the other for a creative art table. You will need shallow containers with red, yellow, and green paints for both tables. For the creative art table, provide a stack of colored construction paper that is big book size and a variety of objects that leave prints of different types and sizes. *Suggestions:* hair roller sponges, carrots cut in half, corks, toilet paper rolls, industrial spools, concentrated juice cans. For the big book table, provide a large stack of white construction paper and objects that will leave large, circular prints. *Suggestions:* large round sponges and grapefruit or orange halves.

Introduction: Before beginning these pages, review the "Traffic Safety Song." As a motivational factor, play one of the games suggested in the Additional Activities section (pages 52–55).

Directions: At the creative painting table, the children can choose pieces of paper and make as many prints as they like.

Note: You may want to save one of each child's page with circle prints for a future long-term shapes book. Make sure their names and the date are on the pages. Then you can send home any additional paperplay pages.

At the teacher-directed table, each child will use three sheets of large white construction paper. Show students how to place the paper so it is laid out the long way. Ask them to show you where the top of the paper is. Once the location is established, have the children print one red circle at the top of their papers. Put those papers aside. Repeat this procedure with the next sheet of paper, having the children make a yellow print in the middle. Then have students make a green print at the bottom of the third piece of paper.

Note: This activity requires a lot of drying space. Perhaps a hallway can be used for this purpose.

Timesaver: It may be easier to staple these three pages together as soon as they are dry.

Making the Book *(cont.)*

PAGE 4

Text: Now you know what three colors mean,

Top, middle, bottom—red, yellow, green.

Activity: Align and glue red, yellow, and green circles to make a traffic light.

Setup: You need black construction paper; scissors; glue; and red, yellow, and green pre-traced or precut circles.

Introduction: Review the "Traffic Safety Song" and positional words. Ask children if they remember where each color appears on a traffic light.

Directions: The circles can be pre-traced for the children to cut or precut and ready for gluing. During this activity, have the children count the circles, review the shape name (circle), colors (red, yellow, green), positional words (above, below, between), and prepositions (under, over).

PAGE 5

Text: One of these colors shining bright

Is what we see on a traffic light.

Activity: Paint with soap bubbles.

Setup: Pour water into three bowls. Add one color of tempera paint (red, yellow, green) to each bowl. Squirt in some clear dish detergent. Experiment to get the right amount of bubbles.

Introduction: Review the "Traffic Safety Song," colors, shapes, numbers, and positional words. As students sing the song, hold up completed book pages.

Directions: Each child inserts a straw into a bowl. Have the youngster blow through the straw to make bubbles. Once the bubbles overflow, lightly place a large sheet of white construction paper over the bubbles. The bubbles will pop, leaving prints on the paper. Repeat with the other two colors on a different area of the paper until it is covered with bubble prints.

Warning: Squeeze the side of the straw and make a slanted slit about 1" (2.5 cm) below the top to eliminate the chance of very young children inhaling any paint.

PUTTING IT ALL TOGETHER

If the first three pages are already stapled, you simply need to add the cover and the last two pages. If the children do this, emphasize the concept of front and back as you assemble the book. For each book, glue the text onto the page that is opposite the illustration.

Additional Activities

Art/Language

Car Creation

Provide a large cardboard box such as the type and size obtained from an appliance store. Let the children paint and decorate it to create their very own car. Bring it outside during playtime.

Straw Painting with Traffic Light Colors

Pour red, yellow, and green tempera paint into separate containers. Add water to each of the paints until they are drippy. For each student, spoon little puddles of paint onto a large sheet of paper. The children create designs by blowing through plastic straws to move the paint around.

Easel Painting

Set up the easel. Add some glue and glitter to red, yellow, and green tempera paint. For a sensory experience, add ground spices or flavor extracts to the paint. For example, shake a little ground cinnamon into the red paint or lemon extract into the yellow.

Math/Language

Traffic Light Necklaces

The children can string o-shaped oat cereal to make necklaces. Have them place red, yellow, and green o-shaped candies in the middle of their necklaces.

Flannel Board Math

Use the patterns (page 63) to create five felt or Velcro cutout cars and trucks. The cars should include one red, one yellow, and one blue for the Our Family Car activity (page 53).

Five Little Cars

Sing to the tune of "Row, Row, Row Your Boat."
(Place all five car cutouts on one side of the flannelboard.)
Five little cars were driving off one day.
Suddenly one ran out of gas. I guess it has to stay.
(Move four of the cars forward.)
There were four little cars driving off one day.
Suddenly one ran out of gas. I guess it has to stay.
(Continue this process until only one car moves forward.)
There was one little car, driving on its way.
It remembered to fill up its tank. It can drive all day.

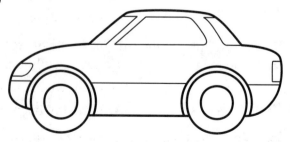

Additional Activities *(cont.)*

Math/Language *(cont.)*

Flannelboard Math *(cont.)*

Truckin' Down the Road

Sing to the tune of "This Old Man."

(Place the first truck on the flannelboard.)

I'm a truck. I am one. I am big and weigh a ton.
With a knick-knack paddy whack, carrying a load,
I keep truckin' down the road.

(Add a second truck.)

We are trucks. We are two. One is old, and one is new.
With a knick-knack paddy whack, carrying a load,
We keep truckin' down the road.

(Add a third truck.)

We are trucks. We are three. We're as clean as we can be.
With a knick-knack paddy whack, carrying a load,
We keep truckin' down the road.

(Add a fourth truck.)

We are trucks. We are four. Listen to our engines roar,
With a knick-knack paddy whack, carrying a load,
We keep truckin' down the road.

(Add the fifth truck.)

We are trucks. We are five. Heading on out for a drive,
With a knick-knack paddy whack, carrying a load,
We keep truckin' down the road.
With a knick-knack paddy whack, carrying a load,
We keep truckin' down the road.

Our Family Car

Sing to the tune of "The Farmer in the Dell."
(Place one car cutout on the flannelboard.)

This is our family car. It's red, yellow, and blue.

Four wheels and a body—roof and bumpers, too.

Mom uses it for work, or drives it to the bank.

Dad takes it through the car wash, and puts gas in the tank.

Someday when I am bigger, I know what I will do.

I will get my license, so I can drive one too.

The above song can also be used as a fingerplay. Follow up by asking students what kind, color, or size of car they would like to drive.

Additional Activities *(cont.)*

Music/Movement

Traffic Train

Materials: red, yellow, and green tagboard circles glued onto craft sticks; large, connecting blocks that are red, yellow, and green

Directions: Line up students to form a train. The leader holds up the appropriately colored circle. Sing, using a quick and snappy tempo for the green circle and a slow tempo for the yellow circle. Depending on which colored circle is displayed, the train moves quickly, slowly, or stops.

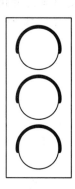 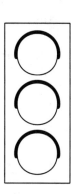

The Traffic Light Song

Sing to the tune of "The Farmer in the Dell."

The light says, "Go." The light says, "Go."
We do what the light says—go, go, go.
The light says, "Slow." The light says, "Slow."
We do what the light says—slow, slow, slow.
The light says, "Stop." The light says, "Stop."
We do what the light says—stop, stop, stop.

Stop-and-Go Singing

Materials: traffic light circles from Traffic Train (above)

Directions: Children are asked to sing a familiar song such as "The Wheels on the Bus." When the designated leader holds up the green circle, the children sing. When the leader holds up the red circle, the children stop singing. The singing continues each time the green circle is displayed.

Variations: (1) Stop-and-Go Musical Instruments—Substitute musical instruments for the singing. (2) Stop-and-Go Movements—The children take turns being the leader. Before holding up the green circle, the leader names a movement such as hopping. Students hop until the leader holds up the red circle.

Seat Belt Song

The children substitute their own nouns to fill in the blanks.

Seat Belt Song

Sing to the tune "For He's a Jolly Good Fellow."

The _____ wore a seat belt. The _____ wore a seat belt.
The _____ wore a seat belt, and we should too.
We should too. We should too.
The _____ wore a seat belt, and we should too.

Red Light/Green Light

Any variation of this old-time favorite children's game can be played.

Additional Activities *(cont.)*

Science/Discovery

Watercolors

Add red, yellow, and green food coloring to separate bowls of water at the water table.

Traffic Light Cookies

Let children decorate sugar cookies with red, yellow, or green frosting. Compare/contrast how many cookies there are of each color. Give each student three cookies, one of each color. Ask them to arrange their cookies in the order of the colors on a traffic light. After the children have decorated their cookies, sing a variation of "Thumbkin." Adapt the following verse for yellow and green lights.

> *Teacher:* Where's a red light? Where's a red light?
> *Children:* Here I am. Here I am.
> *Teacher:* What does red say? What does red say?
> *Children:* Red says, "Stop!" Red says, "Stop."

Fun with Light

Experiment with colored light by placing red, yellow, and green cellophane over flashlights.

Social/Emotional

Stop, Stop, Go

Play a variation of the game "duck, duck, goose" by substituting the word *stop* for *duck* and the word *go* for *goose*. The directions for "duck, duck, goose" are provided on page 205.

Block Center Safety

Add traffic signs to your Block Center. Provide scrap paper and crayons for students to make their own.

Tricycle Safety

Take students outside to ride tricycles. Have the children take turns using the traffic light circles from Traffic Train (page 54) to direct the tricycle traffic.

Directing Traffic

Bring the traffic light circles from Traffic Train (page 54) with you anytime you are walking your class on the school grounds or in the neighborhood.

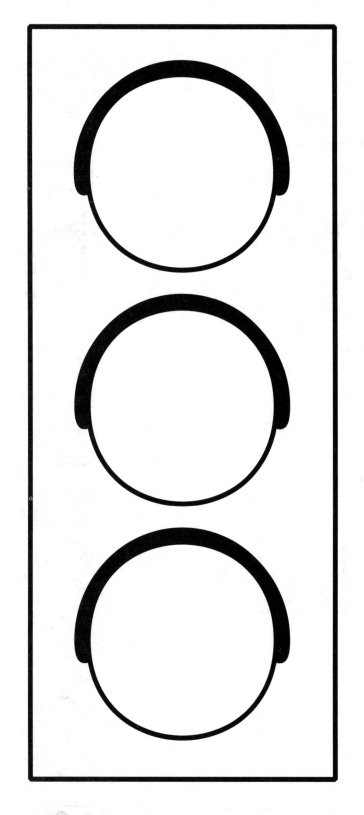

My
Traffic
Light
Book

by _____

Red says, "STOP!" It's up on top.

page 1

Green says, "GO!" It's down below.

page 2

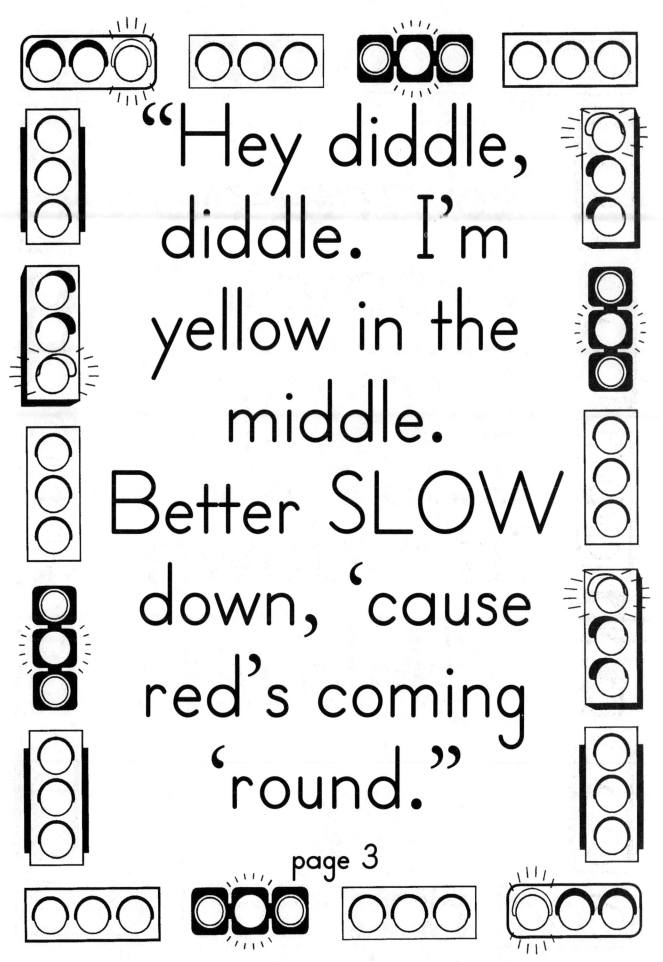

"Hey diddle,
diddle. I'm
yellow in the
middle.
Better SLOW
down, 'cause
red's coming
'round."

page 3

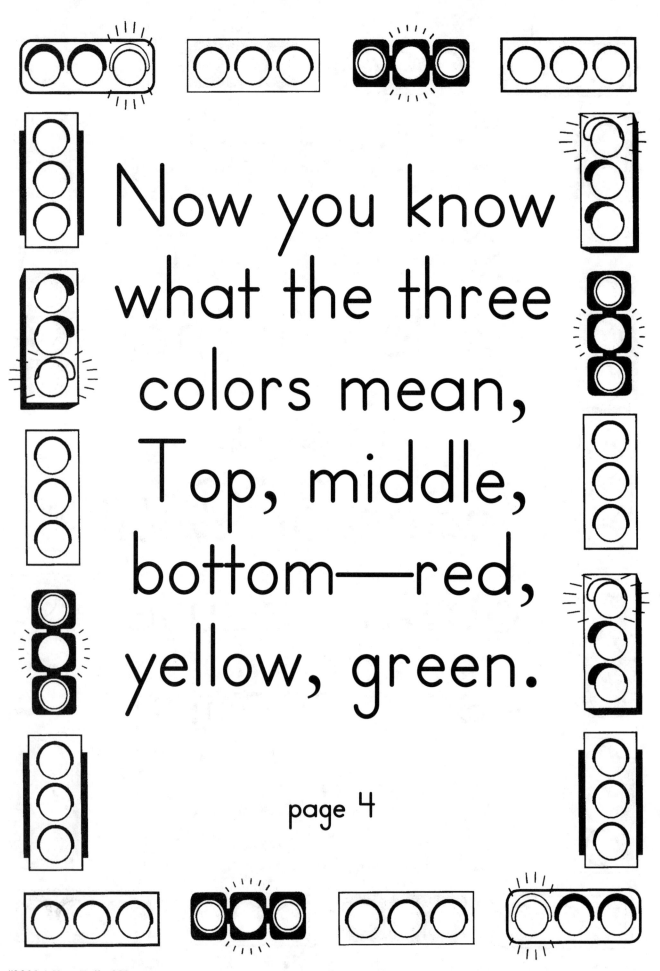

Now you know what the three colors mean, Top, middle, bottom—red, yellow, green.

page 4

One of these colors shining bright
Is what we see on a traffic light.

page 5

 #2311 A Year Full of Themes

Related Resources

Books

Alda, Arlene. *Hold the Bus.* Troll, 1996.

Best, Cari. *Red Light, Green Light, Mama and Me.* Orchard Books, 1995.

Brown, Margaret Wise. *Red Light, Green Light.* Scholastic, 1994.

Chlad, Dorothy. *When I Cross the Street.* Children's Press, 1982.

Courson, Diana. *Let's Learn About Colors, Shapes, & Sizes.* Good Apple, 1986.

Crews, Donald. *School Bus.* Scholastic, 1990.

Dodds, Dayle Ann. *The Shape of Things.* Candlewick Press, 1994.

Dunn, Joyce. *Riding on a School Bus.* SPI, 1989.

Florian, Douglas. *Auto Mechanic.* Greenwillow, 1991.

Griffiths, Rose. *Circles.* Gareth Stevens, 1994.

Hoban, Tana. *I Read Signs.* William Morrow & Co., 1987.

Hoban, Tana. *Red, Blue, Yellow Shoe.* Greenwillow, 1986.

Imershein, Betsy. *Finding Red Finding Yellow.* HBJ, 1989.

Jeunesse, Galimard and Pascale de Bourgoing. *Colors.* Scholastic, 1991.

Klingel, Cynthia F. *Bicycle Safety.* Creative Education, 1986.

McLeod, Emilie W. *The Bear's Bicycle.* Little, 1986.

Scarry, Richard. *Things That Go.* Western, 1987.

Siebert, Diane. *Train Song.* HarperCollins, 1990.

Music

CJ Fundamentals. "Wheels on the Bus." Handy Music Inc., 1995.

Fred Penner Collections. "Car, Car Song." Oak Street Music/Dino Music, 1992.

Palmer, Hap. *Learning Basic Skills Through Music: Health and Safety.* "Buckle Your Seat Belt." Activity Records, 1970.

Palmer, Hap. *Learning Basic Skills Through Music: Health and Safety.* "Stop, Look, and Listen." Activity Records, 1970.

Video

Trains. (Video); 14 min. Coronet/MTI Film and Video, P.O. Box 2649, Columbus, OH 43216; 1-800-321-3106.

Software

Fisher-Price Ready for School. (Kindergarten activities promoting safety such as wearing a helmet while riding a bicycle); CD-ROM for MAC, WIN 95, or WIN 3.1; Davidson & Assoc., Inc., Torrance, CA 90503; 1-800-545-7677.

Car and Truck Patterns

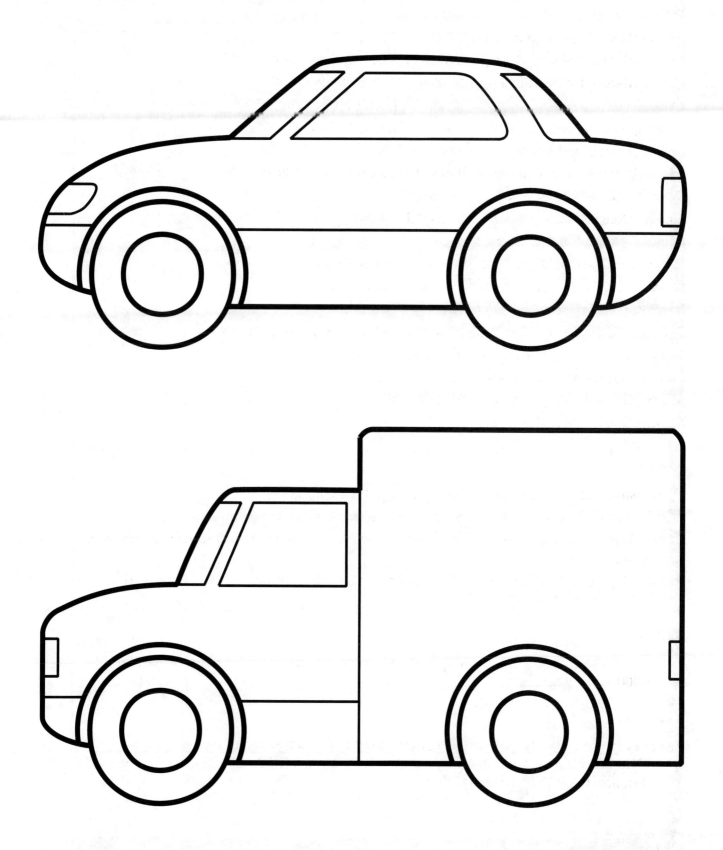

Autumn Leaves Big Book Materials

Unit Materials:

— autumn-colored scraps: yarn, construction paper, felt, tissue, etc.

— glue

— drawing tools: markers, crayons, colored pencils

— construction paper: white and any colors

— dish puffs: the kind that look like a spongy chrysanthemum on a long handle

— paint: red, orange, yellow, green, brown

— shallow paint containers such as cake pans, pie plates, or clean Styrofoam meat trays

— strings of beads

— plastic bubble wrap

— small paint roller or sponge paintbrush

— 3–5 small balloons

— potato or vegetable brush

— Koosh ball (optional)

— five clean, old knee-high stockings

— sand or rice

— white butcher paper

— stapler

Optional Materials for Additional Activities:

— leaves, pine cones, acorns, twigs, bark

— splatter screen: the kind used for frying

— old toothbrush

— old handbrush or scrub brush

— empty spray bottles

— balance scale

— wax paper

— iron

— felt

— fabric paint

Autumn Leaves Big Book

Theme: My World and Me
Topics: Seasons/Autumn Leaves
Duration: One Week
Approach: Adapted Song
             Creative Art Projects

This next big book unit takes advantage of many different creative art methods that are available and brings them together to create the illustrations for this book. Although specific activities are provided below and on the following pages, feel free to incorporate your own creative ideas.

This big book is flexible enough to include as many or as few pages as you choose. All the autumn colors do not have to be included in this project. The beauty of this big book is that each child can have a different number of pages in their individual copies.

If you live in an area where the leaves change colors in the fall, introduce this big book with a Leaf Walk (page 75). Take the children outdoors to explore and observe the different colors, shapes, and sizes of trees and leaves. Point out that some trees do not lose their leaves because they are evergreen. Collect some of the leaves that have fallen on the ground to use in classroom activities.

Note: You may wish to allow the children to listen to music while they create their paperplay book pages. They can brush, dip, dab, swirl, blot, and move to the beat of the music. This can be accomplished by placing earphones on the children at the bookmaking table, or you can play music for the enjoyment of the entire class.

Autumn Leaves

Sing to the tune of "London Bridge Is Falling Down."

Red leaves are falling down, falling down, falling down.

(Hold arms above head; bring hands down while wiggling fingers each time "falling down" is sung.)

Red leaves are falling down, on the ground.
(Use the same gesture, only bring hands all the way down until they are flat on floor.)

Continue in the same way several times, substituting the colors *yellow, orange, green,* and *brown* for each new verse. Then, for the final verse, the word *autumn* replaces the last color name.

Making the Book

COVER PAGE

Activity: Cut and glue scraps to make a collage.

Setup: On a table, place autumn-colored scraps of various materials, a pile of large sheets of construction paper, and some glue. Have students use collage items that will stay glued to the paper but are not so thick that stacking the big books will be difficult.

Note: Those children making a collage for their cover pages will need to glue the title sheet (page 77) on as a first step. Because collages have raised surfaces and some children tend to place most of their items in the center, it is often difficult to glue the title sheet on after the completion of the book.

Introduction: Discuss seasonal changes and read a book about them. See the Related Resources (page 84) for some suggestions. Sing the "Autumn Leaves" song (page 65) in its entirety. Because of its repetition and the familiar tune, the children will quickly learn it. Tell the children that their next big book will be based on this song.

Directions: Explain that throughout the week, there will be a collage table. Let the children know that for those students who decide to make another book, one of their collages will be saved for the cover page. However, assure them that they can make more than one paperplay creation if they wish to take one home. If they do not want to participate in making another book but would like to make a collage to take home, that's okay too.

Alternative: If a child makes several big book pages but did not choose to do the cover page activity (described above), this problem is easily remedied. In the Additional Activities section (pages 72–76), there are suggestions for leaf rubbings and spray bottle painting. Using either one of these techniques for the cover page is another option. Then the title sheet can be glued on as a final step.

Making the Book *(cont.)*

PAGE 1

Text: Red leaves are falling down, falling down, falling down.

Red leaves are falling down, on the ground.

Activity: Make a red painting using a spongy dish puff.

Setup: On the art table, set out some shallow containers of red paint along with a stack of white construction paper. In each paint container, place a spongy dish puff—the kind that looks like a sponge flower at the end of a plastic handle.

Introduction: If you go for a Leaf Walk (page 75), bring out the leaves that were collected. Discuss the different shapes, sizes, and colors. Let the children hold leaves that are the same colors as those in the song. Sing the "Autumn Leaves" song together. While singing, the children can pantomime the action of falling leaves by using the real leaves. Focus on the red leaves, and review the color. Explain that this day's activity will be the first page of their books.

Directions: Direct students to the creative art table. Tell them they are to use the dish puffs to make red leaves on the white paper. Encourage the children to paint creatively by experimenting with these dish puffs.

PAGE 2

Text: Orange leaves are falling down, falling down, falling down.

Orange leaves are falling down, on the ground.

Activity: Make an orange bead painting.

Setup: Set out a stack of white paper and some shallow containers of orange paint. Place a string of large beads that is approximately 10–12" (25.5–30 cm) long on the table near the paints. The beads can be obtained from an old necklace, a piece cut from a beaded Christmas tree garland, or those strung by the children at the classroom Manipulative Center. Some craft stores sell inexpensive strings of plastic beads.

Warning: Beads are a choking hazard. They should not be too small and should be strung together in such a way as to eliminate the possibility of falling apart.

Introduction: Review the "Autumn Leaves" song by using the sample red page described above. Explain to the children that today they will be making the orange page.

Directions: Have students do this activity without any demonstration or instruction aside from letting them know it is a painting activity. Observe how the children manipulate the beads to achieve their works of art.

Making the Book *(cont.)*

PAGE 3

Text: Yellow leaves are falling down, falling down, falling down.

      Yellow leaves are falling down, on the ground.

Activity: Make a yellow bubble wrap painting.

Setup: For this activity, you will need a stack of white construction paper, shallow paint containers of yellow paint, a 3" (8 cm) paint roller or any sized sponge brush, and scraps of bubble wrap (the kind used for shipping).

Introduction: Review the "Autumn Leaves" song. Hold up a sample of the red and orange big book pages (page 67) while singing that part of the song. Explain to the children that today they will be doing page 3 of their books. Ask them to guess which color they will be using.

Note: The Leaf Game (pages 76) is a good way to begin this lesson.

Directions: Before beginning, ask the children if they have any ideas about how to get the paint on the bubble wrap, using the materials provided at the table. Lead them to conclude that they need to roll it on the bubble wrap with the bubble side up.

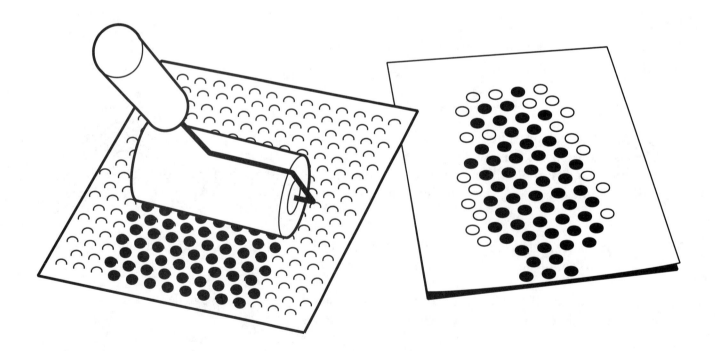

The next question to ask them is how they would get the paint onto the paper. Lead students to conclude that they can either press the painted bubbles onto the paper or press the paper onto the painted bubbles. Using the children's ideas stretches art into a discovery lesson.

Allow the children to experiment with which method works best for them.

Making the Book *(cont.)*

PAGE 4

Text: Green leaves are falling down, falling down, falling down.
     Green leaves are falling down, on the ground.

Activity: Make a green balloon painting.

Setup: You will need a few small balloons. Leave one deflated, for the science experiment described in the Introduction (below), and partially inflate a few for use at the art table. The number of balloons you'll need depends on how many children you would like working together at the art table.

Set out a stack of white construction paper and some shallow containers of green paint. Place a partially inflated balloon into each paint container.

Introduction: Display sample big book pages as you review the "Autumn Leaves" song with students. Integrate a science/discovery lesson by describing objects as light or heavy. Ask the children to guess which is lighter: a leaf or an inflated balloon. Experiment with dropping the two items simultaneously to find out the answer. The children can also experiment with dropping an inflated and a deflated balloon. Then have them try dropping two leaves that are different sizes and/or shapes. Have students compare/contrast the results.

Directions: The children use the inflated balloons for painting by lifting them from the paint containers and lightly pressing down on the paper to make balloon prints.

Warning: When using balloons for any activity, it is of the utmost importance that the children are carefully supervised. Children love balloons, but they can be dangerous if used improperly. Some children are also afraid of the noise balloons make when they are popped. Make sure the balloons are not fully inflated so they do not pop when a child presses down to paint with them.

Making the Book (cont.)

PAGE 5

Text: Brown leaves are falling down, falling down, falling down.

Brown leaves are falling down, on the ground.

Activity: Make brown prints using a potato/vegetable brush and/or Koosh balls.

Setup: Set out some shallow containers of brown paint and a stack of white construction paper. Place the potato/vegetable brush(es) or Koosh ball(s) into the containers of paint.

Introduction: Review the "Autumn Leaves" song, holding up completed big book pages at the appropriate times. Ask children to guess which color they will be using today.

Directions: The children can create different effects and textures on the paper, using the brushes and/or balls to dip and brush, dip and swoosh, or dip and dab.

PAGE 6

Text: Autumn leaves are falling down, falling down, falling down.

Autumn leaves are falling down, on the ground.

Activity: Use autumn colors to make a gravity painting.

Setup: Obtain five clean, old knee-high stockings. You can also use a couple of pairs of pantyhose that have been cut off just above the knee. Fill each stocking or pantyhose leg with sand or rice. Tie the open end into a knot to contain the filler. You may want to knot it again once or twice to form a handle. Place these into the containers of paint.

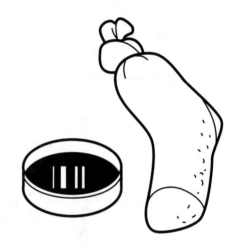

Alternatives: If you don't have extra pantyhose or stockings, clean old socks can be substituted. You can also achieve similar results by funneling sand into deflated balloons and then tying a knot in the open end to contain the sand. Then proceed, using the directions below. Although the end result will be slightly different, it is still a good way to introduce the concept of gravity.

Introduction: Explain that this is the last page of the book. Ask students to tell you which colors they think they will be using for this page. Review the colors and sing the "Autumn Leaves" song, showing previously completed pages as visual clues.

Directions: The children will lift the stockings from the paint and drop them onto the paper. Discuss gravity. Due to the elasticity of hose, the paintings can also be achieved by bouncing the nylon. The children will enjoy stretching and dropping the stockings to create their designs. Allow students to repeat this process until all the autumn colors have been used.

Making the Book *(cont.)*

PAGE 6 *(cont.)*

Bulletin Board: Place a large sheet of white butcher paper on another table. This same sheet will be brought out every time the children do a page for their big books. Each day have students do the same activity twice, once for their big book pages and the other using the butcher paper. This way they add the next color onto the butcher paper as they create each page of their big books. By page 6 of the big book, the end result will be a colorful composition that can be cut into a treetop shape. With the scraps that are left from the butcher paper, trace and cut a variety of leaf shapes. Then, using brown butcher paper, cut out a trunk shape.

For a background, cover your bulletin board with light blue, white, or yellow butcher paper or fabric. Staple the trunk onto the bulletin board. Staple the treetop over the top of the trunk, and attach the leaves at the bottom of the trunk so it looks like they are on the ground. Using a computerized banner or stenciled letters, add a caption of your choice.

Timesaver: You can reuse the trunk from the Apple Tree bulletin board (page 26).

PUTTING IT ALL TOGETHER

Pages 1–6 can be placed into the child-created big book, using one of the following ways.

1. Insert the pages into the book as they are.

2. Draw the trunks in with a crayon or give the children precut tree trunks to simply glue onto the pages.

3. Cut the existing pages into a treetop shape and glue them onto another sheet of construction paper along with tree trunks.

For the children who made collages for their cover pages, the title sheets should already be attached. Otherwise, follow the same procedure as described for assembling other big books.

For this particular book, it is not necessary to have the pages stapled in any specific order. You may wish to allow each student to determine the order of the pages for her/his book.

Take special care to make sure the correct text (pages 78–83) is placed opposite the corresponding illustrations.

Additional Activities

Art/Language

Leaf Dip Painting

Pour a variety of autumn-colored tempera paints into some shallow containers. The children can dip large, sturdy leaves into the paint and then brush them over white construction paper. This process is repeated with all the colors until the children are satisfied with the completed paperplay. Once dry, use these designs to cut out leaf shapes and decorate your classroom with this colorful foliage.

Leaf Rubbings

The children are always amazed at what happens when a crayon is rubbed over a leaf. To make leaf rubbings, have each child place a variety of leaves (bumpy side up) under a sheet of paper. Remove the wrappers from some chunky crayons and tell students to rub the crayons sideways over the leaves. Point out to students that using differently colored crayons for each rubbing, makes the finished product look more attractive.

Note: This activity works best if done on thin paper such as copier or duplicating paper. However, if students do the rubbings on white construction paper, it can be used as an alternate cover page (page 66) for this big book.

Nature Collage

Invite the children to make collages using the leaves, pine cones, etc., which were collected on the Leaf Walk (page 75).

Splattered Leaves

Note: This activity also makes a wonderful cover page, providing you with another alternative.

The children will enjoy making leaf silhouettes by splattering paint around medium-sized leaves that are placed on white construction paper. Here are a couple of suggestions for how to do this project. (1) You may wish to have students take turns using a store-bought splatter screen such as the kind used for frying. Demonstrate how to use the screen. Lean it over the leaf that is on the construction paper. After dipping an old toothbrush into some water thinned tempera paint, rub it across the top of the screen. Encourage students to follow the same procedure using several different colors. (2) There is another option that does not involve a screen at all. The children dip fingernail brushes or flat, kitchen scrub brushes into the paint. As they hold the brushes over the leaves, they run their thumbs over the bristles, causing the paint to splatter. If this is your chosen method, make sure that the tables are covered with newspaper or butcher paper and everyone involved is wearing a paint shirt or smock since it can be somewhat messy.

Spray Bottle Painting

This technique is fast, fun, and creates an effect similar to that achieved by the spattering methods described above. Just take an empty spray bottle and fill it with liquid watercolor paint. Arrange some leaves on a sheet of white construction paper, aim, and spray.

Additional Activities (cont.)

Math/Language

Weighing Leaves

Set out a balance scale and invite students to experiment with weighing leaves and other objects. This is a good activity to do when making page 4 of the big book (page 69), following the discussion about light and heavy. Have the children place some leaves of different sizes into one scale pan and various objects in the other. Ask them to compare and contrast the different quantities and weights on each side of the scale.

Sorting Leaves

Let children sort the leaves collected on the Leaf Walk (page 75) according to shape, color, size, or patterns.

Window Pairs

Collect pairs of different types of leaves. They will need to be fairly supple for this project. For each pair of leaves, cut four pieces of waxed paper that are identical squares or rectangles. Each pair of leaves is pressed in matching shapes which are different from the other pairs of leaves.

Turn on the iron to a medium setting. Place each leaf between two pieces of waxed paper, making sure that the matching pairs are pressed in identical squares or rectangles. Carefully iron each leaf between the two pieces of waxed paper for just a few seconds. Allow the waxed paper to cool, then mix up the pairs of leaves. Invite students to use these window cards for matching the pairs of leaves.

Warning: Never allow students to get near the iron or leaves that have just been pressed.

Puzzle Partners

Enlarge the leaf patterns (page 85). Trace them onto tagboard, and cut as many as you wish to use. Cut each leaf across the center so it looks like two pieces of a jigsaw puzzle. According to the skill you want to develop, place the matching items on both halves of the leaf. You can keep this game simple by placing identical items on both halves, such as a red dot and a red dot. If you wish to increase the degree of difficulty, make pairs that match digits with the correct number of dots or pairs that match concept words. Have the children mix up the puzzle pieces and put the matching pairs together.

Counting Acorns

Sing to the tune of "I'm a Little Teapot."

I'm a little oak tree, straight and tall. *(Hold arms up and out.)*

See my acorns, ten in all. *(Hold up ten fingers.)*

When the wind starts blowing, they fall down. *(Sway arms from side to side.)*

Count them as they hit the ground *(Squat down; tap the floor with each number.)*

1-2-3-4-5-6-7-8-9-10. *(spoken)*

Additional Activities *(cont.)*

Math/Language *(cont.)*

Flannelboard Foliage

Make five leaves (one of each color: brown, yellow, orange, red, green) in one of these two ways: (1) Reproduce the Leaf Patterns (page 85) on cardstock, laminate, cut out, and place Velcro® on the backs. (2) Trace the patterns to make felt leaves. Then do the following math activity with students.

Five Little Leaves

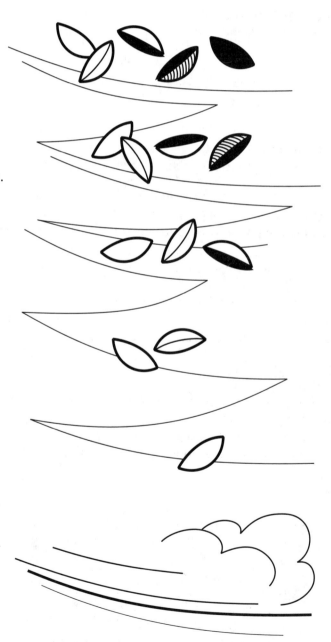

Five little leaves in the autumn breeze,
Fluttered around the nearby trees.
The leaf that was colored brown,
Came gently floating to the ground.

Four little leaves in the autumn breeze,
Fluttered around the nearby trees.
The yellow leaf made a loop.
Then came to a landing with one last swoop.

Three little leaves in the autumn breeze,
Fluttered around the nearby trees.
An orange leaf was flying low,
Then rested on the ground below.

Two little leaves in the autumn breeze,
Fluttered around the nearby trees.
Another leaf fell from overhead,
It was a leaf colored red.

One little leaf in the autumn breeze,
Fluttered around the nearby trees.
The green leaf, close at hand,
Was the last to fly, the last to land.

They're gone for now, but not for long,
They'll be back next fall, where they belong.

Additional Activities *(cont.)*

Science/Discovery

Leaf Walk

If possible, take the children for a walk to look at the fall foliage. Bring along some containers such as plastic pails, buckets, or grocery bags to collect samples of the various leaves that are found on the ground. While on the walk, encourage students to listen to the sound of crunching leaves under their feet. In addition, allow them to crunch some leaves in their hands. Rake together a pile of leaves, and invite students to jump into it. Throw a bunch of leaves into the air so the children can watch them fall. If possible, gather some pine cones, acorns, twigs, and bark. Use these for nature collages (page 72).

Note: If you live in an area where the leaves do not change colors or you don't have access to various leaves, go to a local craft store and purchase some inexpensive fabric leaves in a variety of fall colors.

Discovery Table

Set out some of the leaves, pine cones, etc., at a discovery table along with some magnifying glasses for students to make observations and comparisons. Then play the What's Missing? game by grouping or placing several of the collected objects from nature in a row on a tray. After giving the children a sufficient amount of time to look at all the items, cover them with a large, flat object such as poster board or the lid of a cardboard box. Without the students seeing, remove one of the items. Reveal the items again, and have the children guess which one is missing.

Music/Movement

Fluttering Leaves

Obtain a Hula-Hoop. Cut autumn-colored leaves, using the patterns (page 85) and laminated construction paper. Let every child choose a leaf to hold. Tell the children that when they hear their leaf colors, they should get up and walk through the hoop. Have them keep going around in a circle and pass through the hoop each time until they hear the last line of the song.

Through My Window

Sing to the tune of "Bluebird, Bluebird, Through My Window." Recordings for this music are suggested in the Related Resources (page 84).

Red leaf/leaves fluttering through my window,

Gently dancing as the wind blows.

Red leaf/leaves fluttering through my window,

Oh, my goodness. Now it's autumn.

Additional Activities *(cont.)*

Social/Emotional

The Leaf Game

Have students sing about different colors, using the model verse shown below. Make colored leaves as described for Fluttering Leaves (page 75). Give each child a leaf to hold during the song. Ask students to stand up and wave their leaves in the air when singing about their leaf color. Tell them that after singing the verse that is about their leaf color, they should then place their leaves somewhere in the classroom. To reinforce positional words, ask each child the question, "_____, where did your leaf fall?" Example responses: "My leaf fell behind the milk crate." "My leaf fell on the water table." "My leaf fell next to Paulo."

The Leaf Game Song

Sing to the tune of "The Wheels on the Bus."

The leaves on the tree are red, red, red—red, red, red—red, red, red.
The leaves on the tree are red, red, red, and are falling down, down, down.

Movement Leaves

Using the same leaves that were used for Fluttering Leaves (page 75), have the children play the following game which is another adapted activity song. Repeat the verse shown below, using other colors.

All Fall Down

Sing to the tune of "Ring Around the Rosie."

Red leaves on the trees, swaying in the breeze.
Uh-oh, wind blows—they all fall down.

Home Center

Place winter clothes, such as coats, hats, and sweaters, for the dolls in the center.

  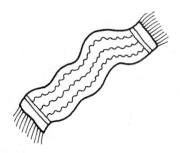  

My Autumn Leaves Book

by _____

Red leaves are
falling down,
falling down,
falling down.
Red leaves are
falling down,
on the ground.

page 1

Orange leaves
are falling down,
falling down,
falling down.
Orange leaves
are falling down,
on the ground.

page 2

Yellow leaves are falling down, falling down, falling down. Yellow leaves are falling down, on the ground.

page 3

Green leaves are
falling down,
falling down,
falling down.
Green leaves are
falling down, on
the ground.

page 4

#2311 A Year Full of Themes

Brown leaves are
falling down,
falling down,
falling down.
Brown leaves are
falling down, on
the ground.

page 5

Autumn leaves
are falling down,
falling down,
falling down.
Autumn leaves
are falling down,
on the ground.

page 6

Related Resources

Books

Arnosky, Jim. *Every Autumn Comes the Bear.* Putnam, 1996.

Carle, Eric. *The Tiny Seed.* Scholastic Big Book, 1987.

Charles, Donald. *Calico Cat's Year.* Childrens Press, 1984.

Dillon, Jana. *Jeb Scarecrow's Pumpkin Patch.* Houghton Mifflin, 1992.

Ehlert, Lois. *Red Leaf, Yellow Leaf.* HBJ, 1991.

Fowler, Allan. *How Do You Know It's Fall?* Childrens Press, 1992.

Fowler, Allan. *It Could Still Be a Tree.* Childrens Press, 1990.

Gavan, Peggy. *Seasons.* Troll, 1994.

Gibbons, Gail. *The Seasons of Arnold's Apple Tree.* Harcourt Brace Children's Books, 1988.

Hirschi, Ron. *Fall.* Cobblehill Books, 1991.

Leonard, Marcia. *Bear's Busy Year: A Book About Seasons.* Troll, 1990.

Maas, Robert. *When Autumn Comes.* Henry Holt & Co., 1992.

MacDonald, Sharon. *We Learn About Fall.* D. S. Lake Publishers, 1988.

Munsch, Robert. *Millicent and the Wind.* Annick Press, 1984.

Schnur, Steven. *Autumn: An Alphabet Acrostic.* Clarion, 1997.

Music

Greg and Steve. *Rockin' Down the Road.* "The Green Grass Grew All Around." Youngheart Records, 1995.

Mattox, Cheryl Warren. *Shake It to the One That You Love the Best.* "Bluebird, Bluebird." JTG of Nashville.

Palmer, Hap. *Folk Song Carnival.* "Blue Bird." Educational Activities Inc., Activity Records, 1970.

Raffi. *The Corner Grocery Store.* "My Way Home." Troubadour Records Ltd., 1979.

Tickle Tune Typhoon. *Circle Around.* "Tree Dancin'." Tickle Tune Typhoon Records, 1983.

Software

Changes Around Us. (software about seasons, plants, and families); CD-ROM for WIN or MAC; Sunburst/Edunetics, 101 Castleton Street, P.O. Box 100, Pleasantville, NY 10570-0100; 1-800-321-5711.

Fisher-Price Ready for School (kindergarten activities and lessons related to a calendar and seasons); CD-ROM for MAC, WIN 95, or WIN 3.1; Davidson & Assoc., Inc., Torrance, CA 90503; 1-800-545-7677.

Sammy's Science House. (software about plants, animals, seasons, weather); CD-ROM for MAC, WIN, or DOS; National School Products, 101 East Broadway, Maryville, TN 37804; 1-800-251-9124.

Leaf Patterns

birch

oak

maple

The Very Hungry_____ Big Book Materials

Unit Materials:

— construction paper: white or light colors
— shallow paint containers
— a variety of fruits and vegetables
— white butcher paper

— drawing tools: markers, colored pencils, crayons, chalk
— magazines
— glue
— scissors
— stapler

Extra:

— watercolor paint
— marbles
— cake pan

— spray bottles
— paper plates
— coloring sheets

Optional Materials for Additional Activities:

— packing Styrofoam
— craft sticks
— pencils
— all sizes of pompoms
— different shapes and sizes of wiggle eyes
— colored cotton balls or craft puffs
— pipe cleaners
— clean egg cartons
— cardboard tubes
— bingo markers or dab-type paint bottles
— newspaper
— foil
— slotted clothespins
— 6" (15 cm) paper plates: white or colored without patterns
— feathers
— craft fur
— cotton batting
— yarn

— plastic eggs
— tagboard
— dark-colored balloons
— flour
— items for health/safety baskets (comb, brush, hat, barrette, ponytail holder, straws, spoons, forks, cups, sports drink bottles, lollipop, etc.)
— clay or play dough
— two large boxes of instant chocolate pudding mix
— two boxes of chocolate sandwich cookies
— milk
— small, soft, round candies
— small paper cups
— sleeves cut from a clean, old, child-sized, stretch knit shirt
— hot glue gun
— glue sticks

The Very Hungry_____ Big Book

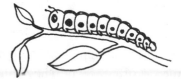

Theme: My World and Me
Topics: Bugs/Insects/Caterpillars/Butterflies
Duration: One Week
Approach: Adapted Story
Combined Illustrations

This next child-created literary effort is a demonstration of how to adapt an existing storybook into big book form. This particular book is an adaptation of Eric Carle's *The Very Hungry Caterpillar* (William Collins & World Publishing Co., 1970).

In Eric Carle's version, the caterpillar nibbles its way through many different foods before it becomes mature and transforms into a butterfly. Since these books should not be lengthy, it is important to keep classroom-made versions of existing stories simple. Try sticking to only one or two changes.

Always pick a favorite story. If you have a specific book in mind but do not get a favorable review from the children, choose another. Once you have a book the children really like and you feel it will be an easy book to adapt, reread the original story to the class. Ask the children what changes they think they would like to make in the story line. The main character is usually a good choice for substitution. In this particular book, the two changes will be the main character and the foods that the main character consumes.

The children can brainstorm the text of the story. You can then adjust the illustrations accordingly. There is a generic, fill-in-the-blanks, pre-written story (pages 97–103) available for you to use. You may wish to reproduce these pages for students, or you can use them as example pages.

If using the text provided, the class should decide as a group what will go in the blanks on pages 2 and 6 of the big book (pages 89, 90, and 91).

Making the Book

COVER PAGE

Activity: Use fruits and vegetables to make prints.

Setup: You'll need a stack of white or light-colored construction paper, shallow paint containers, and a variety of fruits and vegetables. Consider matching the color of paint to the food you are using.

Introduction: Review Eric Carle's story with the children. Explain that since the main character is very hungry, today's activity will involve making prints with food. Show the children the fruits and vegetables. See if they notice whether any of the foods set out for printing are the same as those that were eaten by the caterpillar in the story. You may wish to present a lesson comparing/contrasting fruits and vegetables.

Directions: Ask students if there are other foods that could be used for printing. Inquire which foods might not be good for making prints. Ask them why these types of foods won't work well. Ask them to guess what will happen if you use those foods for printing. As an experiment, try printing with some of the foods that students thought would not make good prints. Have them determine whether their conclusions were correct.

Bulletin Board: Set up a creative art table, layering several sheets of white butcher paper for free printing with the fruits and vegetables. Once covered with prints, the sheets can be attached to a bulletin board as background. After the bulletin board is covered, cut up any remaining pieces to send home and/or add to a Cut, Color, and Glue Center.

Add an attractive border and a banner of your choice. You may wish to use the following poem on the bulletin board.

> One thing that's important to know,
>
> Fruits and vegetables help us grow.

Attach student projects, such as the egg carton or cardboard tube caterpillars (pages 92 and 93), to the bulletin board. Create a banner using Eric Carle's book title *The Very Hungry Caterpillar.*

Note: Save circle prints from fruits and vegetables, such as cucumbers, oranges, and zucchini, for a shape book (pages 227–236).

Making the Book (cont.)

PAGE 1

Text: Once upon a time there was an egg.

Activity: Provide any creative, flat art activity. Some suggestions include felt pen or crayon art, bingo marker art, sponge painting, watercolor painting, marble painting, or spray bottle art. Encourage students to use primary colors.

Setup: Prepare the work area to suit the art activity you have chosen.

Introduction: Review Eric Carle's story *The Very Hungry Caterpillar*. Discuss other living things that come from eggs. Read the book *Chickens Aren't the Only Ones* by Ruth Heller (Putnam, 1981). Discuss the story. Tell children that they will be making egg pictures for page 1 of their big books.

Directions: You can choose to do this activity using one of the following.

1. The art activity can be designed on precut egg shapes that can be glued onto a big book sheet, once dry.

2. Trace an egg shape onto the back of the papers that the children will be using for their art projects. The children can cut out their own egg shapes after their designs have dried. Then glue their pages onto the big book sheets. If large sheets of construction paper are used for the creative art experience, the egg can be traced on one half, and the children can take home the other half.

3. The outline of an egg can be drawn directly on the big book page. Then the children can decorate their eggs by coloring or painting inside the outline. Since this tends to be a difficult task, it may be more appropriate for older students.

Note: Some children may want to make their eggs look cracked. This can be accomplished by either cutting a zigzag line through the egg or using a black crayon or permanent marker to draw a jagged line across the egg. Then glue down the egg.

PAGE 2

Text: One day, out of the egg popped a _____ .

Activity: Have students pick the main character for their stories. For instance, they may want the main character to be a monster. Have students as a group select a word, such as monster, for the blank. Write the word for each child. Then ask students to pick an activity to produce the corresponding illustration.

Setup: Prepare the work area to suit the art activity that the children have chosen.

Making the Book *(cont.)*

PAGE 2 *(cont.)*

Introduction: Review the adapted version of the story with the children. Let them know that on this day they will be illustrating page 2, which shows the main character each of them has chosen for their stories.

Directions: The illustrations for this page and its related activities depend on what kind of main characters the children have chosen. Using the monster character as an example, you can have students do one of the following: make illustrations of monsters using markers, pencils, chalk, or crayons; decorate monsters that are precut or cut and decorate pre-traced monsters; make and decorate paper plate monsters; color outline pictures of monsters; design and paint monsters; trace monster stencils.

The chosen activity can be glued onto or created directly on large pieces of construction paper.

Note: You may wish to play some songs about monsters during this activity. See the Related Resources (page 104) for suggestions.

PAGES 3, 4, and 5

Text:

Page 3—It was a very hungry _____ . On the first day, it ate _____ .
Page 4—On the second day, it ate _____ .
Page 5—On the third day, it ate _____ . Before going to sleep that night, it said,
"_____ ."

Ask the children what words they want to use to fill in the blanks. Then write the words for them.

Activity: Cut and paste magazine pictures.

Setup: Set out scissors, glue, a stack of construction paper, and several magazines.

Note: This activity takes time to do. Although some children can quickly search for and cut out their pictures, others may take much longer. This project is something that can be set out for the entire week or several consecutive days so all students have an opportunity to find the pictures they want to use without feeling rushed.

Making the Book *(cont.)*

PAGES 3, 4, and 5 *(cont.)*

Introduction: Ask students to recall story facts from *The Very Hungry Caterpillar* by asking if they remember what the caterpillar ate. Have them decide what the characters they have chosen might like to eat. Accept all their suggestions. Tell them that they will be looking through magazines to choose pictures of what their characters want to eat. Explain that the pictures they pick will be glued onto the next three pages of their big books.

Directions: Tell the children to look through the magazines and cut out pictures of things they think their characters would like to eat. They can cut and glue as many or as few pictures as they like. Since this is a fictional story, it should be acceptable if students choose pictures of items that are nonedible or silly.

Since every child's big book will have a different main character and set of pictures, it will take some time to write the word choices in the blanks of the text. The easiest way to do this is to fill in the blanks and glue on the text page as you discuss why the child chose his/her particular pictures. You may wish to enlist the help of parent volunteers or older students to do the writing.

PAGE 6

Text: When it woke up the next morning, it found that it had turned into a _____ .

Activity: Have students brainstorm a list of characters for the final illustration. Depending on what the class decides to transform the character into, you can follow the same procedure outlined for page 2 of this child-created big book (page 90).

Setup: Prepare the work area to suit the art activity that is chosen.

Introduction: Discuss reality and fantasy. Point out that caterpillars really do turn into butterflies. Ask the children what is real and fanciful about their main characters. Explain that they will complete their big books with this activity.

Directions: Follow the directions for the activity that is chosen.

PUTTING IT ALL TOGETHER

The assembly of this big book is the same as for the other child-created books. Corresponding text and title can be found on pages 97–103. You can have the children help you or utilize parent volunteers.

You may wish to send a note home to parents, explaining the literature connection for this big book. If parents are aware of the book's author and title, they may borrow it from the local library the next time they visit.

Additional Activities

Art/Language

The activities done in combination with this big book should coincide with the topics of both the original story as well as the adapted version written with the children. Since the example provided on pages 90 and 91 uses a monster as the main character, the Additional Activities (pages 92–96) are based on that topic in addition to butterflies, caterpillars, and foods.

Recycled Caterpillars

Have students glue pieces of packing Styrofoam onto craft sticks. Have them add eyes and antennae to create caterpillars.

Blot-Paint Butterflies

Choose one of the following methods to do this activity.

1. Enlarge the Butterfly Pattern (page 105). Trace butterflies onto construction paper. Make one per child. Squirt tempera paints into small, separate containers and add plastic spoons. Instruct the children to spoon two or three colors of paint onto the blank side of the paper. Help students fold the paper in half and press down to spread and blend the colors. Have them open their papers to allow the pictures to dry. Once the paint is dry, have students cut out the butterfly patterns that were traced on the opposite sides.

2. Give each child a pre-traced butterfly to cut out or give them a precut butterfly. The children then spoon the paint onto the cutouts as described above.

Note: You may wish to use neon colors on black construction paper for these butterflies.

Egg Carton Caterpillars

Note: To collect enough egg cartons for this activity, encourage parents to save them, or ask a restaurant that serves breakfast to save them for you.

Cut out six consecutive sections from the bottoms of clean cardboard egg cartons. The children can paint these any color they choose. Once the cartons are dry, students can draw the facial features and add pipe cleaner or paper antennae.

Recycled Clothespin Butterflies

Using scrap paper, newspaper, or magazine pages, cut 9" x 12" (23 cm x 30 cm) sheets. Help children fold these accordion style. Fold each paper in half to form a V-shape. Place glue in the center of the V-shape on both sides of the folded paper. Then clip a slotted clothespin onto the glue. Allow the glue to dry. Then wrap a pipe cleaner around the top of the clothespin, separating the head and body and forming the antennae. Have students add features with a permanent fine or medium point felt-tip marker.

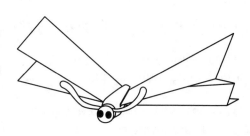

Additional Activities *(cont.)*

Art/Language *(cont.)*

Cardboard Tube Chain Caterpillars

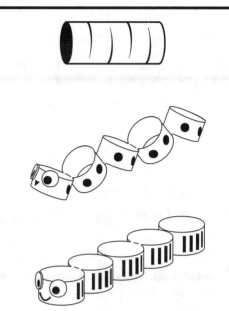

Let the children decorate empty toilet tissue tubes with bingo markers, dab-paint bottles, or felt-tip markers. Once these are dry, flatten the rolls and cut 1" (2.5 cm) slits on alternating sides as shown in the diagram. Fold the rolls accordion style, gluing connected sides together. You may need to use paper clips to hold these in place while the glue dries. Glue the folded rolls onto craft sticks. Have students add beads, wiggle eyes, tiny pompoms, etc., for the eyes. If you choose to keep it simple, all the features can be drawn on, using a felt-tip marker. Pipe cleaners, paper, foil, etc., can be used for the antennae.

Warm Fuzzy Monsters

Set out some inexpensive 6" (15 cm) paper plates and some soft, fuzzy materials such as cotton batting, yarn, colored cotton balls, feathers, fake fur scraps, pompoms, etc. Have the children draw facial features in the center of their plates and glue the soft, fuzzy things around the edge. You may wish to provide wiggle eyes for students to use. Discuss feelings. Ask students what makes them feel warm and fuzzy inside and what makes them feel cold and prickly.

Bulletin Board: Print out or make a banner with a caption of your choice. Arrange all the warm fuzzy monsters on the bulletin board under the banner.

Math/Language

Monster Egg Hunt

Hide some colored plastic eggs around the classroom, and let students search for the monster eggs. Invite students to graph the different colors by taping the eggs onto your flannelboard, wall, or carpet graph (page 15). Using the results, talk about more/less, longer/shorter, and many/few.

Measuring with Monster Feet

Cut out some tagboard monster feet measuring 12" (30 cm) long. Laminate them for better durability. Ask children how many monster feet they think it will take to measure certain items. Then let them use the monster feet to measure the items.

Additional Activities *(cont.)*

Science/Discovery/Language

Health/Safety Concepts

For their individual big books, the children may choose some nonedible items for their main characters to nibble. Those choices are fine for fictional stories, but teach the children about the real dangers of eating these kinds of items. Listed below are some possible health/safety topics you may wish to explore with your class.

- *Poison*—Discuss household items that should not be touched because they are poisonous. Call the Poison Control Center and ask if they can give you some "Mr. Yuk" stickers for your class. Teach the children the universal symbol for "No."

- *Germs*—Talk about coughing and sneezing around food and other people. To illustrate how germs spread, do this activity. Blow up a dark-colored balloon. Sprinkle a little flour on the children's hands. Throw the balloon into the air, and invite students to tap it around the classroom to each other. Ask the children to describe what is happening to the balloon. Discuss how this activity relates to spreading germs.

- *Sharing*—Set out two baskets (red and green, if possible) and various items, some that can be shared and others that can't. Help the children sort the items. Ask them to put items that can be shared in one basket (green) and items that can't be shared in the other (red). Since lice is sometimes a problem at schools, be sure to include a comb, brush, hat, barrette, ponytail scrunchy, etc., in the items for students to sort.

- *Foods That Spoil*—Let the children guess what will happen if certain foods are left out at room temperature for a while. Write down their hypotheses. Leave the foods out, and allow students to observe the changes that take place. Discuss the results.

Clay Creations

Set out some clay or play dough, along with butterfly, caterpillar, monster, and other theme-related cookie cutters. Encourage children to create clay/play dough creatures of their own.

Caterpillar in the Dirt Snacks

Warning: Ask parents if their children have any food allergies or dietary restrictions.

Ingredients: 2 large boxes of instant chocolate pudding mix; 1 box of chocolate sandwich type cookies; milk; soft round candies; small paper cups, one per student

Directions: Finely crush the chocolate sandwich cookies. Pour the pieces into a bowl, place a spoon in it, and set it aside. Tell students that this is the dirt. Using a large bowl, make the pudding mix according to the directions on the box. When the pudding is set, place a spoon in it. Give each child a certain number of candies. There should be enough for each student to make a caterpillar shape by lining up the candies. Help the children spoon some pudding into their cups, and add some crumbled cookies on top. Then have students place the candies in the shape of a caterpillar on top of the "dirt." Now the snacks are ready to eat.

Additional Activities *(cont.)*

Music/Movement/Language

Musical Monster Feet

This activity is played the same way as musical chairs, only instead of sitting on chairs, the children stand on monster feet. This game can be played without losers. Just like musical chairs, a monster foot is taken away after each musical play. Even though there are fewer monster feet, you can still include every child in the game. Have each student not standing on a monster foot touch the actual foot of someone who is already standing on a monster foot.

Note: If you find that children are taking too long trying to decide whose foot they want to touch, try telling them that they only have three seconds. When the music stops, start counting. Depending on the situation, you may want to count faster or slower.

Caterpillar/Butterfly/Monster Dancing

Play music with varying tempos and encourage students to dance like caterpillars, butterflies, and/or monsters.

Follow the Butterfly

If possible obtain a clean, old, stretchy, child-sized long-sleeved shirt. Cut off the sleeves. As an alternative you can cut off the toes from a clean pair of old socks. Cut two pieces of lightweight fabric, like the kind used for curtain sheers, and attach a piece of cloth to each sleeve or sock. You now have butterfly wings. If you can obtain two old square scarves, they also make lovely wings. Instead of sewing, try using a hot glue gun. Choose a leader. The leader inserts his/her arms into the sleeves/socks to become a butterfly and "flies" around the classroom. The other students follow the leader, mimicking his/her movements. Have the children take turns being the leader.

Metamorphosis

Using the butterfly wings described above, have a child pretend to be inside a chrysalis by curling up into a ball and tucking in his/her wings. The rest of the class sings the following song. When the last line is sung, the child can pop out of the chrysalis and pretend to be a butterfly fluttering around. The rest of the class can clap when the word *out* is sung.

Out Comes a Butterfly

Sing to the tune of "Pop Goes the Weasel."

I see a chrysalis,

Hanging up high.

When it is ready,

Out comes a butterfly.

Additional Activities *(cont.)*

Social/Emotional/Language

Caterpillar, Caterpillar, Butterfly

Play the game "duck, duck, goose" by substituting the words, caterpillar, caterpillar, butterfly. The directions for "duck, duck, goose" are provided on page 205.

Egg Piñata

This unit provides many opportunities for egg-related activities, and the following project is sure to be a hit. Set up a center to make an "egg" by covering a balloon with papier mâché. After it hardens, stick a pin in to pop the balloon. Paint the egg-shape whatever colors the children choose. Allow the paint to dry, and then cut a small hole in the egg. Fill it with goodies and replace the piece that covers the hole. Allow students to take turns trying to break it open. Once it is broken, invite the children to get some of the goodies that were inside.

Warning: Be sure to ask parents if their children have any food allergies or dietary restrictions.

Parachute Play

Have one child get under the parachute and pretend to be a caterpillar inside its chrysalis. Everyone else holds the parachute edge loosely against the floor while singing the following song.

Parachute Butterfly

> *Sing to the tune of "Rock-a-Bye-Baby."*
> You are a caterpillar in your cocoon.
> You're getting ready to come out real soon.
> It won't be long before we can spy
> A flittering, fluttering butterfly.

At the end of the song, the parachute is lifted high off the floor, and the child inside comes out and flutters in a circle around the chute once. This can continue with a different volunteer each time for as long as the children show an interest in playing.

The
Very
Hungry

_____

by _____

Once
upon a time,
there was
an egg.

page 1

98

One
day, out
of the egg
popped a

_____

page 2

It was a
very hungry
_____.

On the first
day, it ate
_____.

page 3

On the
second day,
it ate

_____.

page 4

On the third
day, it ate
_____.

Before going
to sleep that
night, it said,
" _____ ."

page 5

102

When it woke up the next morning, it found that it had turned into a

_____.

page 6

Related Resources

Books

Berenstain, Michael. *The Butterfly Book.* Western, 1992.

Carle, Eric. *The Very Hungry Caterpillar.* William Collins & World Publishing Co., 1970.

Gibbons, Gail. *Monarch Butterfly.* Holiday House, 1989.

Heine, Helme. *The Most Wonderful Egg in the World.* Aladdin Books, 1987.

Heller, Ruth. *Chickens Aren't the Only Ones.* Putnam, 1981.

Hoban, Russell. *Monsters.* Scholastic, 1993.

Howe, James. *I Wish I Were a Butterfly.* Harcourt, 1987.

Howe, James. *There's a Monster Under My Bed.* Atheneum, 1986.

Hutchins, Pat. *The Doorbell Rang.* Greenwillow Books, 1986.

Katz, Bobbi. *The Creepy Crawly Book.* Random House, 1989.

Lionni, Leo. *Extraordinary Egg.* Knopf, 1994.

Mayer, Mercer. *A Monster Followed Me to School.* Western, 1991.

Namm, Diane. *Monsters!* Children's Press, 1990.

O'Keefe, Susan H. *One Hungry Monster.* Little, Brown, and Company, 1989.

Sendak, Maurice. *Where the Wild Things Are.* Harper & Row, 1963.

Still, John. *Amazing Butterflies and Moths.* Knopf, 1991.

Watson, Mary. *The Butterfly Seeds.* Tambourine Books, 1995.

Music

Diamond, Charlotte. *10 Carrot Diamond.* "Looking For Dracula" and "Sasquatch." Charlotte Diamond Music, Inc., 1985.

Sesame Street. *"C" Is for Cookie.* "Healthy Food" and "MMM Monster Meal." Children's Television Workshop, 1995.

Tickle Tune Typhoon. *Circle Around.* "The Monster Song." Tickle Tune Typhoon Records, 1983.

Video

Jolly Monsters. (Video about two monster friends); 8 min. Troll Associates, Catalog Sales Dept., 100 Corporate Dr., Mahwah, NJ 07498; 1-800-929-8765.

Very Hungry Caterpillar and Other Stories. (Video version of Eric Carle's story); 25 min. Disney Home Video, 1995.

Software

Jumpstart. (Pre-K activity entitled "Dish Up the Right Order" builds listening, sorting, and sequencing skills using food); CD-ROM for MAC, WIN 95, or WIN 3.1; Knowledge Adventure, Inc., 1311 Grand Central Ave., Glendale, CA 91201; 1-818-246-4400.

Butterfly Pattern

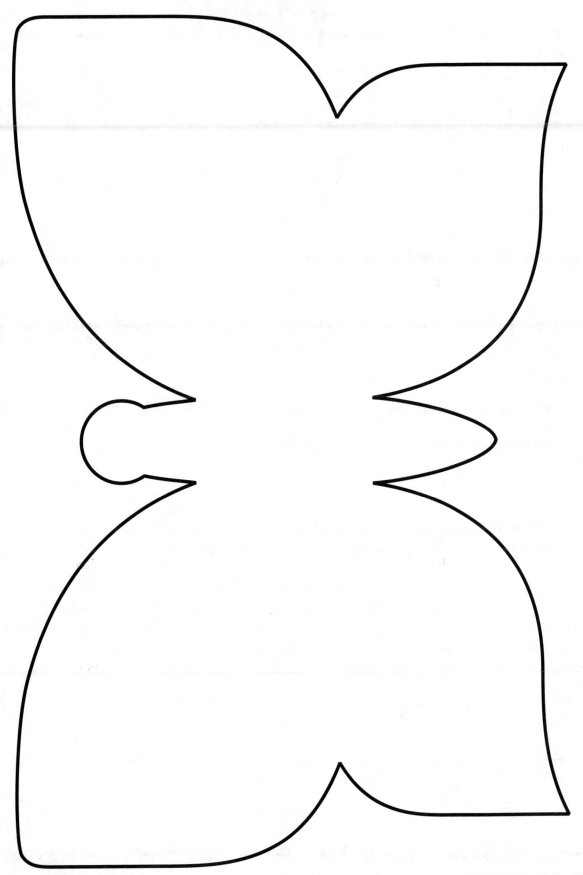

Peanut Butter and Jelly Big Book
Materials

Unit Materials:

— plastic cups
— foil
— grape jelly
— peanut butter
— sliced bread
— light brown, manila, or tan construction paper
— paint: purple, brown, white, red, and blue
— squirt bottles
— crayons: purple and brown
— electric warming tray
— newspaper
— scissors
— glue
— stapler

Extra:

— clean yogurt containers with lids

Optional Materials for Additional Activities:

— unshelled peanuts
— tagboard
— peanut-shaped sponges, like the kind sold for car washing purposes that are wider on the top and bottom and slightly narrower in the center
— drawing tools: crayons, markers, chalk, colored pencils
— felt
— foods with distinct scents, such as coffee grounds, onion, toothpaste, orange, lemon, root beer, cinnamon, mustard, black licorice, peppermint, apples, and celery
— nonedible items with distinct odors such as baby powder, soap, perfume, evergreen sprigs, and flowers
— blender or food processor
— old T-shirt or cloth remnant
— paper grocery bag
— grape juice

Peanut Butter and Jelly Big Book

Theme: Me
Topics: Favorite Foods/Peanut Butter and Jelly
Duration: 3–5 Days
Approach: Original Poem
Creative Art Illustrations

Since the last child-created big book involved foods and monsters, it may have included a discussion about the children's favorite foods. There are many possibilities for creating big books when it comes to the Me theme.

Peanut Butter and Jelly is a quick and easy book about favorite foods. It revolves around the most popular lunchtime sandwich ever. If there were any health activities concerning foods that you did not have time for when creating the last big book, this one provides additional opportunities to complete them.

The following science/discovery activity is a fun way to introduce the topic. Place a little peanut butter in a small cup and a little grape jelly in another. Use foil to cover the cups and poke holes in it with a fork. Yogurt containers with lids can also be used for this purpose.

Warning: If you plan to have the children eat any of the peanut butter and jelly for the big book activities (pages 107–115), be sure to ask their parents if they have any food allergies or dietary restrictions.

Discuss favorite foods with the class. Narrow the conversation down to types of sandwiches. Tell the children that you have some people's favorite foods inside the cups. Invite a volunteer to smell each cup and guess what is inside. Hold the cup containing the peanut butter to the child's nose. You may wish to have more than one child sniff the cup before you reveal its contents. It is interesting to see if all of the students who smelled the peanut butter agree on what they smelled. Take the foil off and show the children what's inside. Do this with the jelly cup as well. You can take it a step farther and ask what flavor of jelly they smell.

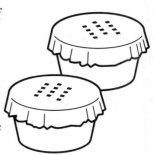

When the above activity is done, tell the children the next big book is only a three-page book, and it is based on the following poem.

Peanut Butter and Jelly

Jelly is purple.
Peanut butter is brown.
Put them together, and hear this sound.
Mmm, mmm, mmm!

Making the Book

COVER PAGE

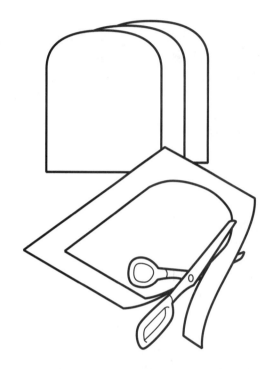

Before beginning this book, take some light brown, manila, or tan construction paper and cut it into the shape of sliced bread. To do this, simply round off the corners on top and narrow the sides a bit. Make sure you have four sheets for each child making a big book.

Activity: Make an easel painting with brown and purple.

Setup: Place small containers of purple and brown paint on the easel tray. The children will paint on the bread-shaped paper.

Introduction: A good way to introduce this page of the big book is to choose a motivational activity, such as Crunchy/Smooth Snacks (page 114), from the Additional Activities section (pages 111–115).

Directions: Tell the children the easel will be set up with paints that are the same colors as peanut butter and grape jelly. Review these colors with them. Let two children paint simultaneously. Give one child the container of brown paint, the other the container of purple. Each child then free-paints, using the given color. After a few minutes, have the children switch colors to complete their paintings.

PAGE 1

Text: Jelly is purple.

Activity: Mix red and blue paints to make purple.

Setup: Set out squirt bottles containing red and blue tempera paints. Turquoise works well for the blue. Bring out the construction paper slices of bread. You may also wish to have some finger-paint paper handy.

Note: You can obtain squirt bottles by recycling empty saline solution bottles. If you do not know anyone who wears contact lenses, go to eye care specialists and ask if they can donate their empty bottles. If you need to enlarge the openings at the tops of these bottles for the paint, use a math compass or the point of a darning needle.

Introduction: Review the "Peanut Butter and Jelly" poem with the children. Explain that they will be finger-painting the jelly page of their books. Ask them what color they think they will be using. Explain that they will be making purple paint for this activity. Do not give them any additional explanation. Let the children's curiosity lead them to the lesson.

Making the Book *(cont.)*

PAGE 1 (cont.)

Directions: Give each child one big book page. Squirt little puddles of blue and red paint side by side on their bread-shaped pages. Invite the children to use their hands to mix the two colors together. Call their attention to the two colors blending together to make the color purple. Have them spread the jelly on the page, leaving a small portion of the paper's edge unpainted.

Some children may want to continue painting once their bread page is done. If this is the case, hand them some finger-paint paper. These sheets, which will not be used for the big book, can be sent home after they dry.

PAGE 2

Text: Peanut butter is brown.

Activity: Mix and paint with a tone. (Tones are colors mixed with white.)

Setup: You will need squirt bottles of brown and white tempera paints, a jar of real peanut butter, and the bread-shaped construction paper.

Introduction: Review the "Peanut Butter and Jelly" poem. Review the jelly page activity described above. Tell the children that they will be making their peanut butter pages. Ask them what color peanut butter is. Bring out some brown paint. Have students compare it to the actual color of real peanut butter. Point out that the peanut butter is a lighter brown.

Remind the children that when they made their jelly pages, they mixed the two colors red and blue to make purple. Explain to students that during this activity, they will not be changing the name of the color; they will just be adding white paint to make it lighter.

Directions: Squirt little puddles of brown and white paint side by side on their bread-shaped pages. Let the children mix the colors together by using their fingers or paintbrushes. Discuss how the brown paint is changing. Ask, "Which color looks more like real peanut butter, the original brown or the light brown tone?"

Making the Book *(cont.)*

PAGE 3

Text: Put them together, and hear this sound. Mmm, mmm, mmm!

Activity: Make melted crayon drawings using purple and brown crayons.

Setup: You need an electric warming tray for this activity. Set out purple and brown wax crayons with the wrappers removed.

Note: Warming trays can be expensive. However, they are sometimes more reasonably priced at yard/garage sales, church bazaars, and flea markets.

Introduction: A good way to begin this project is to start with a peanut butter and jelly snack if students don't have any food allergies or dietary restrictions that would prevent them from doing so. Cut up some sandwiches into small, bite-sized pieces and offer one to each child. If possible, play a song about peanut butter and/or jelly. See the Related Resources (page 120) for suggestions. Ask students to pantomime the actions described in the song. Review the "Peanut Butter and Jelly" poem with the children as they create their last big book pages.

Warning: Cover the warming tray with newspaper to protect the children from the heat. The following activity requires strict supervision. To help avoid accidents, allow only a few students near the warming tray at one time.

Directions: Turn on the warming tray, covered with newspaper, to a low setting. Place a bread-shaped piece of construction paper on the newspaper that covers the tray. A child will hold a crayon on the bread-shaped paper and slowly glide it along the tray. Ask the children what the melted purple and brown crayons look like.

Alternatives: If you are unable to obtain a warming tray or feel that it unsafe to use one in your classroom, blot paintings or straw paintings make good alternatives.

PUTTING IT ALL TOGETHER

Since this big book only consists of three pages and the poem is simple to remember, the children should have an easy time assembling the book themselves. As students put the three pages in order, review how they got the color purple for the first page. Ask if they remember how brown became a light brown for page two. As the children organize the pages according to the sequence of the poem, talk about some of the activities, projects, and experiments that were done during the production of this big book. Ask the children to tell you what their most/least favorite activity was. You may wish to make notes for future reference. Coordinating the title and text (pages 116–119) with the art is the same as for other big books. Once the pages are in order, staple them together. Then read the book with the students.

Additional Activities

Art/Language

Crunchy Collage

Have students arrange empty peanut shells on sheets of tagboard or scrap cardboard. Once they are satisfied with their designs, tell them to glue the shells in place to create a textured collage.

Peanut People

Cut sponges into peanut shapes or purchase the kind used for washing cars. Then invite students to use the sponges and containers of light brown tempera paint to make pictures of a large peanut. Once the paintings are dry, the children can add arms, legs, facial features, hats, bow ties, clothing, etc., to their peanut people. This can be done using any combination of markers, crayons, paint bottles or precut paper shapes.

Math/Language

Velcro® Mat or Flannelboard Peanuts

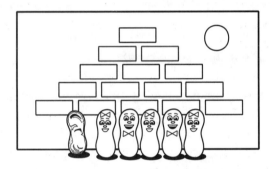

Make a sun by cutting out a yellow circle from felt or poster board. Outline it with either gold, bright orange, or yellow paint. Then cut out fifteen red brick shapes from felt or poster board. Then using the patterns (page 121), make six light-brown felt or poster board peanuts.

If you use poster board for the sun, bricks, and peanuts, decorate them with markers or tempera paints. When the pieces are dry, laminate them and put Velcro® on the backs. You will need to place Velcro® on both sides of the peanut. Try to incorporate the Velcro® as part of the picture so it will not be noticeable. For example, when looking at the front of a peanut, attach the Velcro® so it looks like buttons. On the puddle side, cut black or blue Velcro® so it looks like water droplets.

If you copied the patterns onto felt, decorate them with colored fabric paints. Once the front of the peanuts are dry, flip them over horizontally and turn them into puddles of peanut butter by decorating the backsides according to the patterns.

Note: Use the fabric paint sparingly. If too much paint is used and not enough felt is left exposed, the pieces will not adhere to the flannelboard.

Arrange the bricks on the flannelboard, pyramid fashion, and place the six peanuts in front of the bricks. Add the sun somewhere above the bricks.

Recite the poem on page 112, turning the peanuts over and laying them on their sides when saying the last line.

Additional Activities *(cont.)*

Math/Language *(cont.)*

Peanut Puddles

Use the cutouts to review sizes and shapes. If reinforcing colors is a top priority, consider making the brick wall out of differently colored rectangles instead of red. Ordinal numbers, such as first and second, can be reinforced as you place the peanuts side by side. Depending on where you place the sun, the concepts of left and right can also be emphasized.

Peanut Puddles

A group of peanuts, there were six,
Stood side by side near a wall of bricks.
When all of a sudden, a brick did drop,
Making peanut butter with a plop.
Five little peanuts in a line
Didn't think it would happen a second time,
But another loose brick came tumbling down,
Leaving peanut butter on the ground.
Four little peanuts wondering why,
Upon the ground, their friends did lie.
Then another brick fell. What a sight!
Three peanuts left, all shaking with fright.
Three little peanuts stood near the wall.
Then one more brick began to fall.
It came down fast. It came down hard.

Another splat was heard in the yard.
Two little peanuts stood side by side.
"Hey, watch out!" one of them cried.
Another brick, just like the rest,
Came falling down to leave a mess.
One little peanut stood all alone.
It looked up and let out a groan.
Too late to run, too late to dash,
It's peanut butter with a splash.
It's not terrible, so didn't feel bad.
Peanut butter's good. So smile, be glad.
It's okay, and it's all right,
You can have a taste. You can take a bite.
Nuts are food we're supposed to eat.
Add a little jelly, and have yourself a treat.

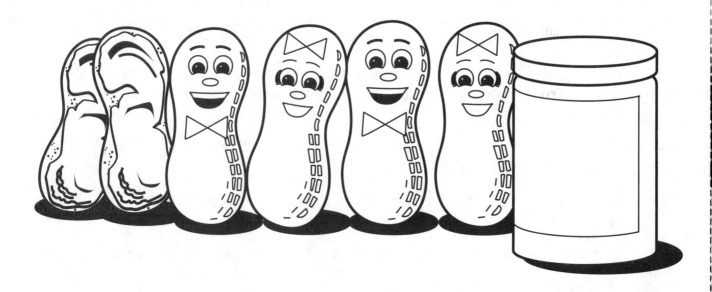

Additional Activities *(cont.)*

Science/Discovery/Language

Guess the Smell

Use the same activity as was described for introducing this big book (page 107), using other interesting foods and scents.

Note: Using small covered yogurt containers with holes poked in the lids makes these sensory cups more durable.

Consider including some or all of the following: coffee grounds, onion, garlic, unwrapped bubble gum, slice or wedge of orange, cinnamon or cinnamon bread, chocolate, mustard, ketchup, relish or pickles, and black licorice jelly beans sliced in half.

You may wish to add some nonfood items such as baby powder, rubbing alcohol-soaked cotton ball, soap, perfume, and pine needles.

Make It Myself Sandwich

Bring in a loaf of bread, a jar of peanut butter, and a jar of jelly. Cut the slices in half and give each child both halves. Discuss the concept of two halves equals one whole. Let them scoop and spread a little peanut butter onto one half and a little jelly onto the other. If students prefer, they can make sandwiches with only one ingredient—peanut butter or jelly. Then allow the children to eat their sandwiches for snack.

Nutty Discoveries

Set out a variety of shelled and unshelled nuts on the discovery table. Leave magnifying glasses on the table also. Discuss sizes, shapes, textures, and colors. Children can observe, compare, sort, categorize, etc.

Make a Venn diagram by overlapping two large circles made from colored tape or drawn with colored chalk. Then students can use this graphic organizer for the sorting task described above.

Peanut Butter from Scratch

Ingredients: 1 cup (225 grams) of nuts, 1–2 tablespoons (15–30 mL) of oil

Optional: salt and/or sugar

Directions: Place the nuts in a blender. Add the oil. Blend the mixture until it is crunchy or smooth. Add a pinch of salt and/or sugar if desired.

Additional Activities *(cont.)*

Science/Discovery/Language *(cont.)*

Will It Stain?

Ask the children what will happen if they drop some peanut butter or jelly on their clothes. Tell them that they will participate in an experiment to find out. Have a child spread a little peanut butter and some jelly on an old T-shirt, cotton rag, or cloth remnant. Leave it there for a day or two. Then try to wash off the food. Discuss what happens.

Crunchy/Smooth Snacks

Help students spread some peanut butter on apple slices or pieces of celery. Serve this snack with grape juice.

Social/Emotional/Language

Color Day

Have a purple and brown day. Send the letter home to parents (page 45) announcing this event. Ask half the class to wear purple clothes and the other half to wear brown clothes on a date that you specify.

Peanut Hunt

Hide some peanuts outside or around the classroom. Have the children pretend they are hungry elephants and send them searching for the peanuts. You can use actual shelled peanuts, candy peanuts, or peanut shapes cut out from paper, using the patterns on page 121. If paper peanuts are used, make them different colors and laminate them.

Theme Bingo

Cut peanut shapes out of a variety of colors. Glue these onto the Bingo Card (page 336) to make a bingo or lotto game to reinforce colors.

Additional Activities *(cont.)*

Music/Movement/Language

Elephant Parade

Play some upbeat music and have the children hold their arms out in front, hands together, and swing their arms like elephant trunks. Instruct them to make elephant noises and lift their legs way up high while moving to the music.

I'm a Little Elephant

Sing to the tune of "I'm a Little Teapot."

I'm a little elephant with lots of spunk, *(Point to self and then place hands on hips.)*

These are my ears, and this is my trunk, *(Place hands on top of head; then hang head down and place arms together in front of head.)*

When I'm feeling happy, I like to jump, *(Point to smile and jump up and down.)*

Watch me stomp and hear me thump. *(Stomp feet while marching in place.)*

Note: With some minimal changes to the lyrics, this song can be used to reinforce numbers. Start with one child at the front of the class, acting out the song.

One little elephant with lots of spunk,

Great big ears and a big long trunk,

When he/she feels happy, he/she likes to jump,

Watch him/her stomp and hear him/her thump.

Then add a second child to the front of the classroom, and use the following lyrics.

Two little elephants with lots of spunk,

Great big ears and big long trunks,

When they're feeling happy, they like to jump,

Watch them stomp and hear them thump.

Continue the song, adding another elephant each time.

Feed the Elephant

Attach a picture of an elephant onto a paper grocery bag. Provide peanuts that are still in the shells. Let the children take turns tossing peanuts into the bag.

Peanut Butter and Jelly

by _____

116

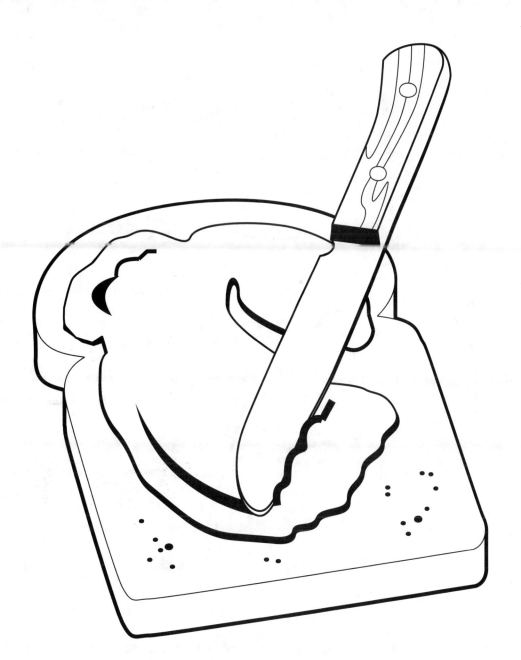

Jelly is purple.

page 1

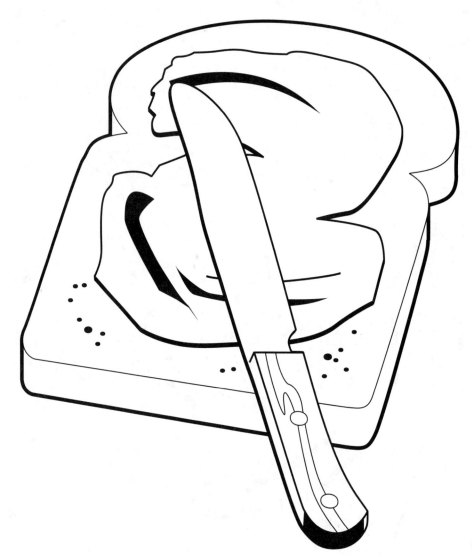

Peanut butter is brown.

page 2

Put them together,
and hear this sound.
Mmm, mmm, mmm!

page 3

Related Resources

Books

Aliki. *My Five Senses.* Harper & Row, 1984.

Baer, Edith. *This Is the Way We Eat Our Lunch.* Scholastic, 1995.

Degan, Bruce. *Jamberry.* HarperCollins, 1998.

Ehlert, Lois. *Eating the Alphabet.* HBJ, 1989.

Ehlert, Lois. *Nuts to You.* HBJ, 1993.

Fechner, Amrei. *I Am a Little Elephant.* Barron, 1984.

Fowler, Allan. *Tasting Things.* Children's Press, 1991.

Hoban, Russell. *Bread and Jam for Frances.* Harper & Row, 1964.

Lord, John V. *The Giant Jam Sandwich.* Houghton Mifflin Co., 1987.

Munch, Robert. *Something Good.* Annick Press Ltd., 1991.

Pluckrose, Henry. *Tasting.* Morrow, 1995.

Smith, Kathie B. *Rand McNally Question Books: The Senses.* Macmillan, 1986.

Westcott, Nadine Bernard. *Peanut Butter and Jelly.* Dutton, 1987.

Music

Fingerplays and Footplays for Fun and Learning. "Peanut Butter." Activity Records, Inc., 1987.

The Learning Station. *Where Is Thumbkin?* "Peanut Butter." Kimbo, 1996.

Penner, Fred. *Collections.* "Sandwiches." Oak Street Music/Dino Music, 1992.

Raffi. *The Corner Grocery Store.* "Going on a Picnic." Troubadour Records Ltd., 1979.

Raffi. *Singable Songs for the Very Young.* "Peanut Butter Sandwich." Shoreline Records, 1976.

Wee Sing Silly Songs. "Peanut on a Railroad Track." Price, Stern, Sloan, 1986.

Video

You and Your Five Senses. (Videotape/Videodisc by Disney Educational Products); 13 min. Available from Coronet/MTI Film and Video, P.O. Box 2649, Columbus, OH 43216; 1-800-321-3106.

Software

Elmo's Preschool Deluxe. (by Sesame Street Learning Series; listening skills, following directions, understanding food groups); WIN 95 or WIN 3.1; Available from Creative Wonders, ABC Electronic Arts, P.O. Box 9017, Redwood City, CA 94063-9017; 1-800-KID-XPRT.

Peanut Patterns

Back

Front

Front

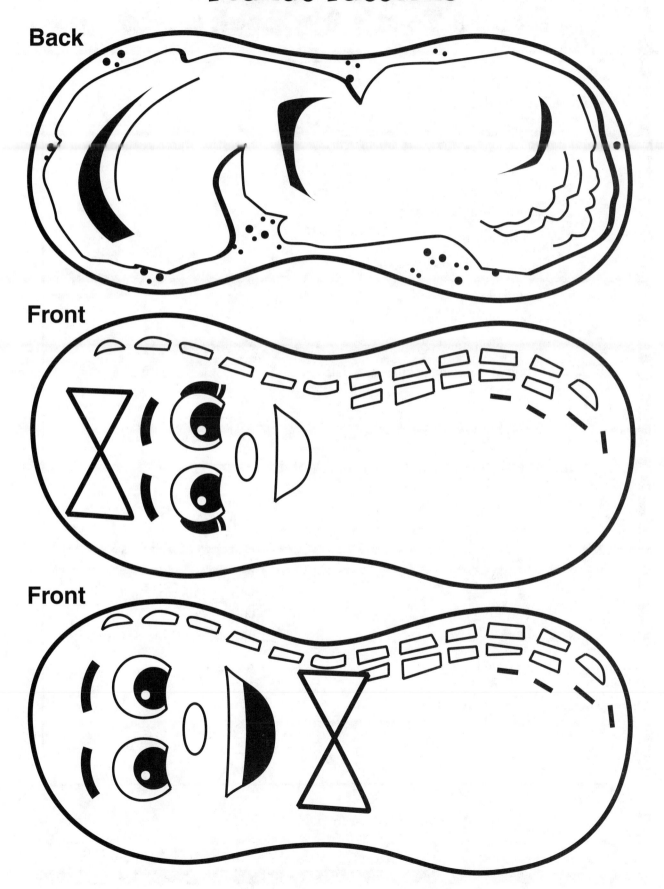

Happy Teeth Big Book Materials

Unit Materials:

— magazines

— scissors

— glue

— construction paper: various colors

— old toothbrushes

— paper craft straws

— tagboard

— paint: white and various colors

— large, black markers

— white Styrofoam packing material

Extra:

— empty roll-on deodorant bottles

Optional Materials for Additional Activities:

— small disposable cups

— empty toothpaste boxes

— paper scraps

— poster board

— 2 small hoops

— baking soda

— hydrogen peroxide

— white/off-white floor or wall tiles

— crunchy/chewy foods: carrot sticks, raisins, etc.

— yarn or thin macramé cord

— buttons

— mouthwash

Happy Teeth Big Book

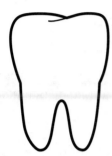

Theme: Me
Topics: Oral Hygiene/Teeth
Duration: One Week
Approach: Original Poem
          Creative-Combination Activities

Since some of the units included in this book deal with foods and contain activities involving sweets, you may want to discuss good oral hygiene and do some or all of the following activities (pages 124–131) with your class. This next child-created big book was designed specifically for that purpose.

You can introduce this unit by having the school nurse or a local dentist come in and talk to your students about proper dental care. In addition, consider showing one of the videos suggested in the Related Resources (page 138).

The poem shown below consists of five lines. Each page of text for the big book is a single line of this poem. At the beginning of this unit, read the poem to the children. Explain to students what this book will include, and ask them to suggest titles. Once the title is selected, print out a title sheet on the computer or make one by hand and reproduce it. If you prefer to skip the brainstorming exercise, give students copies of the title page provided in this book (page 132).

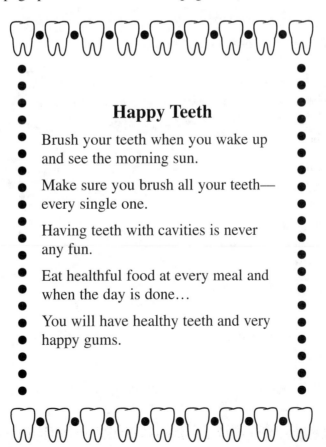

Happy Teeth

Brush your teeth when you wake up
and see the morning sun.

Make sure you brush all your teeth—
every single one.

Having teeth with cavities is never
any fun.

Eat healthful food at every meal and
when the day is done…

You will have healthy teeth and very
happy gums.

Making the Book

COVER PAGE

Activity: Make a smile collage.

Setup: Set out scissors, glue, large construction paper, and several magazines containing an abundance of people pictures.

Introduction: Explain to the children that this book focuses on taking care of teeth and the importance of a good smile. Ask them about their experiences at the dentist's office. Ask if they have toothbrushes at home and what their favorite brand/flavor of toothpaste is. Allow them to share their personal experiences with dental care. Tell them that they will be decorating the cover page of their big books today.

Directions: Have each child point to her/his own mouth and then teeth. Flip through a magazine until you find a closeup of a smiling person. Show students the picture of the person. Ask a volunteer to come up and point to the smile. Do this a few times, having different children point to the people's smiles in a variety of pictures. Tell the children that they will be cutting smiles out of magazines and gluing them onto their cover pages.

PAGE 1 (PART 1)

Text: Brush your teeth when you wake up and see the morning sun.

Activity: Make a toothbrush painting at the easel or a toothbrush splatter painting.

Setup: Set out large sheets of blue construction paper and bright orange paint in small, shallow containers along with some toothbrushes. Splatter painting can be messy, so make sure students have smocks to wear.

Introduction: Explain to the class that one of the best times to brush their teeth is first thing in the morning upon awakening. Recite the "Happy Teeth" poem (page 123). Review the first line of the poem and let the children know those will be the words for the first page of their new big books.

Let them know that toothbrush painting is the activity prepared for the day to make the first part of page 1.

Note: If some children do not want to do the splatter painting, they can skip it and go on to the next step for page 1 of their big books (page 125).

Making the Book *(cont.)*

PAGE 1 (PART 1, cont.)

Directions: For many children, splatter painting may be their chosen activity. For this paperplay, have the children dip their toothbrushes into the paint container. Have them hold their brushes so the bristles are facing down over the paper. Tell them to run their thumbs lightly over the bristles, causing the paint to splatter onto the paper. Allow the paint to dry.

For other children, toothbrush painting at the easel may be their chosen activity. For this paperplay, simply clip the blue paper onto the easel and substitute toothbrushes for paintbrushes. Allow the children to free-paint with the toothbrushes. Let the paint dry before continuing to the next step.

PAGE 1 (PART 2)

Activity: Tear paper to make a sun.

Setup: Set out the previously completed toothbrush paintings along with some yellow scrap paper. You will also need glue and round items such as plastic saucers, margarine lids, and masking tape rolls that can be used for tracing circles.

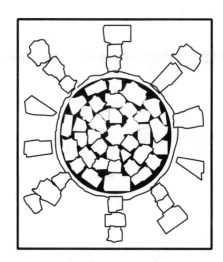

Introduction: Recite the "Happy Teeth" poem (page 123). Restate the first line of the poem and explain to students that they will be using the items on the table to make a sun on their papers. Ask them how they think the round items will be used. Discuss their suggestions.

Directions: Let students choose the items they would like to use to trace their suns. Provide assistance as needed. Explain that they will tear the yellow paper into small pieces and glue these inside the circle that was traced on their papers.

The children will practice their fine motor skills by tearing and gluing the little pieces of yellow paper in order to fill in the circle. Once this is completed, they may wish to add rays of light coming out of their suns, using the same "tear and glue" method. Other options include cutting and gluing small yellow rectangles or simply painting on the rays with rolling or sponge-tip paint bottles.

Timesaver: You can make your own rolling paint bottle. First, pop the ball off the top of an empty roll-on deodorant container. Thoroughly clean and dry the ball and container. Then fill the container with some diluted tempera paint and replace the ball. Tightly screw the lid onto the container until students are ready to use it. Use a permanent black marker to label the outside of the container with the paint color.

Making the Book *(cont.)*

PAGE 2

Text: Make sure you brush all your teeth—every single one.

Activity: Cut and paste a toothbrush.

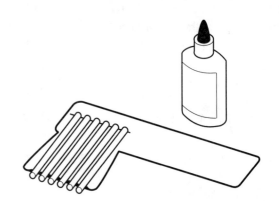

Setup: Using the pattern (page 139), trace and cut one toothbrush per child out of various colors of poster board and draw a line straight across the handle. This designates where the bristles will go. Cut craft straws that are approximately 2.5–4" (6.3–10.5 cm) long, and place these into containers on the paperplay table. Students will also need some glue.

Introduction: Review everything that's been covered thus far about caring for teeth. Recite the "Happy Teeth" poem (page 123). Restate the second line and explain that the paperplay activity scheduled today is based on this line and that it will become page 2 of their big books.

Directions: Give each child a poster board toothbrush and explain that they will be gluing the bristles onto the brush. Direct their attention to the line that was drawn across the handle. Explain that the tip or end of each straw should be glued on that line. Demonstrate for students how to do this. Point out that the bristles will be uneven at the top. Assure students that once the glue is dry, you will help them trim the straws so they are even.

PAGE 3 (PART 1)

Text: Having teeth with cavities is never any fun.

Activity: Make a painting using a toothbrush.

Setup: Set out small containers of white tempera paint and toothbrushes. Trace the Tooth Pattern (page 140) on manila tagboard, making one tooth per child.

Note: For younger children, you may want to precut the teeth. For older children, you may want to improve their fine motor skills by having them do the cutting themselves.

Introduction: Recite "Happy Teeth" poem (page 123), and restate the third line. Explain that lack of brushing or improper brushing can contribute to cavities. Discuss the proper way to brush teeth.

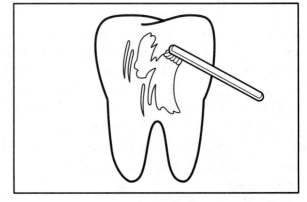

Directions: Tell students that they will be making these teeth the whitest they can be. Have the children dip the toothbrushes into the white paint. Ask them to use up-and-down strokes to whiten the manila-colored teeth. Let the paint dry.

Making the Book *(cont.)*

PAGE 3 (PART 2)

Activity: Draw a sad face.

Setup: Bring out the dry toothbrush paintings. Set out some black markers, glue, and large sheets of colored construction paper.

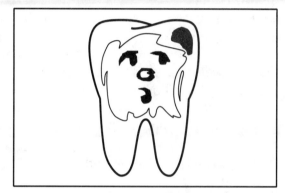

Introduction: Recite the "Happy Teeth" poem (page 123), and restate the third line. Remind the children that cavities are not something anyone would want. Point out that the teeth in today's activity are very sad because they have cavities.

Directions: Have the children glue their teeth onto the big book page. Explain that each one of them should draw a cavity and a sad face on the tooth. This will complete the illustration for page 3 of their big books.

PAGE 4

Text: Eat healthful food at every meal and when the day is done…

Activity: Cut and paste magazine pictures.

Setup: Set out magazines, scissors, glue, and a stack of construction paper.

Introduction: Recite the "Happy Teeth" poem (page 123), and call attention to the fourth line. Talk to your class about food choices that help keep teeth healthy.

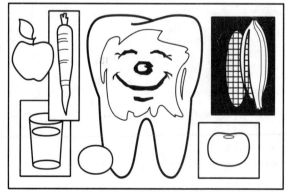

Directions: Tell the children they will be cutting pictures out of magazines for their big books. Explain that they must choose pictures that show healthful foods for happy and healthy teeth.

Variations: These pictures can be glued directly onto the big book page in collage fashion, or they can be glued onto a tooth shape. The pattern on page 140 can be enlarged, cut, and glued onto a large sheet of construction paper. Then the magazine pictures can be glued onto the tooth.

Note: The children may wish to use markers or crayons to draw happy faces on these teeth.

Making the Book *(cont.)*

PAGE 5

Text: You will have healthy teeth and very happy gums.

Activity: Cut and paste a mouth.

Setup: Using the pattern on page 141, trace one mouth per child out of red construction paper. Set out scissors and small, white pieces of packing Styrofoam.

Introduction: Recite the "Happy Teeth" poem (page 123), and restate the last line. Review everything that has been covered thus far concerning good oral hygiene. This is also a good time to do one of the lessons in the Additional Activities section, such as "Strong Teeth" (page 130).

Directions: The children cut and glue the mouth on any color of large construction paper. Once the mouth is glued, have the children add rows of teeth by gluing the individual pieces of Styrofoam onto the the top and bottom rows of teeth.

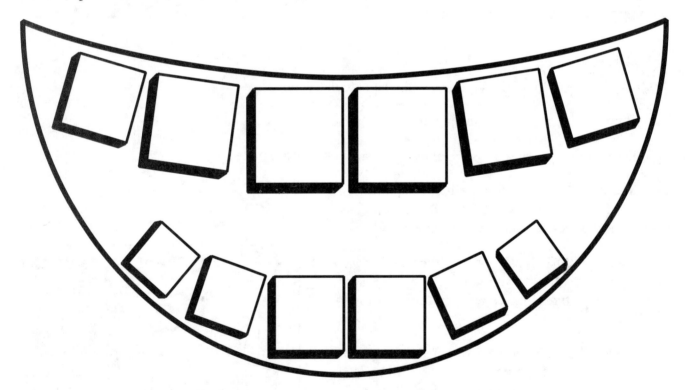

PUTTING IT ALL TOGETHER

Review the "Happy Teeth" poem (page 123), and bring out all Happy Teeth illustrations that students have made for their big books. Sequence the pages, beginning with the cover, as you review the poem. Discuss/review some of the activities that the children did during this unit.

Staple the pages together and glue on the text (pages 132–137) opposite the appropriate illustrations.

Additional Activities

Art/Language

Bathroom Cup Circles

Pour a variety of paint colors into some shallow containers. Place an upside-down bathroom cup in each container. Poke a small hole in the bottom of the cup to allow the passage of air and prevent the cup from sticking in the paint. Have the children pick up the cup from the paint and press the rim lightly onto the paper to make circle paints.

Note: You may want to save these prints for a long-term shape book (pages 227–236).

Painting with White

Since the topic is teeth, set up the easel or a finger-painting table with white paint and let the children free paint on colored construction paper. Once these sheets are dry, bring them out and have students compare them to see which papers have the whitest white. Remind the children that the paint used for the activity was exactly the same. Ask students if some of the paint on the paperplay appears whiter and brighter. See if they can determine what the background color has to do with the whitening quality and appearance of the paint.

Toothpaste Box Instruments

Collect enough boxes from tubes of toothpaste so each child can have one. You may want to ask parents to help with this. Place a few beans or grains of rice inside the box and seal the ends with glue and/or tape. Encourage the children to decorate the boxes in any way they choose. Some ideas include painting the boxes with a mixture of white glue and tempera, gluing tissue paper squares on them, or covering them with colorful scrap collages. Use the instruments for the "Strong Teeth" activity in the Music/Movement/Language section (page 130).

Math/Language

Graphic Organizer

Overlap two small hoops to form a Venn diagram. If hoops are not available, draw a Venn diagram on poster board. Precut and laminate a variety of food pictures. Place all foods in the center of the diagram. On an index card, draw a happy tooth and write the word *happy*. On a separate card, draw a sad tooth and write the word *sad*. Place these at the top of the other sections of the diagram. Review the foods that make teeth strong and happy as well as foods that can contribute to cavities and make teeth weak and sad. In small groups, have a child choose a picture from the center pile, name it, and then decide on which side of the diagram it belongs. Ask her/him to place the picture in the appropriate section of the Venn diagram.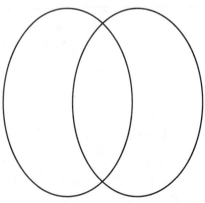

Additional Activities *(cont.)*

Science/Discovery/Language

Homemade Toothpaste

Make toothpaste with the children by mixing together baking soda with a little hydrogen peroxide. Acquire some white or off-white mosaic tiles from your local tile store. Try staining them with various foods. Let the children brush away the stains with the homemade toothpaste.

Crunchy/Chewy

Discuss how teeth help us to eat. Ask the children if they think they could eat a hamburger or celery stick without chewing. Show the class which teeth are used for biting and which are used for chewing. Check for food allergies or dietary restrictions before giving each child a carrot stick and some raisins. Ask them which food will make more noise when it is eaten. Discuss the differences between crunchy and chewy foods. Using the voting/graphing board (page 17), find out if the children like the crunchy carrots or the chewy raisins better. Discuss the results.

Music/Movement/Language

Toothpaste Box Instruments

Make the instruments as directed in the Art/Language section (page 129). The following can be used for parade activities as well. You can substitute the body motions of your choice.

Strong Teeth

Sing to the tune of "The More We Get Together."

Milk has lots of calcium, calcium, calcium.
Milk has lots of calcium. It's good for our teeth.
So clap once *(clap)* and clap twice *(clap twice)*. Milk is very nice.
Milk has lots of calcium. It's good for our teeth.
Nuts have lots of calcium, calcium, calcium.
Nuts have lots of calcium. They're good for our teeth.
So snap once *(snap fingers)* and snap twice *(snap twice)*. Nuts are very nice.
Nuts have lots of calcium. They're good for our teeth.
Cheese has lots of calcium, calcium, calcium.
Cheese has lots of calcium. It's good for our teeth.
So stomp once *(stomp)* and stomp twice *(stomp twice)*. Cheese is very nice.
Cheese has lots of calcium. It's good for our teeth.

Bathroom Cup Catch

Tie one end of a short piece of thin macramé cord or yarn to a button and the other end to a small paper cup such as the kind used in bathroom dispensers. Have the children try to catch the button in the cup by swinging the string slowly and moving the cup into the correct position.

Additional Activities *(cont.)*

Social/Emotional/Language

Dentist Stories

Ask children to share their experiences about visiting the dentist. Discuss the importance of seeing the dentist even when their teeth feel and look fine. Talk about the role of the dental hygienist and the importance of getting teeth cleaned. If possible, show the children actual dental x-rays. Explain how the dentist uses these to see what is going on inside the teeth.

Oral Hygiene

Review what helps keep teeth clean and healthy. Explain that there are other ways to keep the mouth clean. Bring in a mouthwash sample and some small paper cups like those used in a bathroom dispenser. Discuss the importance of not sharing the cups. Explain what mouthwash is for and ask if anyone has ever used it. Let the children smell the mouthwash. Discuss what it smells like. Discuss how gargling does not include swallowing the mouthwash.

Note: Discuss the concept of sharing and explain that in most circumstances sharing is very good. Point out that there are some things that should never be shared. These include things that go into our mouths.

Can You Guess What It Is?

Ask the children if they know what a riddle is. Discuss and clarify the term *riddle.* Let them know you have a riddle for them. Ask them to listen carefully and try to guess what the answer to the riddle is. Read the following poem to the children without saying the last word. See if students can fill in the blank.

A Warm and Friendly Riddle

It's something that you always have,
It's with you night or day.
It's something you should never keep
But freely give away.
It's something people like to get.
I'm sure you will agree.
It's a gift that doesn't cost a thing,
A gift that's always free.
Each person has a different one.
Each person has a style.
So let's all give each other now
A warm and friendly _____ . *(smile)*

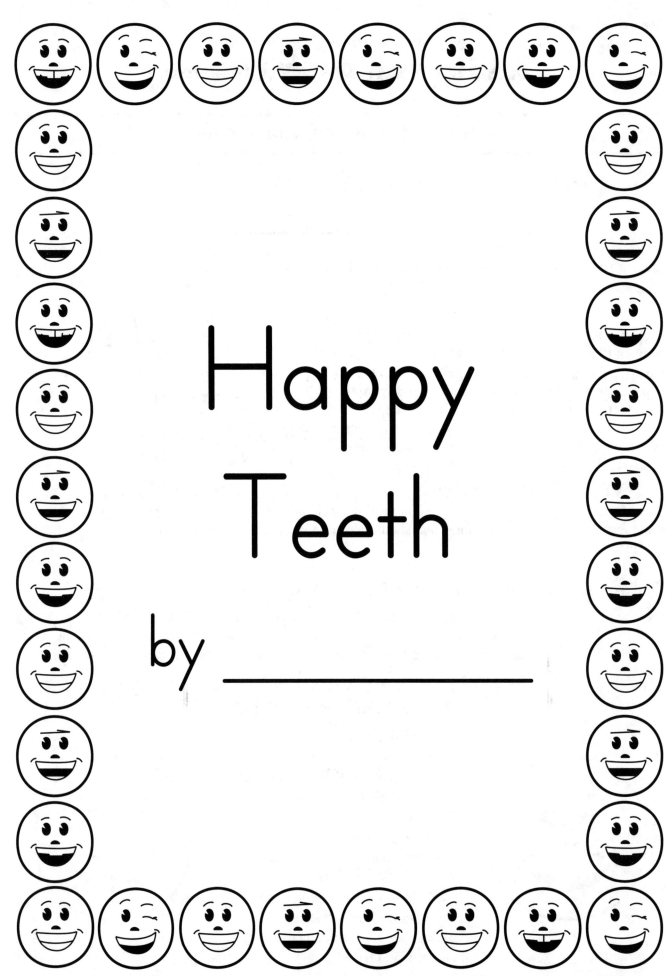

Happy
Teeth

by _____

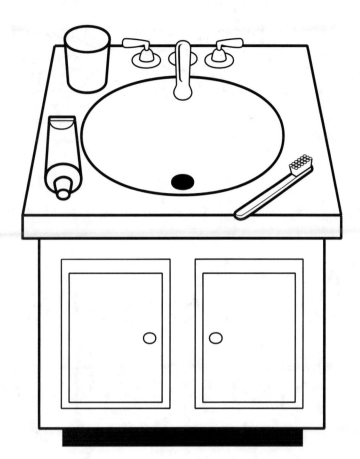

Brush your teeth
when you wake up
and see the morning
sun.

page 1

Make sure
you brush all your
teeth—every
single one.

page 2

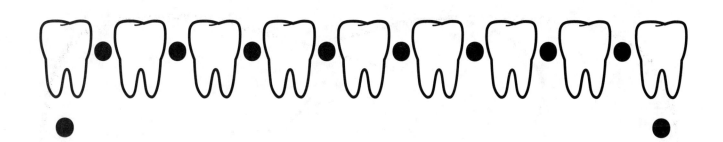

Having teeth
with cavities is
never any fun.

page 3

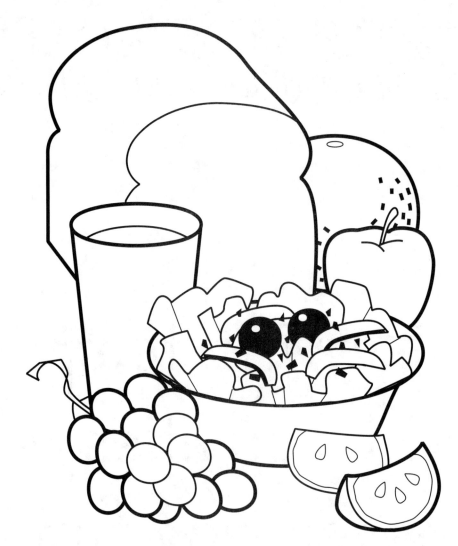

Eat healthful food at every meal and when the day is done

page 4

You will have healthy teeth and very happy gums.

page 5

Related Resources

Books

Behrens, June. *I Can Be a Nurse.* Children's Press, 1986.

Berenstain, Stan and Jan. *The Berenstain Bears and Too Much Junk Food.* Random House, 1985.

Berry, Joy W. *Teach Me About the Dentist.* Grolier, 1986.

Braithwaite, Althea. *Visiting the Dentist.* McClanahan, 1990.

DeSantis, Kenny. *A Dentist's Tools.* Putnam, 1988.

Gillerlain, Gayle. *The Reverend Thomas's False Teeth.* Bridgewater Books, 1995.

Hallinan, P. K. *My Dentist, My Friend.* Ideals Publications, Inc., 1996.

LeSieg, Theo. *The Tooth Book.* Random House Children's Pub., 1981.

Maccarone, Grace. *My Tooth Is About to Fall Out.* Scholastic, 1995.

Mayer, Mercer. *Just Going to the Dentist.* Western, 1990.

Munsch, Robert N. *Andrew's Loose Tooth.* Cartwheel Books, 1998.

Rice, Judith Ann. *Those Icky, Sticky, Smelly, Cavity-Causing But ... Invisible Germs.* Gryphon House, 1997.

Rogers, Fred. *Going to the Dentist.* Putnam, 1989.

Stamper, Judith. *What's It Like to Be a Dentist?* Troll, 1989.

Thaler, Mike. *Fang the Dentist.* Troll, 1993.

Ziefert, Harriet. *My Tooth Is Loose.* Viking Penguin, 1994.

Music

Palmer, Hap. *Learning Basic Skills Through Music: Health and Safety.* "Brush Away." Activity Records, 1970.

Raffi. *Singable Songs for the Very Young.* "Brush Your Teeth." Shoreline Records, 1976.

Video

Junk Food Man. (Video shows how to choose healthful snacks); 10 min. Pied Piper/AIMS Multimedia, 9710 De Soto Ave., Chatsworth, CA 91311; 1-800-367-2567.

Toothbrush Pattern

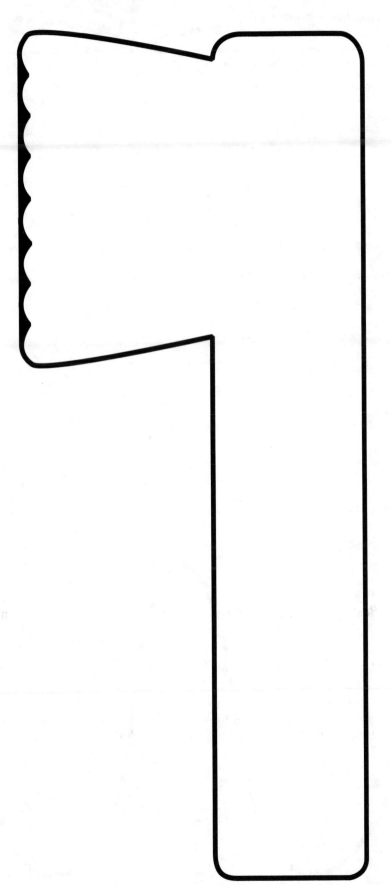

Tooth Pattern

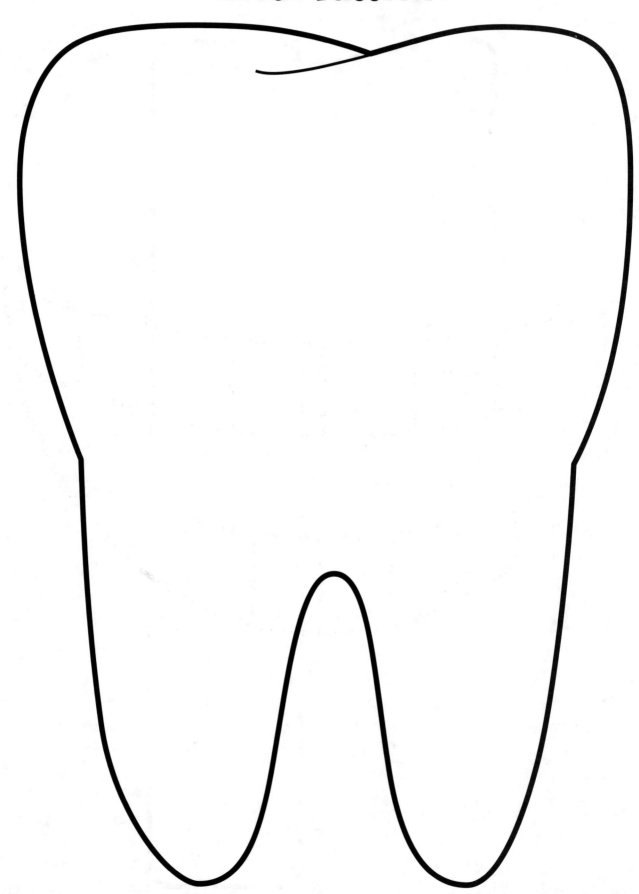

Mouth Pattern

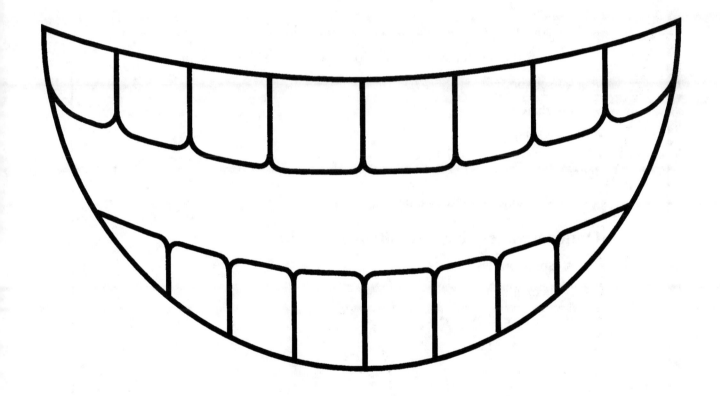

Adhesive Bandages Big Book

Unit Materials:

— various types and sizes of adhesive bandages

— cotton swabs

— sterile gauze

— cotton balls

— tagboard

— drawing tools: various colors, including skin tones

— construction paper: various colors, including white and skin tones

— scissors

— glue

— stapler

Extra:

— skin-tone colored face pads

Optional Materials for Additional Activities:

— spray bottles

— latex gloves

— small candies

— plaster of Paris

— opaque projector

— poster board

Adhesive Bandages Big Book

Theme: Me
Topics: Body Awareness/Health/ Bandages
Duration: One Week
Approach: Original Story
Teacher-Directed Activities

The Me theme has such a wide spectrum that there are hundreds of possibilities for big books. This resource book can be used as a catalyst to integrate self-awareness activities with health lessons in order to promote wellness.

Point out that there are people in the community who care about the health and safety of others and who are available to offer help and direction when needed. The last page of this book includes an emergency phone number for the children to memorize.

Note: This child-created big book can easily branch off into either the theme of My Community and Me (community helpers) or My Family and Me (family responsibilities, illness, aging, special needs).

Help children understand that they can help their bodies function at their best by considering the importance of nutrition, relaxation, exercise, personal hygiene, expression of feelings, and safety. During the course of creating this big book, pay close attention to the contributions the children offer during class discussions. Their comments may give you ideas for future lessons.

Bandages seem to bring about very strong feelings in most children. Some children love them. Others absolutely hate them and will flee at the sight of a bandage box. This book is perfect for both types of children. Those who love bandages will enjoy working with them on this book. In addition, those who hate bandages on themselves don't seem to mind them on something other than their own bodies. It gives them a firsthand opportunity to face their fears in a non-threatening environment.

Note: For your convenience the text (pages 151–153) has been included and can be reproduced for students. However, this is also a great book to do with buddies (page 12). The older child can outline the younger child's body and vice-versa. In addition, the text is so simple for this book that you may wish to have the older children print it on paper rather than photocopying the story pages as suggested for other child-created big books.

Making the Book

COVER PAGE

Activity: Make a collage using adhesive bandages.

Setup: If your school has a nurse, ask for bandage donations. Place these on the art table. Set out other items, such as cotton swabs, gauze, and cotton balls, that can be used as part of the demonstration for how to clean a wound before applying a bandage. Place a stack of differently colored tagboard with a square traced in the center of each. Set out a variety of bandages that are still in their wrappers.

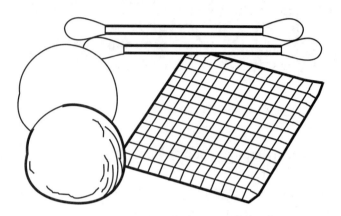

Introduction: Show the children a variety of medical supplies, including different types of bandages. Review body parts. Invite students to compare/contrast the bandages. Talk about what the different bandages are for and how they are designed to fit certain parts of the body.

If possible, invite a doctor or nurse to speak to your class.

Inform the children that today they will have the opportunity to make a collage for their cover pages, using bandages.

Directions: The children will choose the bandages from the available selection, unwrap them, and attach them around the square traced on the tagboard.

PAGE 1

Text: There is a bandage on my _____ . (Insert a facial feature in the blank.)

Activity: Draw a self-portrait.

Setup: You'll need supplies such as markers, chalks, crayons, pencils, scissors, and paper. If possible, provide several mirrors that students can use to look at themselves. If you only have one mirror, discuss the importance of sharing so everyone has a turn to look in the mirror.

Introduction: Ask students to look at themselves in the mirror(s) and comment on their facial features, including hair, eye, and skin color.

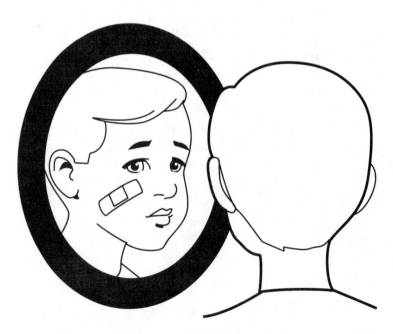

Making the Book *(cont.)*

PAGE 1 *(cont.)*

Directions: This activity can be accomplished in the following ways with or without buddies (page 12).

1. You can have the children draw and color their portraits on large sheets of white construction paper.

2. You can provide precut skin-tone construction paper ovals. Have children choose the oval that best matches their skin colors. Then have them glue their ovals onto large sheets of construction paper and draw/color the facial features.

3. You can trace ovals on skin-tone construction paper. Have the children cut out the ovals and add facial features. Then have students glue the ovals onto large pieces of construction paper.

4. Some companies that sell supplies to school offer multicultural face pads. These are face-shaped pads of paper in a variety of skin-tone colors. They contain approximately forty sheets and are fairly inexpensive. These come in handy for activities such as this one, especially if you are pressed for time. The children can select and glue on the sheet that best matches their skin tones. Then they can use markers, pencils, or crayons to draw the facial features and glue yarn to the top of the oval for hair.

5. If your students are making this book with their buddies (page 12), the older child can be the artist while the younger child poses.

6. Once the portraits are completed, provide each student with an adhesive bandage. Ask the children to choose a place on their portraits to put their bandages. Fill in the blank on page 152 with the name of the facial feature where each student puts the bandage.

PAGE 2

Text: Don't worry. It's all in fun. No need to call 911.

Activity: Outline body parts. Body part suggestions include left hand, right hand, elbow, knee, foot, ankle, leg, and arm.

Note: You can get more specific when applying the bandage by asking students to name the parts of the hand or foot.

Setup: Lay out a stack of light-colored construction paper along with felt-tip markers and crayons.

Timesaver: If it is not possible to do this in a buddy fashion (page 12), you may want to enlist the help of parent volunteers.

Introduction: Review body parts. Play "Simon says" using body parts, or act out the song "Head, Shoulders, Knees, and Toes."

Making the Book *(cont.)*

PAGE 2 *(cont.)*

Directions: The child being outlined can choose the body parts she/he would like drawn. After being outlined, the child may wish to color that specific body part. Some students may choose to retrace the outline with black permanent marker.

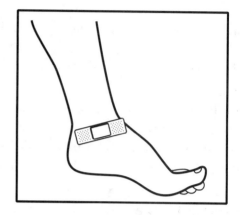

At this point, the child selects the appropriate bandage and sticks it onto the body part where it belongs. For example, a large knee bandage would not be appropriate for a finger. Then indicate the body part on the next page by filling in the blank.

Note: This outlining process can continue as long as there is time and the children remain interested. As a result, the number of pages students have in their completed big books may vary.

LAST PAGE

Text: No text.

Activity: Cut and paste a telephone.

Setup: Pre-trace the Telephone Pattern (page 155) on pieces of construction paper that are all the same color. Photocopy and precut the touch-tone telephone numbers. Set out some scissors and glue along with a stack of large construction paper that is a contrasting color to the pre-traced phones.

Introduction: Review the lesson on germs (page 94). Point out that even though working with bandages has been fun, they are not necessary unless someone is hurt. Tell students that they should never touch another person's blood. Explain that this could make them sick. Tell the children that the adhesive bandages are only for minor injuries. Discuss the differences between minor and major injuries. Help students understand that if someone they know has a medical emergency, it's important to know how to call for help. Stress to students that they should never call 911 unless it is an emergency.

Directions: The children will cut and glue the numbers on the face of the telephone.

PUTTING IT ALL TOGETHER

If these big books were produced with buddies (page 12), then they should be assembled together as well. The buddies can help each other put the pages in the correct order. Then they can read their books together. On the last page of the book, the older children can practice pushing the 911 buttons with the younger children.

Additional Activities

Art/Language

Spray Bottle Bandage Shapes

Remove a variety of bandages from their outer wrappings without removing the waxy protective covering on the adhesive part. Let the children arrange the bandages on pieces of construction paper. Have them spray watercolors or watered-down tempera paints over the bandages. Once the children have covered the entire paper with paint, allow these to dry. Then have them carefully remove the bandages to reveal the shapes left behind.

Surgical Glove Painting

Before beginning this activity, show the children a surgical glove and discuss why it is necessary for medical practitioners and caregivers to use these.

Fill some surgical gloves with water. Then secure the top with a tight knot to keep the gloves from leaking. Set out some shallow containers of paint and let the children dip the fingertips of the surgical glove into the paint. Invite them to create designs by dragging the gloves across their papers.

Cotton Swab Painting

Set out small containers of tempera paint, and allow the children to dip and paint with cotton swabs.

Cotton Ball Designs

Show the children how to stretch a cotton ball into a thin fuzzy strand. Have them stretch and glue the strands for some sensory, fine motor practice.

Math/Language

Emergency Practice

Place a list of emergency telephone numbers in the Home Center near a play phone. Glue pictures of a doctor, police officer, and firefighter onto poster board. Beside each picture, place the real telephone numbers of your local hospital, police station, and fire department. Add 911 to the poster board if this emergency service is available in your area.

Bandage Match-Ups

Stick matching bandages onto 3" x 5" (8 cm x 13 cm) index cards. Then laminate the cards for durability. Mix up the cards and place them on the floor or table. The children can work in pairs to find the matching bandages. You may wish to teach students how to play concentration using the matching cards.

Additional Activities *(cont.)*

Science/Discovery/Language

Candy or Pills?

Explain to students that some candies and pills look very similar. Teach them the difference, and warn them about the dangers of taking candy from strangers or eating candy that has not come from a wrapped package. It is also important for children to know that they should only take medicine given to them by parents, doctors, nurses, and school personnel. Stress that they should never touch medicine bottles.

Note: Some hospitals have poison control programs and have nurses that are available to speak to classes. They teach children about the dangers of household items, including pills. You may want to check into this.

Silhouettes

While experimenting with shadows, you can use the light from a projector to make a silhouette of each child. Outline a child's shadow profile with a white grease pencil on black butcher or construction paper. Cut out the silhouette, and glue it onto white construction paper.

Note: These make great gifts for the children to give to family members or friends. However, they are time consuming and require that the child sitting in front of the projector remain very still for a period of time. You may wish to ask parents for help with this activity so that you can complete more silhouettes in a shorter period of time.

Cotton Ball Pass

Assign partners or allow students to pick their own. Place a cotton ball on the table between each pair of students. Ask the children if they can think of a way to move the cotton ball to each other without touching it. Lead them to conclude that the cotton ball can be passed back and forth across the table by blowing air against it. Then have them try it.

Applying a Cast

Explain that sometimes bandages are not enough to heal a wound. For example, in the case of a broken bone, it is sometimes necessary for a doctor to apply a cast. Make a cast for a doll's arm or leg by dipping medical gauze into some plaster of Paris, and then applying the wrapping around the limb. Set the doll aside and check on the cast periodically. After the plaster has dried, allow students to touch it. Encourage them to tell about experiences they have had with casts.

Additional Activities (cont.)

Social/Emotional/Language

House Calls

In your classroom set up a center that is a hospital emergency room. If possible, include a cot or mat, white shirts for dress-up play, a toy doctor's kit, bandages, pads of paper, pencils, empty plastic medicine containers, etc. The paper and pencils are for students to write out prescriptions and fill out patient charts.

Full Body Outlining

Allow students to outline each other's bodies on large pieces of butcher paper. The children can work with partners from your class or they can work with older students who are buddies. To make the body outline, one child lays on the piece of butcher paper while the other child traces his/her outline. Then the child who was outlined gets up and adds details. Students can use markers or crayons to add facial features, pieces of fabric for articles of clothing, and yarn for hair.

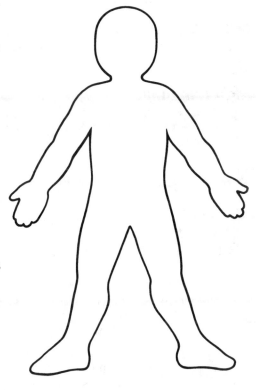

Note: Although these paper people look great displayed on classroom walls, it is difficult to draw a full body outline and add the important details. As a result, this activity is not developmentally appropriate for very young students.

Variations: A better full body tracing for very young children is one that's done outside using chalks. (1) The children can lie down while someone traces the outline of their bodies. (2) Depending on the amount of available sunshine, the children can stand while someone outlines their shadows. When children tire of tracing shadows, they can play shadow tag by trying to touch each other's shadows.

Pin the Nose on the Face

Using an opaque projector and a piece of poster board, trace an interesting cartoon face, omitting the nose. Laminate this picture as well as a blank sheet of tagboard. Use the tagboard to cut out circle-shaped noses. Teach students how to play this game, which is just like Pin the Tail on the Donkey.

Additional Activities *(cont.)*

Music/Movement/Language

Early Childhood Aerobics

Invite an aerobics instructor to visit your classroom and do some movement activities with the children. An alternative is to simply put on some dance music and run your own aerobics class.

Medical Gauze Dancing

Give the children pieces of medical gauze. Play a variety of music and have them dance to the music while waving their gauze strips.

Social/Emotional/Language

Sign Language

Explain why some people use sign language. Invite someone to your classroom to demonstrate sign language for the students. Teach children how to sign some letters, words, or a simple song.

Who Is That?

Blindfold one child. Then designate another child to say something to the blindfolded person, such as, "Hello, _____ (child's name). Can you guess who I am?" The blindfolded child must then guess who is talking by the sound of his/her voice.

Variation: Tape the children's voices on separate occasions while they are playing. When you have a sample of each child's voice, play it back during circle time. See if the children can recognize each of the voices on the tape.

Note: It may be a good idea to jot down a few notes while recording, just in case you may not be able to decipher the voices and forget who's who.

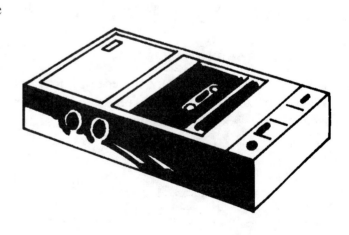

Following Directions

Give simple directions for the children to follow excluding the use of a specific body part. Let the children help each other by offering suggestions.

Examples:

- Get me your library book while using only one leg.

- Open the door without using your hands.

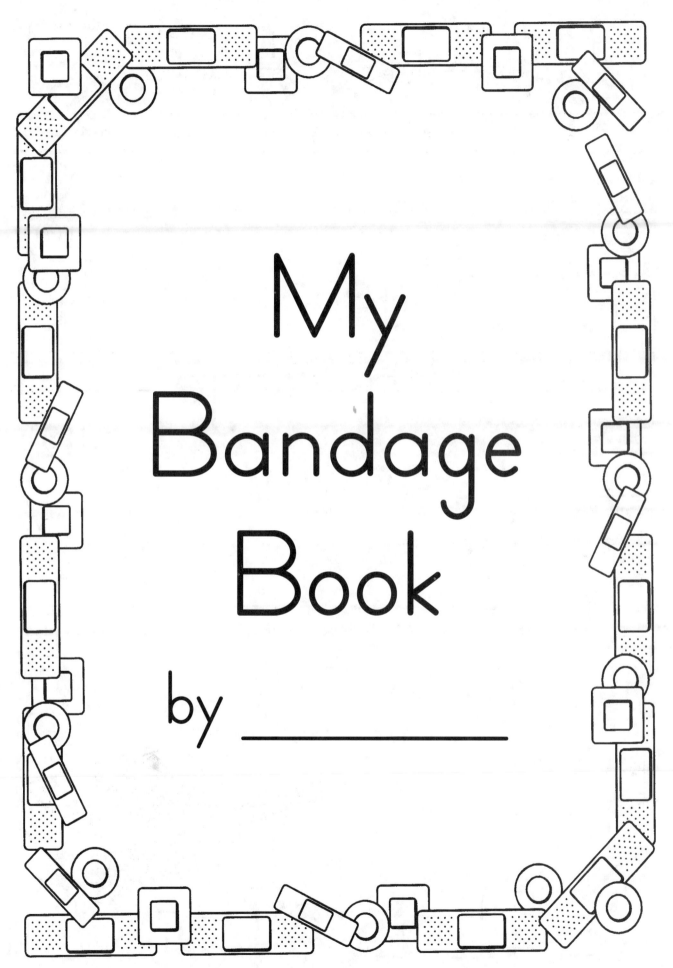

My Bandage Book

by _____

#2311 A Year Full of Themes

There is
a bandage
on my

_____ .

page 1

Don't worry.
It's all in fun.
No need
to call 911.

page 2

Related Resources

Books

Adoff, Arnold, ed. *My Black Me: A Beginning Book of Black Poetry.* Dutton, 1994.

Aliki. *I'm Growing.* HarperCollins, 1992.

Berenstain, Stan and Jan. *The Berenstain Bears Go to the Doctor.* Random House, 1987.

Blegvad, Lenore. *Anna Banana and Me.* Atheneum, 1987.

Brown, Tricia. *Someone Special Just Like You.* Holt, Rinehart, and Winston, 1984.

Courson, Diana. *Let's Learn about Safety.* Good Apple, 1987.

Fassler, Joan. *Howie Helps Himself.* A. Whitman, 1975.

Fleischer, Gary. *First Aid for Kids.* Barron, 1987.

Hallinan, P. K. *My Doctor, My Friend.* Ideal Publications, Inc., 1996.

Hantzig, Deborah. *A Visit to the Sesame Street Hospital.* Random House, 1985.

Mayer, Mercer. *Just My Friend and Me.* Western, 1988.

McCue, Lisa. *Corduroy Goes to the Doctor.* Kestrel Publications, 1987.

Merrifield, Margaret. *Come Sit By Me.* Stoddart Kids, 1998.

Rice, Judith Ann. *Those Mean, Nasty, Dirty, Downright Disgusting But ... Invisible Germs.* Red Leaf Press, 1997.

Showers, Paul. *Your Skin and Mine.* HarperCollins, 1991.

Steel, Danielle. *Freddie's Accident.* Dell, 1992.

Music

Beardon, Libby Core, Camille Core, and Kathleen Patrick Gift. *ABC's in Bubbaville.* Kimbo, 1986.

Greg and Steve. *Kids in Motion.* "The Body Rock" and "Tummy Tango." Youngheart Records, 1987.

The Learning Station. *Tony Chestnut & Fun Time Action Songs.* "Tony Chestnut." Kaladon Publishing, 1997.

Palmer, Hap. *Learning Basic Skills Through Music: Health and Safety.* "Keep the Germs Away." Activity Records, 1970.

Video

Jasper's Hospital Experience. (Video of Jasper the puppet going to the hospital); 20 min. Pied Piper/AIMS Multimedia, 9710 De Soto Ave., Chatsworth, CA 91311; 1-800-367-2567.

Software

Fisher-Price Ready for School. (Kindergarten activities on safety and telephone usage); CD-ROM for MAC, WIN 95, or WIN 3.1; Davidson & Assoc., Inc., Torrance, CA 90503; 1-800-545-7677.

Telephone Pattern

Aikendrum Big Book Materials

Unit Materials:

— one box of spaghetti
— hot plate
— pot or Dutch oven with cover
— oil
— paint: various colors
— construction paper: black, white, yellow, and other light colors
— small and large paint containers
— white chalk
— self-adhesive stars
— ball(s)
— butcher paper: various colors
— sponges for sponge painting
— 6" (15 cm) colored paper plates without designs
— wooden craft spoons
— glue
— scissors
— stapler

Extra:

— craft straws
— yarn, thin macramé cord, or twine
— shredded paper
— hole puncher
— black dab-type paint bottle
— vegetables such as mushrooms and green peppers
— liquid watercolor paint
— food coloring

Optional Materials for Additional Activities:

— white crayons
— various types of uncooked pasta
— food coloring
— plastic combs
— spray bottles
— clothes hanger(s)
— plastic spoons
— plastic sorting tray (like the kind used for dips)
— masking tape
— various colors of felt
— fabric paint
— milk
— vanilla syrup or honey
— vanilla ice cream
— banana(s)
— small pita pockets
— pizza sauce
— shredded Mozzarella cheese
— snack-maker appliance
— sliced bread
— empty shoeboxes
— rubber bands
— empty pizza boxes
— pizza cardboard rounds
— upholstery foam or padding
— various sizes of paper plates
— large cardboard box

Aikendrum Big Book

Theme: Me
Topics: Fantasy/Reality/Body Parts/Foods
Duration: One Week or More
Approach: Adapted Song
                     Combined Illustrations

There are many versions of the song "Aikendrum." This particular child-created big book is based on CJ's version as sung on his *Fundamentals* album (Handy Music Inc., 1995) and Raffi's version as sung on his *Singable Songs for the Very Young* album (Shoreline Records, 1976). The big book text is a shortened version of the song. Although this specific book goes along with the lyrics used by CJ and Raffi, it can easily be adapted to correspond with any version. "Aikendrum" is an easy song to learn, and children love it because it is silly and fun to sing. Learning the song will help very young children remember the text of the big book. However, even if you are unable to obtain any musical version of "Aikendrum," creating the big book will still be a meaningful experience for your students.

This is a good song for the children to brainstorm their own lyrics. If you decide this is what you want to do, then it is just a matter of matching the illustrations to the text your students choose.

Since Aikendrum is a person whose facial features are made from foods, this song fits in nicely with the discussion about foods that started with The Apple Tree big book (pages 21–46). Additional exploration of foods can continue with a unit on pasta and pizza. Although the book itself can be completed in one week, there are so many Additional Activities (pages 163–169) that a two- or three-week unit is possible.

Aikendrum

There was a man who lived in the moon.

His hair was made of spaghetti.

His eyes were made of meatballs.

His nose was made of cheese.

His mouth was made of pizza.

His name was Aikendrum, and he played upon a ladle.

Making the Book

COVER PAGE

Activity: Cook spaghetti, and use it for painting.

Setup: For the first part of this activity, you'll need a box of spaghetti, a hot plate, a pot, and a little oil. Cook ½ box of spaghetti in water with a tablespoon of oil until it is soft and pliable but not mushy.

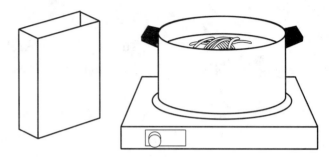

For the second part of this activity, you will need shallow containers of different colored tempera paints and white or light-colored construction paper.

Introduction: While the spaghetti is cooking, show the children some of the uncooked spaghetti. Discuss its appearance and texture. Once the pasta is cooked, run it under cold water and drain. Invite students to compare and contrast the cooked and uncooked noodles.

As a motivational introductory exercise, encourage the children to stand up and move like cooked, floppy, wet spaghetti. Then ask them to move like uncooked spaghetti. You may wish to have students focus on different body parts for this activity. For example, ask them to move their fingers like cooked spaghetti, then their arms, legs, etc. Wrap up the activity with whole body movements.

Teach children the song "Aikendrum." Tell them their next big book project is based on this song. Ask the children if they remember what food Aikendrum's hair was. Explain that the cover page will be made using Aikendrum's hair.

Directions: Give each child fresh noodles before beginning this activity. Discuss how the cooked spaghetti feels and how it must be handled so that it doesn't break. Show the children how to dip a noodle into the paint container until it is covered with tempera, carefully lift it out, and drag it across the paper. Explain that this procedure can be repeated using different colors. After students are finished painting, allow their paperplay to dry. Then reproduce the title (page 170) for students, and glue the copies onto the cover sheets.

Note: If for any reason it is not possible to cook spaghetti in the classroom, you can do this step at home.

Alternative: If your students will not be able to manipulate the strands of spaghetti as suggested, you can easily substitute heavy string or twine for the pasta.

Making the Book *(cont.)*

PAGE 1

Text: There was a man who lived in the moon.

Activity: Cut on a curve.

Setup: Trace the moon pattern (page 175) onto yellow construction paper. For younger children, use a wide-tipped marker to draw a thicker cutting line. Set out glue, white chalk, self-adhesive stars, and a stack of black construction paper.

Introduction: Review the song "Aikendrum" with the children. Explain that the first page of the big book will illustrate where Aikendrum lives. Give each child a pre-traced moon to cut out and glue onto the black construction paper. The children can glue the moon any way they choose. Once the moon is secure, the children can draw stars, using the chalk, and/or arrange the self-adhesive stars around the moon. This can be extended into a math lesson by counting out a certain number of stars to be placed in the background.

PAGE 2

Text: His hair was made of spaghetti.

Activity: Make a collage.

Setup: The setup for this activity depends on the medium you use. For all the choices, you will need a stack of construction paper (any color) and some glue.

Introduction: Review the song "Aikendrum." Ask the children what it would be like to have spaghetti for hair. Encourage them to think of other things that are long and stringy like spaghetti. Explain that there will be a collage table for illustrating this page of their big books.

Directions: Described below is a variety of options for illustrating this page. All the paperplay for these illustrations should be done vertically on large sheets of construction paper.

1. Uncooked Spaghetti Collage—Give each child a small bundle of uncooked spaghetti. Have the children break the noodles into the desired sizes and then glue them onto the paper.

2. Craft Straw Collage—Compare white craft straws to uncooked spaghetti. Let children cut the straws into the desired sizes and then glue them onto the paper.

3. Yarn or Twine Collage—Compare yarn or twine to cooked spaghetti. Set out small containers of watered-down glue. Older children can cut the yarn the desired lengths. Provide precut yarn for younger children. Have the children dip the yarn into the glue and then arrange it on the construction paper.

4. Macramé Cord Collage—Craft stores may be able to donate scraps of macramé cord. To make a macramé cord collage, have the child dribble glue onto the paper, place the cord over the glue, and press down lightly on the cord.

Making the Book *(cont.)*

PAGE 3

Text: His eyes were made of meatballs.

Activity: Print with a ball.

Setup: Gather some balls that can be used for printing. Rubber, sponge, and foam balls all work well. Make sure the balls used at the teacher-directed table are small enough that two prints will fit on the same paper, side-by-side.

Set up the teacher-directed bookmaking table with a stack of white or light-colored construction paper. You'll need a shallow container of brown tempera paint with some red drizzled on top, but not mixed into the brown. Be sure to use a paint container that is large enough to fit the size of ball you are using. Pour just enough paint for one or two children at a time. Fresh paint should be added often to keep the colors in the prints separate. Otherwise, the red and brown will mix together and the sauce-on-meatballs effect will be lost. Place one of the balls in the paint container. When the children come to this table, remind thems that they will only be making two prints to illustrate Aikendrum's eyes.

At a child-directed table, layer several large sheets of butcher paper. At this table, at least three containers of brightly colored paint should be available for use. Primary colors or neon colors are good choices for this activity. Place any size of ball in each container of paint. Different-size balls will add to the total look of the finished product. As each sheet of butcher paper is filled with prints, remove it to reveal a blank sheet underneath. Allow the completed butcher paper to dry. These sheets can be saved for a bulletin board, which is described below.

Introduction: Review the song "Aikendrum" with the class. Ask the children to describe what a meatball is, including color, shape, and texture. Tell them that they will be producing the illustration for page 3 of their child-created big books. Explain that they will be printing with balls today. Let them know that there are two tables, one for the children making big books and another where they can freely print using a variety of colors.

Directions: At the child-centered table, the children can freely paint and print using the different colored paints and the variety of balls available. At the teacher-directed table, remind the children they will be making two prints only for Aikendrum's two eyes. Once these prints have dried, you can add a white circle with a dot of black in the middle or glue some wiggle eyes in the center to make them look more like actual eyes.

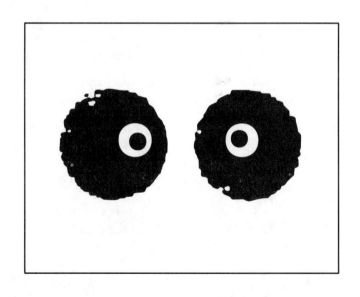

Bulletin Board: Cover your bulletin board with the print-covered butcher paper. Add a clever caption such as We Have a Ball in Our Room, Having a Ball in Art, or In School, We Have a Ball.

Making the Book *(cont.)*

PAGE 4

Text: His nose was made of cheese.

Activity: Older children fold and cut or use a hole punch. Younger children make dab paintings.

Setup: Set out some scissors, glue, hole puncher, a black dab-type paint bottle, and large black construction paper. For older children, set out yellow construction paper, measuring approximately 9" x 12" (23 cm x 30 cm). Each child needs one sheet. You can also provide 3" (8 cm) squares of yellow construction paper.

Introduction: Review the song "Aikendrum." Tell the children that they will be adding page 4 to their big books today. Ask them what they think the next page should be. If possible, bring in a variety of cheeses, including Swiss cheese, for the children to look at, smell, touch, and taste. Ask the children to compare/contrast the cheeses.

Warning: Check with parents to see if their children have any food allergies or dietary restrictions before allowing students to eat any cheese.

Directions: Tell the class that Aikendrum's nose will be made out of Swiss cheese and today's activities include illustrating page 4 of their big books.

If you have older children, explain that they will be cutting holes in yellow paper to make it resemble Swiss cheese. Show the children that by folding the paper and cutting out a small portion on the fold, they will have Swiss cheese holes when they open the paper. This process is repeated until there are enough holes in the paper to make it look like cheese. You may want to help students round out the corners and curve some edges to give it an even more realistic look. Once this is done, glue the cheese onto a sheet of large black construction paper.

Another option is to give the older children 3" (8 cm) squares and a hole puncher. Let them randomly punch holes until they are satisfied with the effect. Once these have been completed, glue them onto a large sheet of black construction paper.

For very young children, give each student one of the 9" x 12" (23 x 30 cm) sheet squares of yellow construction paper, and let them dab and dot the paper with the black paint bottle to simulate the holes. After the paint is dry, glue the cheese onto large sheets of black construction paper.

Note: If you do not have the dab-type paint bottles, simply pour some tempera into a small shallow container and have the children use their thumbs or index fingers to paint the holes.

Making the Book *(cont.)*

PAGE 5

Text: His mouth was made of pizza.

Activity: Make vegetable prints on circles or triangles.

Setup: Put out some scissors and large sheets of colored construction paper. For the pizza, trace large circles (approximately the size of a dinner plate) or large triangles onto red construction paper. Set out small containers of paint to match the colors of the vegetable toppings you decide to use. Use real vegetables or sponges cut into the shapes of vegetables.

Directions: Cut out the circles and triangles yourself or have students do it. Once the shapes are cut out, have the children glue them onto large sheets of colored construction paper. Have students make prints on red circles or triangles. Shredded yellow paper or felt can be added onto the circles or triangles as a finishing touch.

PAGE 6

Text: His name was Aikendrum, and he played upon a ladle.

Activity: Add facial features to a paper plate head and make hand prints.

Setup: For this page, you will need small paper plates, glue, markers, crayons, and sponge-tipped bottles with red, yellow, and brown paint. Yarn, macramé cord, craft straws, or shredded paper are needed for Aikendrum's hair. In addition, you will need flat wooden craft spoons. Plastic spoons can be substituted, but the books will not close properly or lay flat.

Introduction: Review the song "Aikendrum." Inform the children that they will be making the final page of their big books today.

Directions: Have students choose from the available materials and sequentially draw and assemble Aikendrum's head. One at a time, brush paint onto a child's hands, turn the sheet with the paper plate head upside down, and press her/his hands onto the paper just below the head and a few inches apart to make Aikendrum's hand prints. After the paint dries, turn the papers right side up and let students glue the spoons between the hand prints.

PUTTING IT ALL TOGETHER

Reproduce the text (pages 171–173), cutting where indicated. If your class came up with an original version, write or use a computer to print out your own text to reproduce. Once this is done, review the song with the children, and then organize the big book pages and staple them together. After the pages are secured, help the children glue down the corresponding text.

Additional Activities

Art/Language

Starry Night

The first page of this big book illustrates that Aikendrum lives in the moon. Discussions about day and night can precede or follow the making of page 1.

To make a starry sky, give the children white crayons and have them draw stars on yellow construction paper. Have them press down hard on the crayon as they draw. With very young children, you may want to do this part yourself. Provide some containers of diluted black tempera paint and paintbrushes. Instruct the children to brush the paint across the paper. Ask them to observe what happens to the paint when they try to cover the crayon.

Pasta Collage

Gather a variety of pastas. Invite the children to make collages by arranging and gluing the shapes on small sheets of tagboard.

Note: To dye the pasta different colors, place it in food coloring or liquid watercolor paint mixed with rubbing alcohol in a resealable plastic bag. Soak the pasta until the desired color is achieved. Allow the pasta to dry before using for the collages.

Bulletin Board: Save the above collages and arrange them on a bulletin board with a caption such as We Really Use Our Noodles in School, We Use Our Noodles in _____ 's Class, or We Learn to Use Our Noodles at _____ School.

Comb Paintings

Since page 2 of the big book is about hair, allow the children to use combs as painting tools. Add a dollop of fingerpaint to some fingerpainting paper. Then have the children glide the combs back and forth over the paint to create unique patterns and designs.

Spray Paint Ladles

Have one child at a time arrange wooden craft spoons on a sheet of white or light-colored construction paper. Fill a spray bottle with liquid watercolor paint and let the child spray the entire paper. Allow the paint to dry. Then have the student remove the spoons. The same spoons can be reused for the next child's painting, but be sure to use fresh spoons when changing colors. When students are finished with this project, you can recycle the wooden spoons by making a mobile (page 164) for the classroom.

Additional Activities *(cont.)*

Art/Language *(cont.)*

Mobiles

Cut different lengths of elastic thread, thin string, yarn, or dental floss. Tie one end to the wooden craft spoons and the other to the bottom part of a clothes hanger. Write or print out two copies of a single-page caption such as Smiles by the Spoonful, Spooning Out Lots of Surprises, or Spoonfuls of Giggles Is Our Recipe for Fun.

Place one copy of the caption facedown on a table. Cover the back with glue. Place the clothes hanger on top of the glue, making sure the hook part of the hanger is above the top edge of the paper and the strings are straight. Cover the back of the other copy with glue. Then align it with the first copy, faceup, directly over the hanger. Firmly press down on the papers to glue them in place.

Bulletin Board

Ask each child to bring in one disposable plate and one plastic spoon, any size and color. Compare and contrast the various plates and spoons that are brought to class. These can be grouped and graphed according to size and color. Different types of disposable products (paper, plastic, Styrofoam) can also be discussed.

Have some white paper plates set out at a Creative Art Center. Let the children use markers, crayons, and dab-bottle paints to come up with their own original designs. If possible, purchase an inexpensive, red and white checkered plastic tablecloth. Use it to cover a bulletin board. Staple both the commercially decorated plates and the child-created designs onto the board. Fill in spaces between the plates by attaching the plastic spoons as well as any painted wooden spoons that might be left over from the Spray Paint Ladles activity (page 163). Complete the bulletin board with a banner that reads Dishing Out Some Kindergarten Fun, Dishing Out Some Early Childhood Fun, or Food for Thought.

If your bulletin board is situated at a Skills Center, possible captions could be: Dig into Some Block Building, The Latest Scoop on Math Skills, or Stirring Up Science Surprises.

If your bulletin board is located near your classroom library or quiet area, have the children draw their favorite book characters on the plates and/or write their favorite book titles and use the caption Taste Our Delicious Books.

Additional Activities *(cont.)*

Math/Language

Sorting Pasta

Obtain an inexpensive plastic serving tray, such as the kind used for dips. In the center compartment, place pasta of various shapes. Have the children sort the pasta according to type.

Matching Noodles

Stick a thick piece of masking tape onto the table. Using a permanent marker, write the numbers 1, 2, 3, etc., directly on the tape. Be sure to leave spaces between the numbers. Place a container of pasta on the table. Ask the children to count out and place the appropriate number of noodles above the corresponding number.

Pizza Pie

Using the Pizza Triangle Patterns (page 176) or the pizza rounds (page 168) as props, recite the following poem.

Pizza Pie

Sing to the tune of "Twinkle, Twinkle Little Star."

Count these slices. There are eight.
Put one slice on your plate.

Now there's seven ready to eat.
Take another. Have a treat.

Six left now, but they won't last.
Grab another slice real fast.

Five to go. Eat one more.
Look! Now there's only four.

It's so good. It's so yummy.
Another slice goes in the tummy.

Three are left, but don't worry.
You'll still get more if you hurry.

Here's another slice for you.
Take one now. There's only two.

Have another. They're almost gone.
All that's left is a single one.

Eat it now, and you'll be done.
You ate it all, and now there's none.

It was so good. It was so nice.
You ate a pizza—every slice.

Additional Activities *(cont.)*

Math/Language *(cont.)*

Pasta Necklaces

Set out pasta, such as ziti, rigatoni, and wheels, that can easily be strung. Encourage the children to make patterns by counting out three of one kind, one of another. This activity can also be done by alternating pasta with cut-up plastic straws, beads, or o-shaped cereals.

Block Building

Encourage students to use blocks and buildable toys to design and build new homes for Aikendrum.

Counting Pepperoni

Make at least six pizza triangles (page 176) out of red felt or construction paper along with 21 brown circles. Number the triangles 1 through 6. Have the children arrange the pizza wedges in numerical order and then place the corresponding amount of pepperoni on the slices.

The Missing Cheese

Using the patterns (page 177), make a mouse and several cheeses for a felt or Velcro® kit. The mouse can be made out of any color, but the cheeses should be yellow. Place the mouse on the flannelboard and tell the children to carefully watch the cheese shapes as you recite the limerick shown below. As you say the last two lines, cover the felt or Velcro® pieces with a poster board (or something similar) and remove one of the cheese shapes. After taking away a chunk of cheese, put the poster board aside and ask the children if they can name the shape of the cheese that was eaten by the mouse.

The Missing Cheese

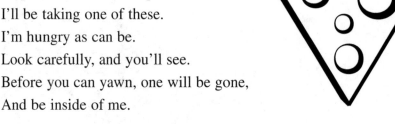

I'm out to get some cheese,
And always do as I please.
Stop and think, 'cause quick as a wink,
I'll be taking one of these.
I'm hungry as can be.
Look carefully, and you'll see.
Before you can yawn, one will be gone,
And be inside of me.

Additional Activities *(cont.)*

Science/Discovery

Night and Day

Overlap and glue together two pieces of construction paper, one dark blue or black and the other yellow. Label one side *Night* and the other *Day*. Have the children look through magazines and cut out pictures displaying daytime and nighttime activities. Tell them to glue their pictures under the appropriate headings on the construction paper.

Moon Shakes

Discuss how cheese is made. Then make moon shakes with your students.

Warning: Be sure to ask parents if their children have any food allergies or dietary restrictions.

Aikendrum's Favorite Moon Shake

Ingredients: 2 cups (500 mL) milk, 2 tablespoons (30 mL) vanilla syrup or honey, 10 drops of yellow food coloring (optional), 1 scoop of vanilla ice cream, $^1/_2$ banana

Directions: Blend all of the ingredients until the mixture is smooth. Pour the shakes into small paper cups, and serve with cheese squares or crackers and cheese.

Note: If you are unable to use a blender, this drink can be made without the ice cream and banana. Place the other ingredients in a large, plastic container and let the children shake it until it's done. Add some music to the movement by putting on a peppy tune and passing the shaker jar around a circle. Continue until everyone has had a turn.

Making Pizza

Pizza is a favorite, and there's no better way to wrap up this unit than to make some classroom pizzas. The following directions make it quick and easy.

Pita Pizza

Ingredients: 1 package of pita pockets, 1 small jar of pizza sauce, 1 large package of shredded Mozzarella cheese

Directions: Place the pita pockets on a cookie sheet. Spread some sauce on top of them. Then sprinkle cheese over the sauce. Place in a 350° F oven for about 15 minutes or until done. If you prefer to make individual pizzas, use mini pita pockets or sliced English muffins.

Pizza Pockets

For these, you'll need a snack maker that toasts triangle-shaped snacks and pastries. Preheat the snack maker. Place sliced bread in the appliance. Spoon on some pizza sauce and cheese, and cover with another slice of bread. Close the cover of the appliance and cook the pizza pocket until it is done, approximately two minutes.

Additional Activities *(cont.)*

Social/Emotional/Language

Pizzeria

Set up a pizza parlor near the Home Center, if possible. If you have a puppet stage in your classroom, you can transform it into a pizza restaurant. If not, you can use a small table or a couple of desks pushed together to make a countertop. Don't forget to include a small table and a few chairs to be the dining area.

Make menus, signs, and a price list. The price list should reflect the numbers students are currently learning or reviewing. "No Smoking" and "Open" signs can also be added.

Some pizza restaurants will donate empty pizza boxes and cardboard rounds. Pizza crusts can be made by cutting thin upholstery foam or carpet padding into circles. This type of material usually comes in rolls and is spongy to the touch. Sometimes carpet warehouses or building supply stores will donate samples or leftover pieces. Bear in mind the foam should be white, yellow, or a manila color. To give the outside edge of your pizza that baked-in golden brown look, dust some powdered bronze colored blush or eye shadow along the rim.

Use cardboard rounds as the pattern for cutting red felt. Cut the felt in an uneven circle slightly smaller than the crust so it can be the sauce. Toppings can be cut out of felt or craft foam. There should be at least two of these pizzas.

There should also be a pre-assembled pizza with toppings that cannot be removed. This can be accomplished by using a hot glue gun to secure each of the toppings. If you prefer, you can use fabric paint to add the toppings and drizzle on the cheese. You may even consider using both methods.

The pizza should then be cut into eight slices to be sold by the slice.

Note: By placing a small piece of Velcro® on the cardboard pizza round with the partner piece underneath each slice, it will be easier to keep track of the slices and prevent them from sliding off and getting lost. This cardboard round can also be clipped onto the easel or flannelboard with a clothespin and used to teach a math lesson on fractions.

Add a toy cash register and telephone to this center, along with a pencil and small pad of paper or a few sheets stapled together for taking orders. Encourage the children to make money at the Cut and Color Center. Allow the children to help set up the restaurant. Let them design and create some of their own signs and decorations for the center. Have the children join forces to transform a cardboard box into a pizza oven by painting the box and gluing on knobs and handles, using wooden craft pieces or craft foam. In addition, you may wish to have students make a pizza delivery car out of a cardboard box.

Additional Activities *(cont.)*

Social/Emotional/Language *(cont.)*

Cat and Mouse

Choose one child to be the mouse and one to be the cat. The mouse is given a piece of cheese. This can be anything—play cheese, felt, paper, or even a yellow wooden block can be used.

Have the children sit in a circle with their hands cupped behind their backs. The child chosen as the cat must step into the circle and cover his/her eyes. The mouse then walks around the circle and chooses someone to give the cheese to. As the mouse is walking around the circle, the children recite the poem shown below. When the poem ends, the cat uncovers his/her eyes and guesses who has the cheese. Another cat and mouse can be chosen and the game can continue until everyone has had a turn or as long as interest lasts.

Cat and Mouse

Be it night or be it day,
The mouse will give the cheese away.
I wonder when. I wonder who.
Will it be me, or will it be you?

Music/Movement

Strum and Play

Since Aikendrum strummed his ladle, students may enjoy creating stringed shoebox instruments. Encourage parents to send shoeboxes to school. Extra shoeboxes may be obtained at some shoe stores.

Cut a hole in the center of each shoebox lid, leaving at least 2" (5 cm) on either side. Set out containers of tempera paint mixed with a little white glue and some paintbrushes. If you have foam brushes, this activity provides an opportunity to use them. However, any paintbrushes can be used for this purpose. Have the children brush on the paint and let the shoeboxes dry. Once the paint is dry, stretch some thick elastic strings or large rubber bands the long way across the shoebox. Students are now ready to play along with some music or have a parade.

Moving Like Noodles

Play music with different tempos and encourage the children to move and dance like cooked and uncooked pasta, including spaghetti noodles, wheels, bow ties, lasagna, and spirals.

Moon Walking

Have students pretend to take a spaceship ride to the moon. Once there, play slow, soft music. Ask students to walk on the moon as if they are weightless. You may wish to have students play follow the leader in slow motion.

Aikendrum

by _____

There was
a man who lived
in the moon.

---Cut---

His hair
was made of
spaghetti.

His eyes
were made of
meatballs.

page 3

- Cut -

His nose
was made
of cheese.

page 4

172

His mouth
was made
of pizza.

- - - - - - - - - - - - - - - - Cut - - - - - - - - - - - - - - - -

His name was
Aikendrum, and he
played upon a ladle.

Related Resources

Books

Asch, Frank. *Happy Birthday, Moon.* Prentice-Hall, 1982.

Barrett, Judi. *Cloudy with a Chance of Meatballs.* Aladdin Paperbacks, 1982.

Branley, Franklyn. *The Moon Seems to Change.* HarperCollins, 1987.

Brown, Margaret Wise. *Goodnight Moon.* HarperCollins, 1991.

Carle, Eric. *Papa, Please Get the Moon for Me.* Picture Book Studio, 1986.

dePaola, Tomie. *Strega Nona.* Simon & Schuster, 1988.

Fowler, Allan. *So That's How the Moon Changes Shape.* Childrens Press, 1991.

Gilchrist, Jan Spivey. *Indigo and Moonlight Gold.* Black Butterfly Children's Books, 1993.

Grossnickle, Anna. *Daddy Makes the Best Spaghetti.* Clarion, 1988.

Ivimey, John W. *Three Blind Mice.* Clarion, 1987.

Lundell, Margo. *The Wee Mouse Who Was Afraid of the Dark.* Platt and Munk, 1990.

McDonnell, Janet. *Mouse's Adventure in Alphabet Town.* Childrens Press, 1992.

McMillan, Bruce. *Eating Fractions.* Scholastic, 1991.

Murphy, Stuart J. *Give Me Half.* HarperCollins, 1996.

Numeroff, Laura Joffe. *If You Give a Mouse a Cookie.* Harper & Row, 1985.

Peterson, Cris. *Extra Cheese, Please!: Mozzarella's Journey From Cow to Pizza.* Boyds Mills, 1994.

Stevens, Janet. *The Town Mouse and the Country Mouse.* Holiday, 1987.

Thurber, James. *Many Moons.* HBJ, 1990.

Ungerer, Tomi. *Moon Man.* Delacorte, 1991.

Yaccarino, Dan. *Zoom. Zoom. Zoom. I'm Off to the Moon.* Scholastic, 1997.

Yolen, Jane. *Owl Moon.* Philomel, 1987.

Music

CJ Fundamentals. "Aikendrum." Handy Music Inc., 1995.

CJ Fundamentals. "On Top of Spaghetti." Handy Music Inc., 1995.

Diamond, Charlotte. *10 Carrot Diamond.* "I Am a Pizza." Charlotte Diamond Music Inc., 1985.

Grammer, Red. *Teaching Peace.* "See Me Beautiful." Red Note Records, 1986.

The Learning Station. *Where Is Thumbkin?* "Mister Moon." Kimbo, 1996.

Raffi. *Singable Songs for the Very Young.* "Aikendrum." Shoreline Records, 1976.

Sesame Street. *"C" Is for Cookie.* "If Moon Was a Cookie." Children's Television Workshop, 1995.

Video

Cloudy with a Chance of Meatballs. (Video); Live Oak Media, 1990.

Moon Pattern

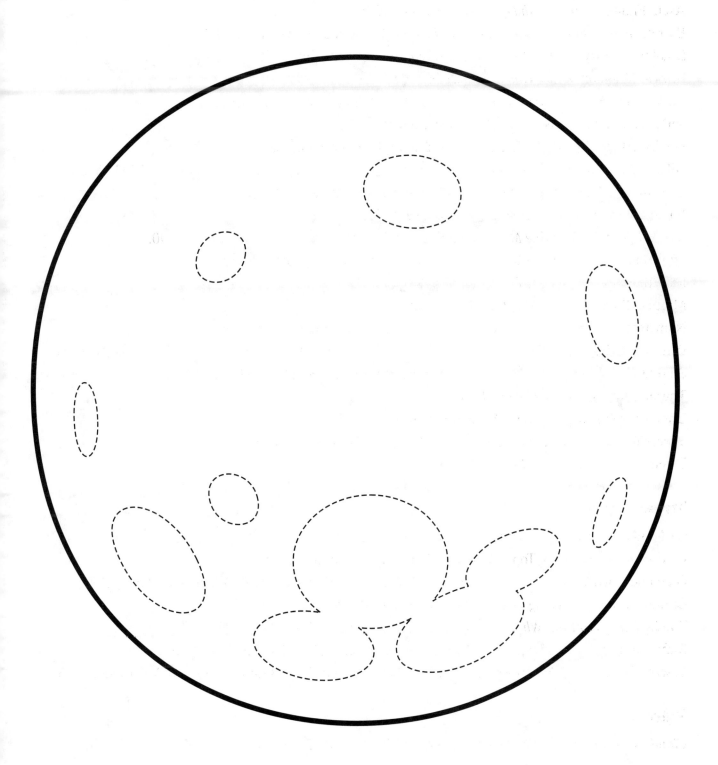

Pizza Triangle Patterns

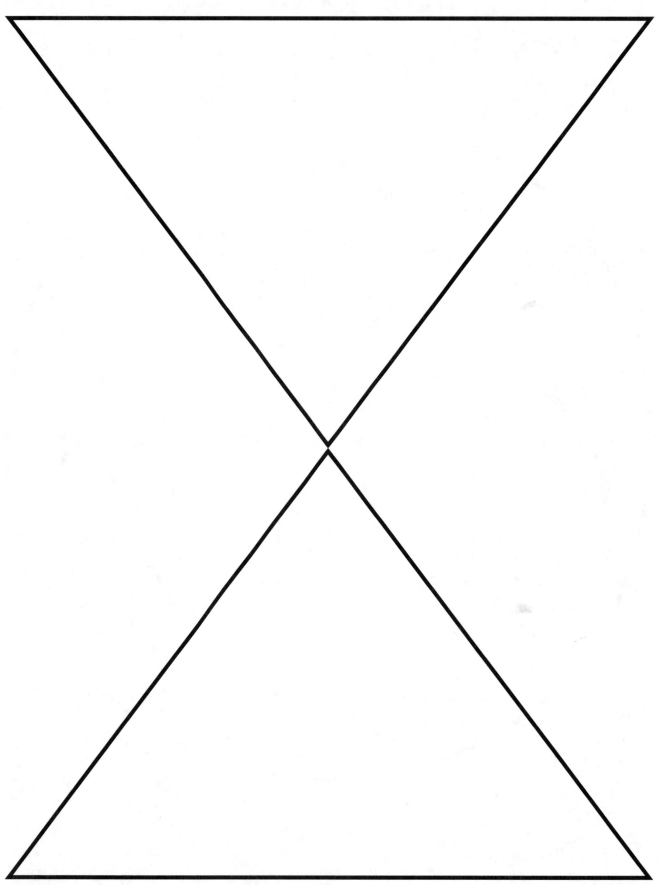

Mouse and Cheese Patterns

Families Big Book Materials

Unit Materials:

— coffee filters
— construction paper: various colors, including green
— drawing tools
— paint: various colors
— newspaper
— food coloring
— eyedropper
— butcher paper: light blue or aqua
— sticky dots
— tissue paper: all colors
— cardboard tubes
— glue
— scissors
— stapler

Extra:

— paper towels
— rolling or dab-type paint bottles
— plastic bag
— family photos
— tagboard

Optional Materials for Additional Activities:

— play dough
— craft sticks
— 3" x 5" (8 cm x 13 cm) index cards
— flower stickers
— garden shop flyers or gardening catalogs
— felt
— fabric paint
— one or two towels
— soda pop
— clean, empty, 12 oz. (360 mL) bottle
— vinegar
— funnel
— baking soda
— balloon
— lightweight sports equipment: plastic horseshoes, large rubber balls, soft football, plastic golf clubs, ring toss game, etc.
— baby food or applesauce
— large blanket or vinyl tablecloth
— large paintbrushes: 1.5" (3.8 cm) or larger

Families Big Book

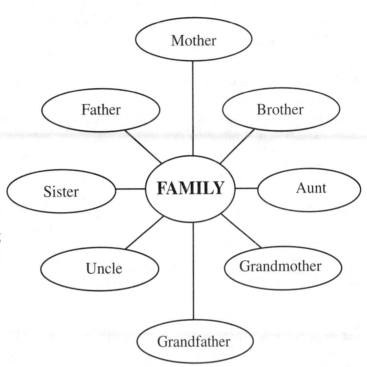

Theme: My Family and Me
Topics: Relatives/Family Members/Flowers
Duration: One Week
Approach: Original Story
Combined Illustrations

This next child-created big book helps make children aware of the similarities and differences among families. It gives them a topic they are most familiar with, thus making it something about which they are more apt to share their experiences. This particular big book approach to families is very lighthearted and basic, comparing families to flower gardens. It's up to you and your class what route to take from there.

For many children, talking about their families is one of their favorite subjects. Unfortunately, for some this topic can bring about painful memories. This is a sad reality, and it is important to be aware of special circumstances. It is necessary to be sensitive to any unpleasant family experiences children may have had or are having. However, it should not prevent you from discussing the topic. The My Family and Me theme is an extension of the Me theme. The children can easily continue with their self-exploration while becoming more aware of those around them. It gives them the chance to learn about other children and their siblings as well as opportunities to tell about grandparents, great-grandparents, and other relatives. Working parents, relatives with special needs, and divorce and remarriage are just some of the issues many children face within their families that affect them on a daily basis. Children experience many emotions they don't quite understand or know how to express. This theme allows for the continuing exploration of self that includes feelings and emotions.

Cultural Awareness

It is important to give the children opportunities to become aware of cultural differences and similarities. Some teachers make the mistake of generalizing cultures and stick to typical cultural activities such as serving tortillas for a "Mexico Day." Very young children are not immediately interested in people they don't know and who live far away. Eating with chopsticks is a great dexterity activity, but if no one in your class eats with chopsticks at home, then the activity is not a culturally relevant one for the children you are teaching. They are interested in themselves, their families, and their friends—in that order. The best way to teach cultural awareness is to explore the cultures within your school or classroom. The best resources you have available to teach students about cultures are the children themselves and their families. Send home the letter (page 197) to invite parents/guardians to share activities and information about their cultures.

Families Big Book *(cont.)*

Cultural Awareness *(cont.)*

If you decide to explore the different cultures in your classroom, you may wish to send home a letter inviting parents and other family members to come to school in order to share information about their cultures, using pictures, videos, songs, dances, foods, etc. As an alternative, you might find it more effective to call specific parents and personally ask them to share stories and information about their cultures. Some parents may not feel comfortable speaking in front of the class. However, they may be willing to send items, such as music or recipes, to share with students. It takes a little research and networking, but it can be well worth the trouble it takes to set up these activities.

Note: You can also introduce information about other lands, using books, videos, and television shows.

The guidelines for making this big book (pages 181–185) list specific illustration suggestions for each page. As emphasized throughout this resource book, please do not feel that you are limited to doing only these designs. You may have a particular flower printing or flower pattern that you have used in the past that would work well in place of a suggested activity. As long as the illustration matches the text, you can use any flower art activity you desire. Also, you might consider making this book so that it is held horizontally rather than vertically. This will allow more space for the illustrations.

There is reproducible text included (pages 191–195), but you may prefer to involve the children in brainstorming sessions to come up with an original collaboration. Ask students to tell how they think families are like flower gardens. Some very young children may have some trouble with this abstract idea and will need help. Older children may come up with some very creative suggestions.

Note: Students may wish to illustrate the last page of this book with a collage of family photographs. If this is what they decide to do, it will be necessary to write parents a letter telling them about this big book and asking them to send photographs that can be glued onto the last page.

Families Are Like Flower Gardens

Just like flower gardens, families are different colors.

Just like flower gardens, families are different shapes.

Just like flower gardens, some families are big.

Just like flower gardens, some families are small.

Just like flower gardens, families are special.

Making the Book

COVER PAGE

Activity: Create art with a coffee filter.

Setup: There are three kinds of filters available: basket style, cone shaped, and flat circles. Any type of coffee filter will work for this activity. If you are using the basket-style or cone-shaped filters, you will need to flatten them out and precut them in halves or quarters. If they are cut in halves, hold them so the straight edge is on the bottom and the curved side is on top. Gather up the bottom before gluing it onto the page.

Note: Paper towels can be cut into the desired shape and substituted for coffee filters.

Make sure you have extras if you intend to create a bulletin board (page 182).

You may also want to provide the children with long strips of green paper for the stems and precut leaves. If you simply do not have enough time or help to precut these items, the children can draw leaves and stems with crayons, markers, and colored pencils. As an alternative, students can add stems and leaves by printing with sponges that are cut into the appropriate shapes. The children can also paint on the details, using paintbrushes and rolling-paint or dab-type paint bottles. If you are able to precut the leaves and stems, you can give the children a choice as to what they want to do. The children may decide to use a variety of techniques.

Lay out some newspaper and place small containers of food coloring mixed with a little water or undiluted liquid watercolor paints on a table. The primary colors are a good choice for this activity. Place an eyedropper in each container.

Introduction: Any book about families can be read as an introduction to this unit. See the Related Resources (page 196) for suggestions. Ask the children questions about their families. Discuss similarities and differences among families. Tell the children the title of the next big book, and discuss how families are like flower gardens. The children are bound to mention some of the things described in the text of the book.

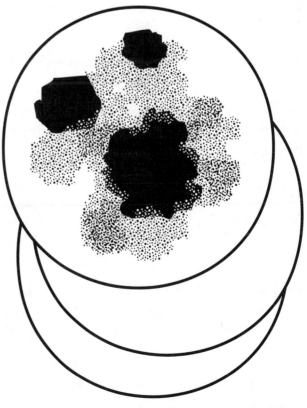

Note: If you choose to use photographs on the last page, you can have the children present these pictures at Show and Tell each day.

Directions: Have the children use the eyedroppers to drop and dot the paint or food coloring onto the coffee filters. When the filters are dry, glue them onto the big book pages. Tell students to add the stems and leaves.

Making the Book *(cont.)*

COVER PAGE *(cont.)*

Bulletin Board: Cut sheets of blue or aqua butcher paper that are large enough to fit on your bulletin board. Each day place the butcher paper on a table. Invite volunteers to glue and paint some of the flowers they make for their big books on it. By the end of the week you will have a nice arrangement of flowers on the butcher paper. Draw stems and leaves. Then glue some green shredded paper or cellophane grass around the flowers. You can also place a sun in the corner. Then hang the butcher paper on the bulletin board.

Play Charlotte Diamond's song entitled "Each of Us Is a Flower" on her *10 Carrot Diamond* album (Charlotte Diamond Music Inc., 1985). The title of this song also makes a wonderful caption for your bulletin board.

PAGE 1

Text: Just like flower gardens, families are different colors.

Activity: Make flowers using sticky dots and bingo markers or dab-type paint bottles.

Setup: Set out different-colored sticky dots, bingo markers or dab-type paint bottles, and a stack of large construction paper. Thumbprints made with paint can be used instead of using the sticky dots or the paint bottles. Provide markers, crayons, and colored pencils for children who choose to add extra details.

Introduction: Continue the discussions about families.

Directions: You may wish to allow the children to design their own flowers all over the page. If you prefer to use a teacher-directed art activity, show students how a sticky dot can be the center of a flower and the bingo markers can print the petals surrounding the sticky dot. Remember, this page is about different colors, so encourage the children to use as many colors as possible.

PAGE 2

Text: Just like flower gardens, families are different shapes.

Activity: Use tissue paper to make flowers.

Setup: Set out some tissue paper that has been cut into 1–2" (2.5–5 cm) squares. The tissue paper should be a variety of colors. On this big book page, the center of the flower is a shape, and the petals are made with the squares of tissue paper. To achieve this design, you can do one of the following: (1) Cut simple geometric shapes out of sponges and let the children sponge-paint the centers of the flowers. (2) Have precut geometric shapes for the children to glue onto their big book pages. (3) Let the children use geometric shape stamps or stencils to make the middles of the flowers.

Making the Book *(cont.)*

PAGE 2 *(cont.)*

Timesaver: When working with large numbers of students, it is usually necessary to cut quite a bit of tissue paper. For this reason, it is easier to cut several layers at once. However, by doing this, the squares have a tendency to stick together. The children find it frustrating to take these apart before using them. In order to prevent this from happening, place the cut-up tissue in a large plastic bag that is free of holes or tears. Blow up the bag balloon style, twist the top to keep the air inside, and shake the layers of tissue apart.

Introduction: Continue with the discussions about families. Discuss height and weight with the children. This may be a good time to measure the children and chart their heights. Don't forget to save the information for the All About Me books (pages 215–226).

Directions: Have the children start their flowers by gluing shapes onto the large construction paper. Then have them surround the shapes with the squares of tissue. To do this, students take individual pieces of tissue paper, crumple them, and glue them around the perimeters of the shapes. Details such as stems and leaves can be added.

PAGE 3

Text: Just like flower gardens, some families are big.

Activity: Make flower prints with cardboard tubes.

Setup: Set out a stack of construction paper and some shallow containers of different-colored paints. Snip ³/₄" (1.8 cm) slits all around the edge of an empty toilet tissue tube. Fold the sections out and flatten them by pressing the tube down on the table.

Introduction: Discuss family sizes. Encourage the children to talk about how many members are in their immediate families. Ask if students have relatives who live with them. This may be a good time to discuss family responsibilities. Find out if the children have any special chores that they do around the house. Examples include setting the table, making beds, getting the newspaper or the mail, and feeding the family pet. You may also wish to take this opportunity to discuss pets and how to care for them.

Directions: Have the children place the cut portion of the tube in the paint and press it down on the paper to make flower prints.

Note: Since the text refers to large families, this is a good time to review the concept of few and many. Make sure the children have many flowers when they're done. If the children lose interest before they have many flowers, they can add flower stickers or use flower stamps to add to their illustrations. These additions do not need to be done on the same day.

Making the Book *(cont.)*

PAGE 4

Text: Just like flower gardens, some families are small.

Activity: Make circle flowers.

Setup: For this activity, the children will be making two flowers on the page. This activity reinforces the circle shape and conceptual development, as well as counting, ordering, and size recognition skills.

According to your goals and students' abilities, you will need to either trace or precut three different sized circles (one small, one medium, one large) in various colors. The largest circle should not be much bigger than a compact disc. Each child will need two circles of every size. Set out some glue.

Before beginning, draw a three-column chart on a piece of butcher paper. Write the headings *Small, Medium,* and *Large.* Place the differently sized circles in the appropriate columns.

Small	Medium	Large
○	○	◯

Introduction: Continue the discussion about family sizes.

Directions: Have the children choose one circle from each of the columns on the chart, making sure they are three different colors. Ask students to count to three when they get their circles. Show them how to assemble their flowers according to size, beginning with the largest. Emphasize the order (first, second, and third) as well as size. Review the colors of the circles as the children are gluing their flowers. After the children have made two flowers on their big book pages, they can add stems and leaves.

Note: Craft sticks painted green make great stems.

PAGE 5

Text: Just like flower gardens, families are special.

Activity: Draw family portraits or make photo collages.

Setup: Place glue, drawing tools, and a stack of construction paper on the table. Photographs are optional.

Note: If actual photographs are going to be used, ask for them early so you can receive them all before beginning this page.

Making the Book *(cont.)*

PAGE 5 *(cont.)*

Note: Make sure parents know their photographs will be glued onto the big book page. If you decide to use photographs but some children don't bring any, you can explain that many families keep their photographs in special places at home. Point out that photographs are sometimes shared with friends and relatives so some families may not have extras they can spare.

Introduction: It's up to you whether or not students use actual photographs for this page. If you think parents will be hesitant to give up family photographs for this activity, have students make drawings of their families instead.

Directions: Have the children talk about their pictures as they glue them onto the book pages. The children who do not use photographs can draw family portraits, using markers, crayons, and colored pencils. Write the names of the family members beside the drawings and photographs. If the child elaborates on what the person in the drawing or photograph is doing, you can write that too. Children who use photographs may also want to add hand-drawn pictures of relatives and pets that are not shown.

Occasionally, teachers have extra copies of student photographs that were taken on Picture Day. If you have any of these extras or if you have taken pictures of your students, these can be glued onto the center of the children's big book pages and surrounded by their drawings and/or personal photographs.

Note: Make sure you make a copy of this big book for the classroom library. Use one or more photographs of the class for the last page. You may wish to have students sign the last page of the class book.

PUTTING IT ALL TOGETHER

This big book is fairly lengthy compared to some of the others that students have made, so it will be time consuming for the children to assemble it. However, since this book is based on the My Family and Me theme, you may wish to ask parents for help with putting this book together. By now, parents know what these child-created big books are all about, and they may be interested in lending a hand.

This book is put together the same way as the others. Reproduce the title and text (pages 190–195), or have students make up their own version. Be sure to review each page with the children as you go along. After the pages are secured, read the book aloud with students.

Additional Activities

Art/Language

Place Mats

Have students design place mats on tagboard. Laminate them for durability.

Playdough Families

Let the children sculpt family members out of clay or play dough.

Craft Stick Families

Set out some craft sticks, crayons, markers, and glue. Ask the children to make people by arranging and gluing the craft sticks on sheets of construction paper. Encourage students to decorate these figures to represent people in their families. They can add details to the sticks by drawing facial features, hair, arms, fingers, shoes, etc. When the stick people are completed, have the children glue them onto sheets of construction paper or tagboard. Ask the children to tell you about their families. Write down what they say next to their stick people. You may wish to save this for the All About Me book (pages 215–226).

Hand Print Tulips

Brush paint onto each child's hand, omitting the thumb. Have the children press their painted hands on construction paper to make tulips. Tell them that they can add a stem and leaves if desired.

Music/Movement/Language

Good Sports

This is a perfect time to engage in recreational sports. Discuss favorite sports within families, including those that are watched and those that are participated in by family members.

Ask if anyone has ever participated in outdoor sports activities such as baseball, badminton, and/or soccer. Play some of these games outdoors with your class. Consider organizing a kickball game on the school playground or using chalk to draw a hopscotch game on the sidewalk. Some indoor sports that can be done inside the classroom include bowling, lightweight plastic horseshoes, ring toss, and golf.

Neighborhood Walk

Read your favorite version of *The Three Little Pigs*. Discuss helping family members. Talk about the houses in the story. If your school is in a residential area, take a walk around the block and look at the different kinds of housing. Talk about building materials, size, design, color, etc.

Additional Activities *(cont.)*

Math/Language

Flower Matching

Use 3" x 5" (8 cm x 13 cm) index cards and flower stickers or pictures cut from gardening catalogs or garden shop flyers to make identical pairs. Have the children match the pictures.

Theme Bingo

Use the Bingo Card (page 336) and flower stickers to make a bingo game.

Where We Live

Encourage children to build houses, garages, etc., in the Block Center. Add dollhouse figures and furniture for this purpose.

Flower Math

Cut and glue five flowers made of felt, using the circle patterns from page 4 of the big book (page 184). Glue on wiggle eyes and paint on noses and mouths. Make a yellow circle for the sun and a white circle for the moon. Place the flowers on the flannelboard according to the following poem.

A Family of Flowers

Sing to the tune of "Five Little Ducks"

One little flower, lonely as can be,
Called out to a member of his family,
"Come on over and sing with me.
The sun is shining splendidly."

Two little flowers singing in the sun,
Called for another sister to come.
They said, "Two is nice, but three's more fun.
The sun feels good. Come on, get some."

Three little flowers stood side by side,
When another little flower suddenly cried.
"It's time for me to grow and not to hide.
I'd like to sing and stand with pride."

Four little flowers joined in song,
And called a brother to come along,
He said, "Our singing is loud and strong,
And I know this is where I belong."

Five little flowers sang that noon,
And although they don't sing in tune,
They're a family of flowers, all in bloom,
Singing until the light of the moon.

Additional Activities *(cont.)*

Science/Discovery/Language

Baby's Bath

Note: You will need dolls and towels for this activity.

Take some plastic dolls from the Home Center over to the water table. Explain that bathtime is an important part of a baby's day. Show the children how to bathe a baby. During the bath, review body parts and the concept of right and left. Allow each child to bathe a doll. After the bath, have the children dry, dress, feed, and put their babies in beds. If you choose to do this activity, a lesson on evaporation using the towels can follow.

What Dries Our Clothes?

Discuss how the towels feel after giving baths to the babies. Ask how you should dry them. Accept all answers. Let the children pick places to put the towels to dry. Encourage students to think about these questions: *Is it better to put the towels outdoors or keep them indoors? Why? Is it better to lay the towels on a flat surface or hang them up? Why?* Place towels in different spots to see which dry fastest. Periodically check on the towels. Discuss the results.

Soda Bubbles

Ask students what their families drink at breakfast, lunch, snack, and dinner. Point out that many families drink sodas. Give each child a small cup of soda. Let them observe the bubbles and listen to the fizz. Explain that there is air in the bubbles. To demonstrate this further, clean out a 12-ounce (360 mL) soda bottle and pour vinegar in it. The level of the vinegar should measure about 1" (2.5 cm) from the bottom of the bottle. Using a funnel, add a tablespoon of baking soda. Quickly remove the funnel, and fit the open end of a balloon snugly over the top of the bottle. The gas formed by the mixture will expand the balloon.

Social/Emotional/Language

Classroom Community Center

Set up a center of places in the community where families go together, such as a grocery store, shoe store, restaurant, hairdresser/barbershop, clothing store, bank, and gas station. The children may enjoy setting up a fast-food restaurant. If you go to a fast-food restaurant and explain to the manager that you would like to set up a replica of the restaurant in your classroom, they are often willing to donate some paper products.

Note: Thin, beige sponge foam, like the kind used for upholstery, makes great French fries when cut into strips. To make fish patties and/or chicken nuggets, cut various thicknesses of foam into the desired shapes and dust them with powdered, brown-tone blush makeup. In addition, this type of foam makes good pizza crust (page 168) when cut into a circle.

Additional Activities *(cont.)*

Social/Emotional/Language *(cont.)*

Baby Food

Check to see which children have food allergies or dietary restrictions. Then, one day for snack, serve only baby food such as applesauce.

Family Picnic

Have an outdoor or indoor picnic. Pick a day when the school lunches can be easily boxed or bagged, and/or have the children bring lunches from home. To set up for the picnic, lay out a large blanket or vinyl tablecloth. During the picnic, encourage students to pretend that they are somewhere other than the school. You may wish to play environmental music such as beach sounds or birds chirping.

Painting the House

Cut pieces of butcher paper to make the shape of a house. Mount the paper house on the wall or bulletin board. Provide paint and large paintbrushes. Invite the children, one or two at a time, to paint the paper house.

Parents as Resources

Explain to parents that the children are exploring different occupations. Invite them to visit your class and talk about their work. Ask them if they can donate any materials that they use in their jobs. For example, an office worker might have scrap computer paper or shredded paper, a carpenter might have extra roof shingles and wood scraps, and a textile factory worker might have fabric remnants and empty spools.

Role-Playing Occupations

Have the children pretend to be people performing various jobs or duties. Suggested role-playing activities include professional athletes playing different games, painters painting a house, circus performers doing their acts, farmers tending to their fields and/or animals, carpenters constructing buildings, bakers making bread, car wash attendants cleaning cars, police officers directing traffic, firefighters extinguishing a blaze, car mechanics fixing vehicles, seamstresses sewing clothes, dry cleaner workers pressing clothes, custodians cleaning the school, cafeteria workers/restaurant workers preparing food, office workers filing papers, salesclerks running cash registers. The children will enjoy guessing who's who.

Family Celebrations

You may wish to help students research specific family celebrations. Have them investigate the food, music, clothing, games, decorations, etc.

Families Are Like Flower Gardens

by_____

Just like flower gardens, families are different colors.

page 1

#2311 A Year Full of Themes

Just like flower gardens, families are different shapes.

page 2

Just
like flower
gardens, some
families are big.

page 3

Just like flower gardens, some families are small.

page 4

Just like flower gardens, families are special.

page 5

Related Resources

Books

Bunting, Eve. *Flower Garden.* Harcourt Brace & Co., 1994.

Corey, Dorothy. *Will There Be a Lap for Me?* Albert Whitman & Co., 1992.

Crews, Donald. *Big Mama's.* Greenwillow, 1991.

Dorling Kindersley Editors. *My First Look at Clothes.* Random House, 1991.

Ehlert, Lois. *Planting a Rainbow.* Harcourt Brace Children's Books, 1992.

Hausherr, Rosemarie. *Celebrating Families.* Scholastic, 1992.

Henkes, Kevin. *Jessica.* Mulberry Books, 1998.

Kissinger, Katie. *All the Colors.* Redleaf Press, 1997.

Mallett, David. *Inch By Inch: The Garden Song.* HarperCollins, 1995.

Mayer, Gina and Mercer. *This Is My Family.* Western, 1992.

Tamar, Erika. *The Garden of Happiness.* Harcourt Brace Children's Books, 1996.

Music

Charlotte Diamond. *10 Carrot Diamond.* "Each of Us Is a Flower" and "The Garden Song." Charlotte Diamond Music Inc., 1985.

Greg and Steve. *Playing Favorites.* "The Three Little Pigs Blues." Youngheart Records, 1991.

Hallum, Rosemary, Ph.D. & Henry "Buzz" Glass. *Fingerplays and Footplays for Fun and Learning.* "I'm a Little Teapot." Activities Records, Inc., 1987.

The Learning Station. *Tony Chestnut & Fun Time Action Songs.* "Shiny Clean Dance." Kaladon Publishing, 1997.

Raffi. *One Light, One Sun.* "In My Garden." Shoreline Records, 1985.

Raffi. *Singable Songs for the Very Young.* "Down By the Bay." Shoreline Records, 1976.

Videos

Are You My Mother? (Video); 25 min. Random House Video, 1992.

Brave Little Toaster. (Video); 90 min. Disney Home Video, 1994.

Software

Elmo's Preschool Deluxe. (by Sesame Street Learning Series; teaches problem-solving skills as students search for missing items in the count's castle); WIN 95 or WIN 3.1; Available from Creative Wonders, ABC Electronic Arts, P.O. Box 9017, Redwood City, CA 94063-9017. 1-800-KID-XPRT.

Reader Rabbit's Reading 1. (basic phonics, letter patterns, basic spelling, memory and concentration skills, vocabulary building); CD-ROM for MAC and WIN; TLC Properties, Inc., The Learning Company, 1 Athenaeum Street, Cambridge, MA 02142. 1-800-227-5609.

Teddy Finds a Family. (software about the importance of belonging to a family); PC; National School Products, 101 East Broadway, Maryville, TN 37804. 1-800-251-9124.

_____

(Date)

Dear Parent/Guardian,

On _____ , we will begin studying about families. During this unit, we will be exploring the various cultures represented in our classroom. I would like the children to share experiences related to their backgrounds. I would greatly appreciate any information you would like to share about your culture.

I am also looking for volunteers who would like to do activities and/or tell about experiences that reflect family histories and cultural backgrounds. Some suggestions are listed below.

- music—Teach us a traditional song or send a cassette for us to hear.

- dance—Teach us the steps to a traditional dance.

- art—Display traditional art or craft work.

- literature—Read aloud or tell a story that reflects your culture.

- food—Prepare a favorite family recipe for students to taste.

- clothing—Show some traditional clothing from your culture.

- celebrations—Tell about special days and events celebrated by your culture.

If you would like to volunteer to share or send something related to your family's culture, please sign and return the form at the bottom of the page.

_____

(Teacher)

_____

(School)

_____

(Phone)

- -

☐ Yes, I would like to volunteer to share or send something related to our family's culture.

Your Name: _____

Your Child's Name: _____

Work Phone Number: _____

Home Phone Number: _____

Long-Term Big Books

This type of child-created big book entails saving paperplay over a long period of time. The pages do not necessarily have to be completed in consecutive order. Examples of long-term theme activities are provided on pages 200–261. These big books are great to assemble during the last few months of school. By the end of the year, you have these books that are practically complete and just need to be stapled together.

Although these are called long-term books because the pages may be made anytime throughout the year, you can still teach a specific thematic unit. If you decide to build a unit around a long-term book, such as the farm unit (pages 199–214), you really only need one or two days to make a cover and add the text. For the duration of the unit, you can concentrate on other activities that revolve around the topic of farms as shown in the graphic organizer below. Use your own ideas or the suggestions provided in the Additional Activities sections to supplement the pages in the big books.

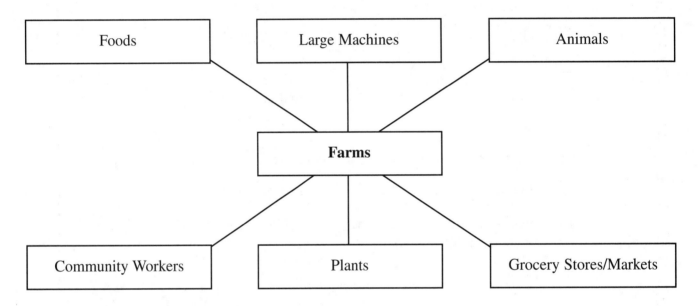

If you decide you want to do a long-term book, it's important to have a special out of the way place to store all the pages. Since these books take time to complete, you may have big book pages in storage for quite a while. The procedure is simple, but it does require planning. The important question you need to ask is "What paperplay activities from each week's lesson plans can I save for the purpose of creating a big book that focuses on a particular theme?"

Note: The activities for each theme should be filed separately. Depending on what you are using for storage, you may opt to use colored tagboard as thematic dividers.

There are no limitations. If you do the art anyway and it happens to be something that goes along with a specific unit, use it for a long-term big book. A project doesn't have to be completed in a certain amount time, be a lot of work, take up the majority of your instructional time, or be stressful to you to count as a real lesson. Once these books are completely assembled, they become a learning package designed for repeated use. Since the children have ownership, they'll want to review these independently and share their accomplishments time and time again, reinforcing all the skills they have learned.

On the Farm Big Book Materials

Unit Materials:

— glue

— scissors

— drawing tools: crayons, markers, chalk, colored pencils

— stapler

— construction paper: all colors

— tagboard

— paint: all colors

— scrap and collage items

Extra:

— stamps and stamp pads

— stencils

— sponges cut into shapes

Optional Materials for Additional Activities:

— feathers

— eggshells

— yarn

— instant chocolate pudding mix

— milk

— bowl

— plastic or rubber horseshoes

— rubber bands

— buttermilk

— clay or play dough

— plastic eggs

— wool remnants

— carrots or apples

— goat's milk or goat cheese

— heavy cream

— grains and grain cereals

— popcorn

On the Farm Big Book

Theme: My Family and Me
Topics: Farms/Farmers/Occupations
Duration: Long-Term
Approach: Adapted Song
Teacher-Directed Activities

Farms and farm animals are popular topics. This theme can be approached from a variety of angles and can be done at different times each year. Some connections to the theme are suggested below.

Me—animals I like, places I like to visit, farm foods I eat

My Family and Me—family members who own or work on a farm, animal families, buying farm products at stores/markets

My Community and Me—farms in the community, stores/markets that sell farm products

My World and Me—worldwide use of farm products, environmental issues, dirt, water cycle, sun, earthworms, gardening, fertilizing, recycling

This child-created big book is an adapted version of the song "Down on Grandpa's Farm," sung by Raffi on his *One Light, One Sun* album (Shoreline Records, 1985). There is reproducible text (pages 209–210) if you wish to use it, but you'll need to brainstorm the name of the farm with the children. Students may need to vote to pick one person's name for the farm. After the children select the name of the farm, write it in the blanks and reproduce the text pages. This way the name of the farm will be the same in every child's book. As an alternative, you may wish to ask each child to name the farm. Then write the child's suggestion on his/her big book pages.

PUTTING IT ALL TOGETHER

Once you have saved all the pages related to the farm theme that you want for your big book, it's just a matter of pulling them out of your files and assembling the book. Since the children may not have seen some of their artwork in a while, it is a good idea to review the pages with them.

A reproducible title sheet can be found on page 208. As the text (pages 209 and 210) is glued onto the page opposite the illustration, review the animal names and the sounds they make.

Don't forget to make a copy of this book for your classroom library. Be sure to write your name in the blanks for the name of the farm. The children will enjoy singing this song about their teacher. It may prove to be one of their favorite books to read over and over again.

Additional Activities

Warning: Check to see if children have any food allergies or dietary restrictions that would prohibit them from eating any of the snacks described on pages 201–207.

Art/Language

• *Chickens/Turkeys/Ducks*

Painting with Feathers

Rather than using paintbrushes at the easel, let the children use feathers instead.

Feather Crayon Rubbings

The children can rub a crayon over feathers that are placed underneath a thin sheet of paper.

Eggshell Art

The children can glue colored eggshells onto tagboard to create an original, textured design.

Note: This activity needs preparation because it takes time to save, wash, dry, and dye enough eggshells for an entire class. Sometimes restaurants will save eggshells for you, along with the egg cartons that you can use for other projects.

• *Sheep*

Yarn Collage

Set out different colors and thicknesses of yarn and some glue. Let the children create collages.

Yarn Painting

Thick, heavy yarn is required for this project. Have the children create designs by dipping the yarn in small containers of paint and dragging it back and forth across their papers.

• *Pigs*

Yummy Mud Paintings

Make chocolate pudding according to the directions on the package. Ask students if it looks like mud. Have them pretend to be piggies and finger-paint with this edible delight. Encourage the children to sound like pigs rolling in the mud as they paint with the pudding.

Pink Piggies

Show pictures of pigs/piglets. Discuss the colors of these animals. Ask students how the color pink is made. Remind them about how they made the light brown tone by mixing brown and white paint (page109). Explain that the color pink is also a tone. Mix red and white tempera paint to make the color pink. Allow students to free-paint at the easel, using the pink.

Additional Activities *(cont.)*

Art/Language *(cont.)*

• *Horses*

Horseshoe Printing

Using small, rubber horseshoes, have the children brush some paint on the flat side and make horseshoe prints.

• *Goats*

Grass Collage

Read your favorite version of the story *The Three Billy Goats Gruff.* This story might spark students' interest in an adapted big book version. Then let the children gather some grass or provide cellophane grass. Have them use it to create collages.

• *Cows*

Buttermilk Art

Brush a thin layer of buttermilk over some art paper. Before the buttermilk dries, have the children use colored chalks to draw pictures on the paper. Allow the buttermilk to dry.

• *Farms*

Invite students to sculpt animals out of clay or play dough.

Math/Language

• *Chickens/Turkeys/Ducks*

Egg Hunt

Have an egg hunt as described on page 93.

Sorting Feathers

Have the children sort feathers by size and/or color.

• *Pigs*

Circle Pig

Enlarge the Pig Pattern (page 212). Have students cut and glue the pattern together to make the pig. This activity can be used to reinforce the circle shape and review sizes. While assembling the pieces, discuss which should be glued on first, second, third, etc.

Additional Activities *(cont.)*

Math/Language *(cont.)*

• *Sheep*

Matching Wool Remnants

Cut wool scraps into 3" (8 cm) squares and let the children match the sets. Compare the woolly feel of the cloth and yarn.

• *Horses*

Poem

Using the Horse Pattern (page 213), make a felt or Velcro® kit by cutting out eight brown horses. Cut matching manes and tails in red, orange, yellow, green, blue, pink, black, and white. Place the horses on the flannelboard and give each child either a mane or a tail. As you read aloud the poem, have the children place their manes or tails on the horses in the order specified.

Eight Brown Horses

Eight brown horses grazing on hay,
Noticed something missing one sunny day.

They looked out across the grassy land,
Their manes and tails were in children's hands.

The first horse said, "If you're holding black,
I'd like you to bring my tail and mane back."

The second horse knew just what to do,
"Please bring me mine. They're colored blue."

The third horse asked, "Do you think —
I can have my mane and tail of pink?"

The fourth one looked, then called, "Hello.
You've got mine, and they're yellow."

The fifth horse spotted the orange hair.
"Please bring my mane and tail from there."

The sixth horse said, "If you might,
Return my mane and tail of white."

The seventh heard what the others said,
And called out, "Mine are colored red."

The eighth horse asked, "Has anyone seen,
My mane and tail that are colored green?"

Their manes and tails are what they got.
Then those horses left the field with a happy trot.

Additional Activities *(cont.)*

Science/Discovery/Language

• *Chickens/Turkeys/Ducks*

Light as a Feather

Have students use balance scales to compare/contrast the weight of feathers with other objects.

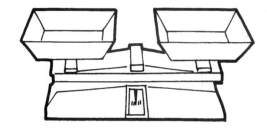

Sinking/Floating

Fill each egg with items of different weights. Have the children hold each egg in their hands and state whether it is light or heavy. Ask students if they think each egg will sink or float. Invite volunteers to put one egg at a time into the water at the water table. Have the children determine if their hypotheses were correct. Remove the items from inside the eggs; ask volunteers to put the eggs back in the water. Ask the children to compare/contrast the results.

• *Sheep*

Wool

If possible, place some sheep's wool on the discovery table for the children to examine.

Note: Many teachers use cotton puffs or batting to decorate lamb crafts. If you have a really cute lamb pattern that you'd like to use, perhaps the children can glue on appropriately colored yarn rather than use the cotton since it does not come from sheep.

From Wool to Yarn

If possible, invite a guest to spin yarn, knit, or crochet.

• *Pigs*

Sand Table Fun

Mud protects the coats of hogs because their tails are too short to fan away the flies. Add water to the sand table and make mudpies. If you prefer, go outside with a bucket of water and make real mudpies.

• *Horses*

Horse Food

Set out some hay, carrots, and apples on the discovery table.
You may wish to serve some carrots and apples for snack one day.

• *Goats*

Food Made from Goats

Let the children try a little goat's milk or goat cheese.

Additional Activities *(cont.)*

Science/Discovery/Language *(cont.)*

• *Cows*

Discovery Table

Set out some grains such as corn, wheat, oats, buckwheat, barley, and wheat bran. Let the children touch and compare these foods. Allow students to taste cereals made out of these grains. Have them examine corn kernels. Make popcorn as a treat or for art projects.

Make Butter

Pour heavy cream into an empty peanut butter jar until it is about half full. Let each child take a turn shaking the jar. Point out how the cream changes in texture and appearance. After a while, the cream will separate. Have students keep shaking the jar. The liquid is the buttermilk (page 202); the clump that remains is the butter. You may wish to blend a little salt into the butter. Then scoop it out and serve it on some crackers or bread.

Cheese and Milk

Serve some cheese, milk, or ice cream. You can add food coloring or flavored syrup to the milk.

Music/Movement/Language

• *Chickens/Ducks/Turkeys*

Feather Blowing Relay

Make two lines of children across a room or down a hallway from each other. Place a small feather on the floor. The first child in line crawls on the floor and blows the feather to the first child in line on the opposite side. When the feather reaches that child, he/she then crawls and blows it back the other way to the second child in line on the opposite side. This continues until all children have had their turn.

Duck Songs

Have students act out all the duck songs you know.

Duck, Duck, Goose

The children sit in a circle. One child is the goose and walks around the outside of the circle, tapping each child on the head while saying, "Duck." At some point, the goose taps someone and says, "Goose." This child gets up and chases the goose around the circle. The goose must run to the seat of the child who was tapped "Goose" and sit down before getting caught. If the goose gets caught before reaching the vacant seat, he/she must quack like a duck from one to ten times, depending on the number specified by the child who caught the goose. If the goose is not caught, the child left standing becomes the new goose. He/She walks around the circle, tapping heads just as the first child did.

Variation: Have the children quack as they run around the circle.

Additional Activities *(cont.)*

Music/Movement/Language *(cont.)*

• *Sheep*

Yarn Shapes

You will need plenty of open space for this activity. Arrange the children in a circle. Using a skein or ball of thick yarn, give one child the end of the yarn. Moving around the circle, let each child take hold of a section of the yarn as it unravels. Once the yarn has made its way around, cut it and tie the two ends together. Have students stretch the yarn to form a circle. Ask them if they can move to make a triangle, square, rectangle, and oval with the yarn.

Baa, Baa, Black Sheep

Teach children the nursery rhyme "Baa, Baa, Black Sheep." If possible, play Raffi's version from his album *Singable Songs for the Very Young* (Shoreline Records, 1976). For an additional math and science/discovery lesson, ask the children how many bags are in the song.

• *Pigs*

Pig Poem

Have students act out the following adaptation of "Five Little Monkeys."

Dancing Pigs

Five little piggies dancing in the dirt,

One fell down, and he got hurt.

Mama came running from across the farm,

And put that piggy inside the barn.

Four little piggies dancing in the dirt, …

(Using the previous verse as an example, continue until there aren't any piggies left.)

No more piggies dancing in the dirt,

They all fell down; they all got hurt,

Outside, no piggies can be found,

They're all indoors, safe and sound.

• *Farms*

Music

Have students sing and act out "Old MacDonald Had a Farm." Play music and encourage them to move like farm animals.

Additional Activities *(cont.)*

Music/Movement/Language *(cont.)*

• *Horses*

Horseshoes

Play this game using the plastic, lightweight horseshoes. If possible, show a real horseshoe.

Trotting

Play music that has a variety of tempos. Have students gallop or trot to the rhythm.

Social/Emotional/Language

• *Sheep*

Poem

Using the patterns (page 214), make a felt or Velcro® kit for the following poem.

Sheep Family

Baa, baa, I'm a ewe,
And I'm a mommy, too.
Baa, baa, I'm a ram.
I'm a daddy. Yes, I am.
We are lambs. We are small,
But someday we will grow up tall.
I'm a girl, and when I do,
I'll grow up to be a ewe.
I'm a boy. That's what I am.
I'll grow up to be a ram.
Our wool is used for cloth and yarn.
We're gentle animals on a farm.
If people cannot get to sleep,
They close their eyes and count us sheep.

• *Ducks*
Watch the video *The Ugly Ducking* (page 211). Discuss the feelings of the characters.

• *Pigs*
If your class has a long attention span, watch the Disney video *Babe* (page 211).

• *Farms*
Have a "Farm Day." Play country-western music, serve barbecue, wear bandannas, and do some simple country-western dances. Add farm clothes and items to the Home Center.

My
Farm
Book

by _____

Down on

_____'s

farm, there
was a little

_____

that made
a sound like this,

"_____".

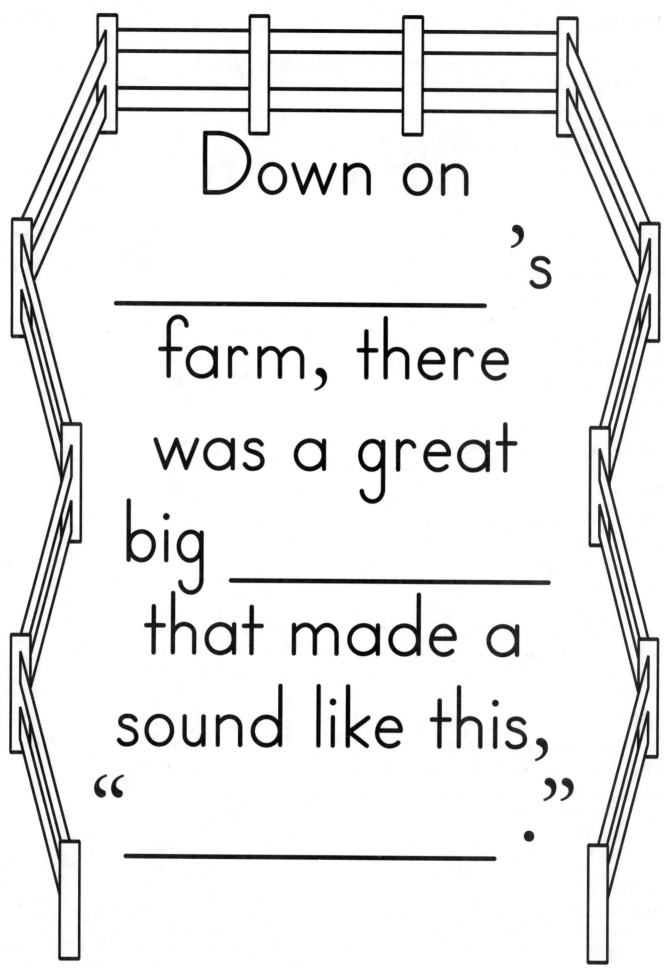

Down on

's

_____

farm, there

was a great

big _____

that made a

sound like this,

" _____ ".

Related Resources

Books

Aliki. *Milk from Cow to Carton.* HarperCollins, 1992.

Aubinais, Marie. *The Farm.* Abbeville Press, 1996.

Booth, Eugene. *On the Farm.* Raintree, 1985.

Brown, Margaret Wise. *Big Red Barn.* HarperCollins, 1989.

Ehlert, Lois. *Color Farm.* Lippincott, 1990.

Fass, Bernie. *Old MacDonald Had a Farm.* Clarus Music, 1985.

Fleming, Denise. *Barnyard Banter.* Henry Holt & Co., 1994.

Fowler, Allan. *Horses, Horses, Horses.* Childrens Press, 1992.

Fowler, Allan. *Thanks to Cows.* Childrens Press, 1992.

Hinds, P. Mignon. *Baby Calf.* Longmeadow, 1988.

King-Smith, Dick. *The Spotty Pig.* Ferrar Straus Giroux/HBJ, 1997.

Kitamura, Satoshi. *When Sheep Cannot Sleep.* Ferrar Straus & Giroux, 1988.

Krementz, Jill. *Holly's Farm Animals.* Random House, 1986.

McQueen, Lucinda. *The Little Red Hen.* Scholastic, 1987.

Nakatani, Chiyoko. *My Day on the Farm.* Crowell, 1986.

Music

All-Time Favorite Dances. "The Chicken." Kimbo Educational, 1991.

CJ Fundamentals. "Farmer in The Dell." Handy Music Inc., 1995.

Grammer, Red. *Teaching Peace.* "Barnyard Boogie." Red Note Records, 1986.

Greg and Steve. *We All Live Together, Vol. 5.* "Down on the Farm." Youngheart Records, 1994.

The Learning Station. *Tony Chestnut & Fun Time Action Songs.* "How Much Is That Doggie?" Kaladon Publishing, 1997.

Raffi. *The Corner Grocery Store.* "Cluck, Cluck, Red Hen." Troubadour Records Ltd., 1979.

Raffi. *One Light, One Sun.* "Down on Grandpa's Farm." Shoreline Records, 1985.

Video

Babe. (video about a pig that learns to herd sheep); MCA Home Video Inc., 1996.

Charlotte's Web (video of E.B. White's classic tale); Paramount Home Video, 1972.

Copycat Dog. (video about a dog who acts like other farm animals); 9 min. Troll Associates, Catalog Sales Dept., 100 Corporate Dr., Mahwah, NJ 07498. 1-800-929-8765.

The Ugly Duckling. (video of Hans Christian Andersen's classic tale); 11 min. Troll Associates, Catalog Sales Dept., 100 Corporate Dr., Mahwah, NJ 07498. 1-800-929-8765.

Software

Mother Goose's Farm 4 Learning. (includes Barnyard Counting, Farmhouse Rhythm & Shapes, Playground Reading, and Picnic Pond Reading); CD-ROM for MAC or WIN. Forest Technologies, 514 Market Loop, Suite 103, West Dundee, IL 60118. 1-800-544-3356.

Pig Pattern

Horse Pattern

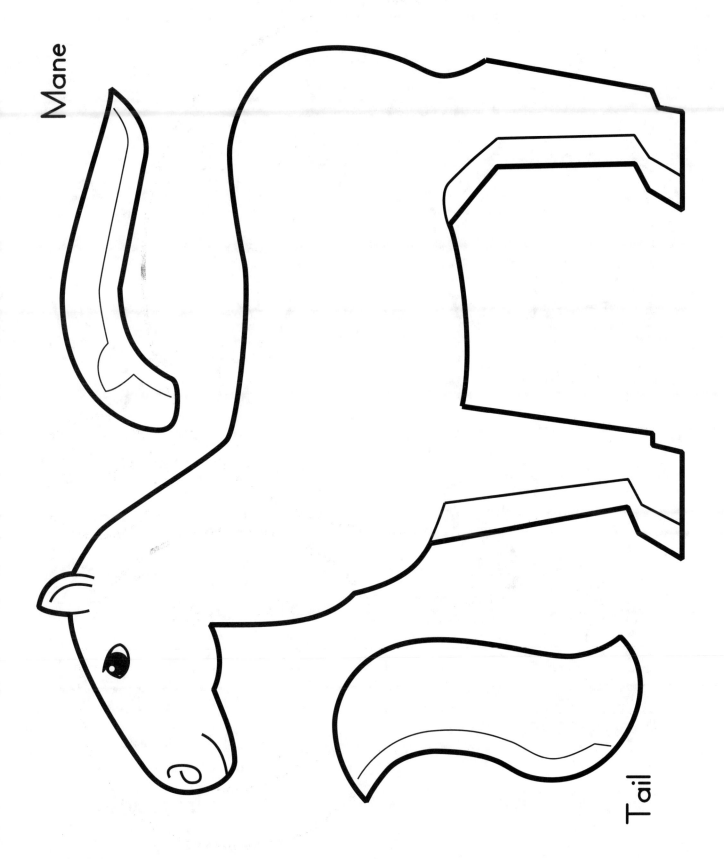

Mane

Tail

Sheep Patterns

Ewe

Ram

Boy Lamb

Girl Lamb

All About Me Big Book Materials

Unit Materials:

— glue
— scissors
— drawing tools: crayons, markers, chalk, colored pencils
— stapler
— construction paper: all colors
— tagboard
— paint: all colors
— scrap and collage items

Extra:

— stamps and stamp pads
— stencils
— sponge-painting shapes

Optional Materials for Additional Activities:

— buttons
— ribbons
— 5" x 8" (13 cm x 20 cm) blank index cards
— fabric paint
— parachute or old, flannel-backed vinyl tablecloth
— clean, old pairs of socks
— zippers

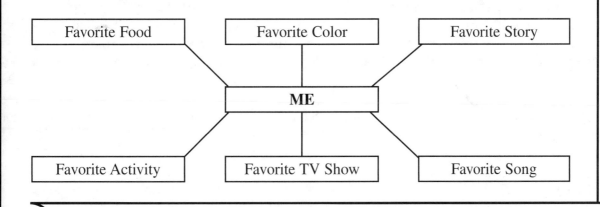

All About Me Big Book

Theme: Me
Topics: Individual Uniqueness/Personal Profiles
Duration: Long-Term
Approach: Original story
Combination

A reproducible title page and sample text are included (pages 220–223) for this long-term big book. You can read it over and reproduce any/all of the pages that coincide with paperplay activities that you would like to do with your students throughout the year.

Some examples of paperplay that can be saved throughout the year include easel paintings or any creative artwork done in using each child's favorite color, hand prints, collages using magazine pictures of favorite toys or favorite foods, people stencils, drawings of favorite television characters, and self-portraits.

If students make paperplay houses, write the children's addresses and add these pages to the big books. If you make paperplay balloons, cupcakes, or candles during the school year, save them and glue them onto big book pages with the children's birthdates. Sometime during the school year, measure and weigh the children. Write this information as part of the text for this big book and have the children draw corresponding pictures or use boy/girl stencils for the illustrations.

Print the first letter of each child's name on a sheet of construction paper using a wide-tipped marker. Have the children glue yarn, macramé cord, or crumpled tissue squares directly on the lines. Sticky dots or notebook paper reinforcements can also be used for this purpose. This paperplay activity can be used as the illustration. As an alternative letter activity, tell students to use letter stamps and stamp pads to decorate their big book pages.

The above activities can also be used to illustrate each child's age. Simply substitute a number for the letter.

PUTTING IT ALL TOGETHER

For this particular big book, you may want the children to begin by making self-portraits and then doing a name activity. The rest of the book can be assembled in whatever order you choose. The pages containing other information about the children and the corresponding paperplay activities can be added according to your preferences. All subsequent pages depend on the activities that are done and saved throughout the year. If only a couple of pages were saved during the year but you would still like to put together a big book, this topic can easily be explored as a separate unit.

Additional Activities

Art/Language

Buttons and Bows

Follow up a discussion about dressing with an activity using dress-up items. Set out a variety of buttons and ribbons and let the children make a collage using these things.

Zipper Rubbings

Set out a variety of zippers. Have students make designs by placing sheets of thin paper on top of the zippers and rubbing crayons over them.

Pocket Puppets

Try not to wear pockets the day you do this activity; that way, if there are any children who are not wearing pockets, they can identify with you. Before beginning this activity, ask everyone who is wearing clothes with one or more pockets to stand up and show them to the class. Talk about the different types of pockets there are.

Then round the top corners of 5" x 8" (13 cm x 20 cm) blank index cards. Provide two cards to each student. With younger children, have them glue the top and sides together. If you have older children, have them punch holes and use yarn to lace their cards together. Be sure students leave the bottom ends open so that they can insert their hands. Once the top and sides are fastened, the children can add hair and facial features with markers, crayons, buttons, pompoms, yarn, shredded paper, or other scrap items.

Self-Portraits

Encourage students to draw self-portraits.

Math/Language

Sorting Socks

Make a collection of clean old pairs of socks that includes different lengths, colors, sizes, and fabrics. If you prefer, use the Sock Patterns (page 225) and construction paper to make the pairs. Mix up the pairs. Then have students work independently or with partners to match the pairs.

Color Buttons

Take a small group of children and let each child pick a different color of crayon from a pack. Place a pile of buttons on the floor or table and instruct the children to find only the buttons that match the color of the crayon they picked.

Sorting Buttons

Invite the children to sort buttons according to shape, size, or color.

Additional Activities *(cont.)*

Math/Language *(cont.)*

Sock Matching

Using the Sock Pattern (page 225), cut out and decorate pairs of socks. Make sure to face the pairs in opposite directions for left and right socks. The designs on each matching pair should be the same. Keep one sock from each pair and give the matching sock to a child. Place one sock at a time on the flannelboard as you sing the song below. Have the child holding the matching sock place it on the flannelboard next to its mate.

Sock Pairs

Sing to the tune of the "Alphabet Song."

I have two feet on which I walk,
But I can only find one sock.
Here's a sock I like to wear,
But I need a matching pair.
Bring one up so we can see,
If it matches perfectly.

Science/Discovery/Language

My Shadow

Shine a light against a plain, light-colored wall, and let children experiment with hand shadows.

Music/Movement/Language

Shoe Drop

This activity can be done using a parachute, a round flannel-backed tablecloth, or a piece of cloth cut into a large circle. If a tablecloth or fabric is used, cut in the center a small hole that is large enough for a child's shoe to drop through. Lay the open, cloth circle on the floor. Have the children sit around the circle. While reinforcing the concept of left and right, have each child remove one shoe. Tell the children to toss their shoes onto the circular cloth, stand up, and firmly hold the edges of the cloth. Ask them to carefully bounce the cloth up and down until one of the shoes falls through the hole in the center. When a child sees her/his shoe fall through, she/he must run under the cloth, retrieve it, sit down, and put it on. Point out that only one child can be under the cloth at a time. Once the child has the shoe back on, she/he should stand back up and continue bouncing the remaining shoes until everyone has had a turn.

Note: Tell students that they do not have to tie their shoes. At the end of this activity, have the children who are able tie their own shoes do so and then help others who can't. Make notes about who can and cannot tie shoes for future reference.

Additional Activities *(cont.)*

Music/Movement/Language *(cont.)*

Body Parts

Act out the song "Head, Shoulders, Knees, and Toes." The Learning Station has a good version of this song on its *Where Is Thumbkin?* CD and cassette (Kaladon Publishing, 1997).

Sock Toss

Use the same socks as Sorting Socks (page 217). Show the children how to form a ball from the socks by holding the tops together, stretching one sock open, folding the top over, and pushing the remaining socks inside. Have students toss the socks into a laundry basket or milk crate.

Social/Emotional/Language

Zip

Cut zippers out of a variety of old clothing. If possible, ask tailors if they have any zippers they could donate for your classroom. Let the children practice zipping and unzipping these.

Button Up

Before doing this, color-code large buttons and buttonholes on an old jacket or sweater, using fabric paint. Use different colors for each button, but make sure each button and matching hole is the same color. This will make it easier for students to correctly align the buttons. Hang the jacket or sweater backwards on a chair. Let the children practice buttoning and unbuttoning it.

Tie It in a Bow

Have students practice doing things that Little Critter says he can do in Mercer Mayer's book *All By Myself* (Western, 1983). Bring in an old pair of shoes or sneakers to give the children practice with tying shoes. Be sure to use new laces.

Birthday Cake

Make a birthday cake (page 226) for students to sign after they learn their birth dates. This cake will be an extra incentive as well as enable you to determine who still needs help with this skill.

Families

Share one of the stories about families with the class. See the Related Resources for suggestions (page 224). Ask students to tell what a family is and what the word *related* means. Have them tell about their families: who the members are that live with them, who the members are who do not live with them, who the oldest and youngest members are, where they live, what they like to do together, and how they help each other. Then have students draw pictures and dictate stories about their families.

All
About
Me

by _____

My name is _____ .

- -

I am _____ years old.

- -

I am _____ inches tall and weigh _____ pounds.

- -

This is my handprint.

This is me.

page _____

My birthday is on _____ .

page _____

I live at _____ .

page _____

My favorite color

is _____ .

page _____

My favorite food

is _____ .

page _____

My favorite television show

is _____ .

page _____

My favorite thing to do

is _____ .

page _____

Related Resources

Books

Aliki. *My Feet.* HarperCollins, 1990.

Aliki. *My Hands.* HarperCollins, 1990.

Anholt, Catherine. *What Makes Me Happy.* Candlewick Press, 1996.

Fox, Mem. *Whoever You Are.* Harcourt Brace Children's Books, 1997.

Harris, Robie H. *Happy Birth Day.* Candlewick Press, 1996.

Hoffman, Mary. *Amazing Grace.* Dial Books for Young Press, 1991.

Mayer, Gina and Mercer. *This Is My Family.* Western, 1992.

Mayer, Mercer. *Just Me and My Puppy.* Western, 1985.

Mayer, Mercer. *Just My Friend and Me.* Western, 1988.

Munsch, Robert. *Moira's Birthday.* Annick Press, 1987.

Munsch, Robert. *Stephanie's Ponytail.* Annick Press, 1996.

Murphy, Stuart J. *A Pair of Socks.* HarperCollins 1996.

Pearson, Susan. *My Favorite Time of Year.* HarperCollins, 1988.

Wildsmith, Brian. *My Dream.* Oxford University Press, 1986.

Wood, Audrey. *Silly Sally.* HBJ, 1992.

Music

Diamond, Charlotte. *10 Carrot Diamond.* "Four Hugs a Day." Charlotte Diamond Music, Inc., 1985.

Greg and Steve. *Kids in Motion.* "Can't Sit Still." Youngheart Records, 1987.

Greg and Steve. *Rockin' Down the Road.* "Can't Sit Still." Youngheart Records, 1995.

Hallum, Rosemary, Ph.D. & Henry "Buzz" Glass. *Fingerplays and Footplays for Fun and Learning.* "Where Is Thumbkin?" Activity Records, Inc., 1987.

The Learning Station. *Tony Chestnut & Fun Time Action Songs.* "One Two, Buckle My Shoe." Kaladon Publishing, 1997.

The Learning Station. *Where Is Thumbkin?* "Head, Shoulders, Knees, and Toes." Kaladon Publishing, 1997.

Palmer, Hap. *Learning Basic Skills Through Music: Health and Safety.* "Exercise Every Day." Activities Records, 1970.

Raffi. *Singable Songs for the Very Young.* "I Wonder If I'm Growing." Shoreline Records, 1976.

Software

Elmo's Preschool Deluxe. (by Sesame Street Learning Series; game dealing with emotions and activities that build social skills such as sharing, cooperating, and taking turns); CD-ROM for WIN 95 or WIN 3.1; available from Creative Wonders, ABC Electronic Arts, P.O. Box 9017, Redwood City, CA 94063-9017. 1-800-KID-XPRT.

Sock Patterns

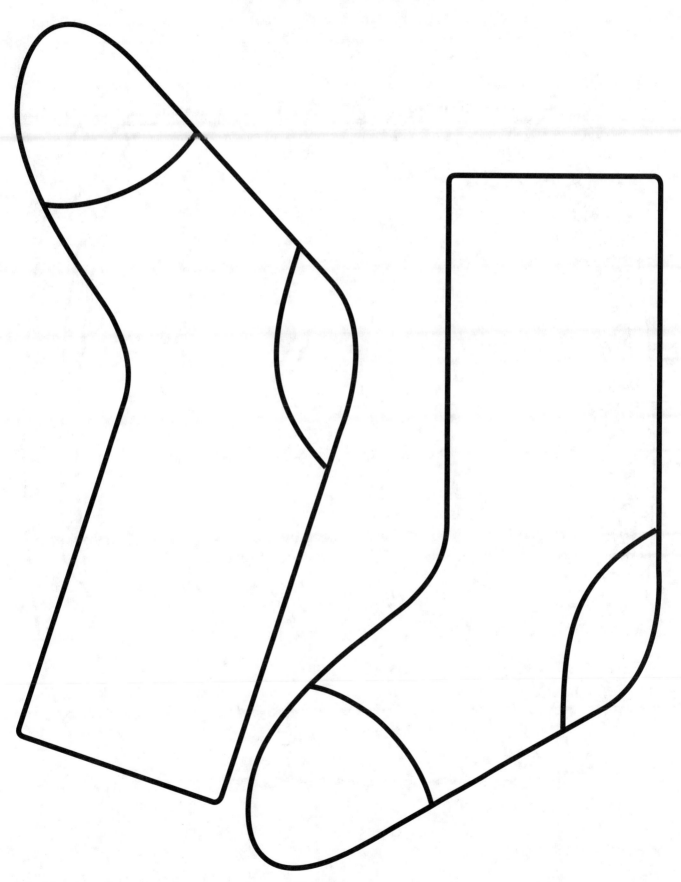

Birthday Cake Pattern

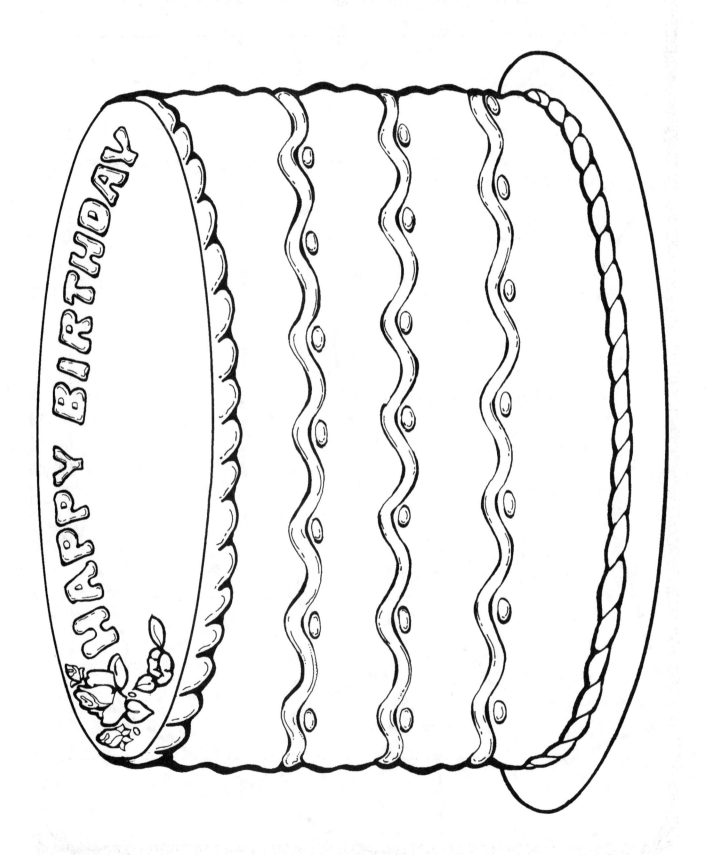

Shapes Big Book Materials

Unit Materials:

— glue
— scissors
— drawing tools: crayons, markers, chalk, colored pencils
— stapler
— construction paper: all colors
— tagboard
— paint: all colors
— scrap and collage items

Extra:

— stamps and stamp pads
— stencils
— sponge-painting shapes

Optional Materials for Additional Activities:

— sand
— confetti
— cotton batting
— glitter
— pompoms
— oatmeal
— plastic bottle caps
— macramé cord
— clean tongue depressors
— crackers
— cheese
— parachute or large blanket
— glue gun/gluesticks
— cotton balls

— rice
— tissue paper
— cornmeal
— feathers
— Styrofoam packing
— small posters
— stickers
— cereal
— fruits and vegetables
— play dough
— felt or pellon
— 1" (2.5 cm) wide dressmaker waistband elastic

Shapes Big Book

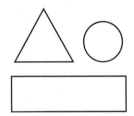 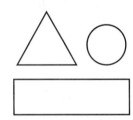

Theme: My World and Me
Topics: Shapes—Circle, Square, Triangle, Rectangle, Heart, Diamond, Oval
Duration: Long-Term
Approach: Original/Adapted Poem
Combination Illustrations

For this big book, save any moderately flat paperplay dealing with shapes. Shape activities may include rubbings, cutouts, prints, stamp art, stencils, sponge-painting, and crumpled tissue paper or thick yarn glued onto pre-drawn shapes. You may have saved circle-shaped pumpkins in October, triangular evergreens in the winter, hearts in February, circles for the Traffic Light book (page 51), fruit prints for The Very Hungry _____ book (page 88), the cup prints for the Happy Teeth book (page 129), and the buttons and bows collage for the All About Me unit (page 217).

If the entire page is filled with the same shape, such as circles, you can use the following text.

This page is full of circles.

Circles all around.

The shape's the same no matter what—

Even upside down.

If the shape you are focusing on is only one part of the whole picture or illustration, you can use the following adapted poem taken from Bill Martin, Jr.'s *Brown Bear, Brown Bear, What Do You See?* (Henry Holt & Co., 1996).

I spy a shape. What do I see?

I see a _____ (name of shape) looking at me.

If you want to include math skills, have students specify numbers as in the following example.

I spy two shapes. What do I see?

I see two circles looking at me.

Alternative: Have students sing the following to the tune of "Mary Had a Little Lamb."

There's a _____ (name of illustration) on this page, on this page, on this page.

See the _____ (name of shape) on this page. Can you find it?

PUTTING IT ALL TOGETHER

Reproduce the title and text (pages 232–235). The above text for this Shapes big book and the text for the Colors big book (pages 242–243) can be interchangeable by making minor adjustments. Fill in the blanks accordingly and proceed to assemble the book in any order that you and your students choose.

Additional Activities

Art/Language

Fold-Over Kites

Precut diamond-shaped kites out of construction paper. Show the children that a diamond shape folded in half becomes two triangles. Help them squirt small amounts of paint, one color on each triangular half of the kite. Have the children fold the kite and press down to blend the colors. Unfold the kites and allow the paints to dry.

Note: If these kites are used for a big book, they can be glued onto large sheets of construction paper. Then have students draw the tails with markers or crayons. If they are used as wall decorations, the tails can be added by gluing strips of paper that have been folded accordion style.

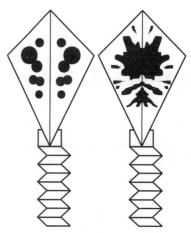

Bulletin Board: Cover the bulletin board with light blue or yellow butcher paper or fabric. Place the kites described above on the bulletin board with a banner of your choice. Some ideas include Flying High in _____'s Class and Reach for the Sky.

Textured Shapes

Provide a variety of materials that have different textures such as sand, rice, glitter, small feathers, pompoms, Styrofoam packing pieces, shredded paper, yarn, macramé cord, crumpled tissue paper, confetti, oatmeal, cornmeal, and cotton fluff or batting. Draw the outline of a shape on pieces of construction paper. Have the children add textures to the shapes by gluing any of the materials inside the outlines.

Printing with Blocks

Using the blocks in your Block Center, have students choose different shapes and make prints with them. They can do this by dipping the blocks in some paint and then pressing them on sheets of construction paper.

Math/Language

Circle Patterns

Save an assortment of colored flat, plastic bottle caps, such as the kind on milk and juice, to use with the following patterning activity.

Trace the caps side by side on large, blank white index cards. Color the circles according to the colors of the bottle caps you traced. Encourage the children to reproduce the patterns they see on the cards, using the actual bottle caps.

Additional Activities *(cont.)*

Math/Language *(cont.)*

Shape Puzzles

Cut small posters into geometric shapes. For example, when the pieces are put together, one poster might make a triangle. The number of pieces will depend on the age and ability level of your students. For very young children, four pieces might be enough. These puzzles can be stored in large manila envelopes. Draw a picture of the shape enclosed on the outside of each envelope.

Shape Lotto

Reproduce the Bingo Card (page 336) to make a game using shape stickers or stamps. If there is room, put two or three shapes in some of the bingo squares. This will help reinforce number concepts as well as shapes.

Matching Textured Shapes

Cut pairs of different shapes out of a variety of textured materials and glue them onto blank index cards. Ask the children to match the shapes as well as the textures.

Shape Dominoes

Place about 24 craft sticks vertically on a table. Draw a line horizontally across the center of each stick. Start with one stick and draw different shapes on opposite ends using, different colors. Take another stick. On one end draw a shape that matches one end of the first stick. On the other end, draw a new shape. Continue this process until the game is complete. Then allow students to match the ends of the shape dominoes.

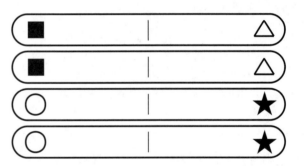

Science/Discovery/Language

Shape Snacks

Set out an assortment of foods in a variety of shapes. For example, cereals and crackers come in many shapes. Other choices include orange and cucumber slices (circles), watermelon wedges (triangles), cheese strips (rectangles), and saltines (squares).

Dough Shapes

Set out some soft play dough and use ordinary items as cutters. Empty toilet paper tubes, cardboard or plastic boxes, empty and cleaned school milk cartons, and yogurt containers work well as cutters.

Note: You may need to cut some of the boxes to reduce the sizes and make them more manageable. Poke holes in them to prevent the dough from getting stuck.

Additional Activities (cont.)

Music/Movement/Language

Parachute Shape Exchange

You'll need a parachute or a large sheet or blanket for this activity. Pairs of children will need matching shapes. You may wish to consider using the shape bracelets described below.

Trading Places

Sing to the tune of "Yankee Doodle."

Shapes go walking round and round with smiles upon their faces.

_____ (shape name) without a sound—quick, change places.

(Hold it high until the shapes are ready.)

(Spoken) "Are you ready? Bring the chute down."

(Continue until all of the children have had a turn.)

Musical Shapes

Set up chairs in rows. Be sure there is one for every child. Begin by giving each child a shape bracelets as described below. Place a shape on every chair. The shapes on the chairs should match those that the children have. Play music as the children move around the chairs. Tell students that when you stop the music, they must sit in the chair with the shape that matches theirs. A chair is then taken away, and the music and movement resumes. Then next time the music stops, the child without a chair should sit on the floor next to a chair that has his/her matching shape.

Social/Emotional/Language

Shape Hunt

Ask the children to find something in the room that matches the shape on their bracelets (below).

Shape Bracelets

Make matching pairs of bracelets out of construction paper or waistband elastic. If you have a large class, identical shapes can be made in different colors.

Materials: waistband elastic, approximately 1" (2.5 cm) wide; glue; sturdy fabric such as felt, pellon, or craft foam or fabric paints; hot glue gun (optional)

Directions: Cut the elastic strips to comfortably fit your students' wrists. For each bracelet, zigzag stitch the two ends together. Cut 2" (5 cm) shapes out of felt or draw them directly onto the center of the bracelets using fabric paints. The children can wear these bracelets for a variety of activities.

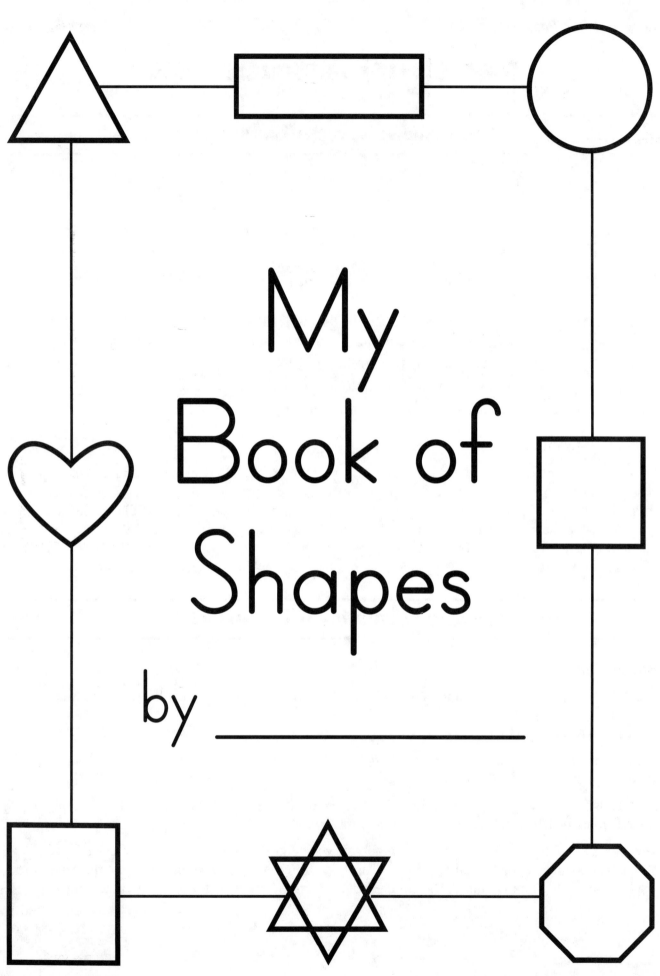

My Book of Shapes

by _____

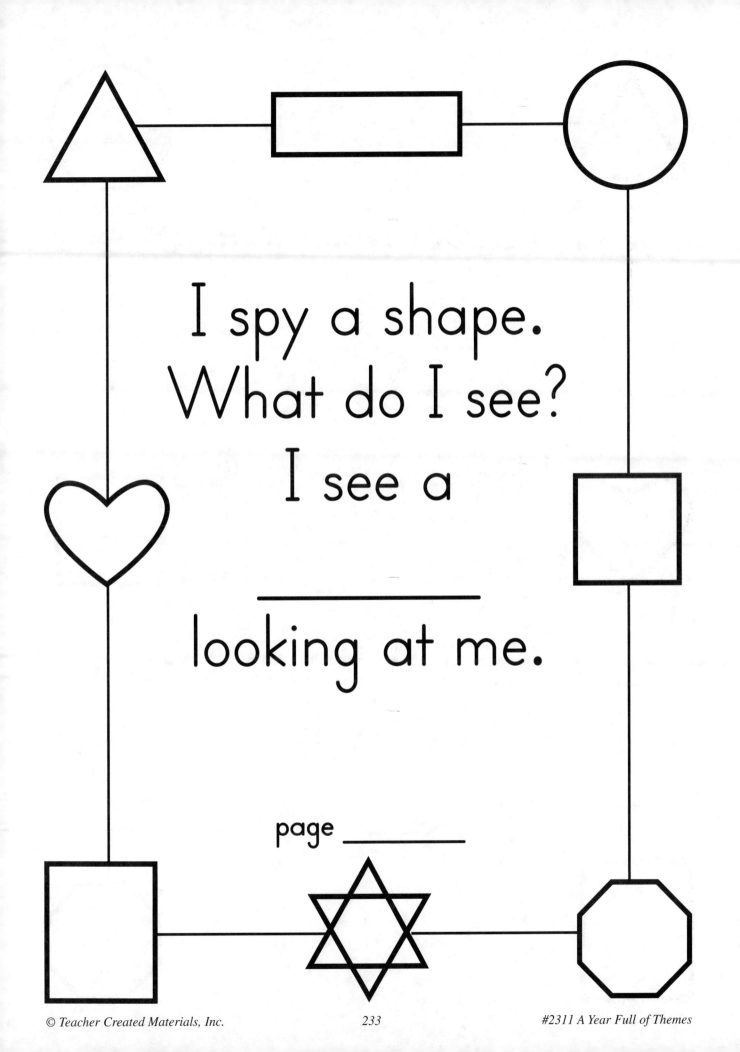

I spy a shape.
What do I see?
I see a

_____

looking at me.

page _____

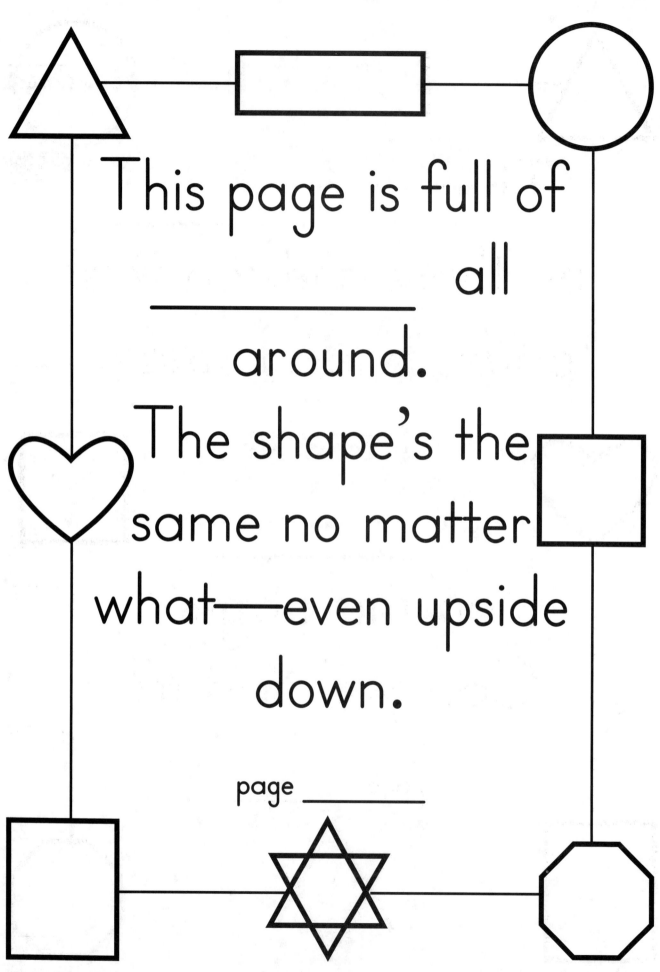

This page is full of all

_____

around.
The shape's the same no matter what—even upside down.

page _____

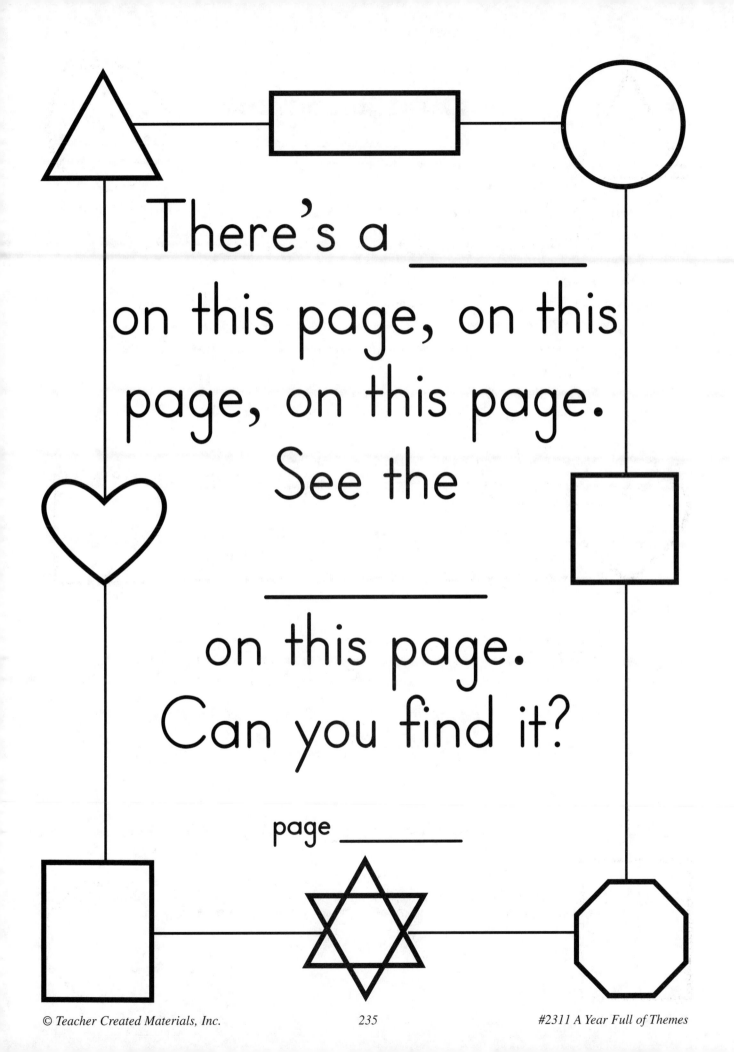

There's a _____
on this page, on this
page, on this page.
See the

_____
on this page.
Can you find it?

page _____

Related Resources

Books

Allington, Richard L. *Shapes.* Raintree, 1985.

Brown, Margery W. *Afro-bets: Book of Shapes.* Just Us Books, 1991.

Carle, Eric. *Draw Me a Star.* Paper Star Books, 1998.

Courson, Diana. *Let's Learn About Colors, Shapes, & Sizes.* Good Apple, 1986.

Crews, Donald. *Ten Black Dots.* Mulberry Books, 1995.

Dodds, Dayle Ann. *The Shape of Things.* Candlewick Press, 1996.

Forte, Imogene. *I'm Ready to Learn About Shapes.* Incentive Publications, 1986.

Greene, Rhonda Gowler. *When a Line Bends, a Shape Begins.* Houghton Mifflin Co., 1997.

Griffiths, Rose. *Circles.* Gareth Stevens, 1994.

Hoban, Tana. *Shapes, Shapes, Shapes.* William Morrow, 1986.

Moss, David. *Shapes.* Outlet Book Company, 1989.

Pienkowski, Jan. *Shapes.* S & S Trade, 1989.

Rogers, Paul. *Shapes Game.* Holt, 1990.

Ross, Shirley and Cindy McCord. *Shape Creatures.* Monday Morning Books, 1987.

Taulbee, Annette. *Shapes & Colors.* Schaffer Publications, 1986.

Thomson, Ruth. *All About Shapes.* Gareth Stevens, 1987.

Worth, Bonnie. *Muppet Babies Shape Machine.* Checkerboard Press, 1988.

Yenawine, Phillip. *Shapes.* Delacorte, 1991.

Music

Greg and Steve. *We All Live Together, Vol. 3.* "Shapes." Youngheart Records, 1979.

Palmer, Hap. *Learning Basic Skills Through Music, Vol. 2.* "One Shape, Three Shapes." Activity Records.

Palmer, Hap. *Learning Basic Skills Through Music, Vol. 2.* "Triangle, Circle or Square." Activity Records.

Sesame Street. "C" Is For Cookie. "Circles." Children's Television Workshop, 1995.

Video

Barney's Shapes & Colors. (Two videos about shapes and colors); 30 min. The Lyon's Group, 1997.

Software

Elmo's Preschool Deluxe. (by Sesame Street Learning Series; develops cognitive skills using shapes and colors); WIN 95 or WIN 3.1; available from Creative Wonders, ABC Electronic Arts, P.O. Box 9017, Redwood City, CA 94063-9017. 1-800-KID-XPRT.

Colors Big Book Materials

Unit Materials:

— glue

— scissors

— drawing tools: crayons, markers, chalk, colored pencils

— stapler

— construction paper: all colors

— tagboard

— paint: all colors

— scrap and collage items

Extra:

— stamps and stamp pads

— stencils

— sponge-painting shapes

Optional Materials for Additional Activities:

— vinegar

— spray bottle

— squeeze bottles

— rubber bands

— white butcher paper

— cardboard circles

— spring clothespins

— pistachio instant pudding mix

— milk

— bowl

— sugar and/or honey

— mild laundry soap

— food coloring

— ice cube tray

— powdered tempera: any color

— aluminum foil

— craft sticks

— empty seasoning/spice containers or old salt and pepper shakers

— cardboard tubes

— wax paper

— variety of fruits

Colors Big Book

Theme: My World and Me

Topics: Colors: Primary and Secondary, Light and Dark Colors

Duration: Long Term

Approach: Original Poem

Combination Illustrations

Creating a long-term book about colors requires planning and storage of any paperplay that can be used as a big book page. Here are a few suggestions. Use red apple prints that were left over from the Apple Tree book (page 25) for red pages. Save fruit prints (page 88), such as those done with oranges, for orange pages. Use the purple paperplay activity from the Peanut Butter and Jelly big book (pages 108 and 109) for purple pages and the pink piggies paintings (page 201) done for the On the Farm big book for pink pages.

This is also a perfect opportunity to justify the use of crafts or dictated art in your classroom. These types of paperplay activities are perfect for a book about colors. Make an inventory of the activities that you normally do throughout the year and note which ones can be used as part of a long-term color book. If you're doing these activities anyway, you can give them an extended purpose by including them in this type of book.

The text (page 243) can be duplicated for each page of the big book. Simply fill in the blank to match the corresponding illustration as shown in the following example.

> There are many colors in this book
> Here's an orange pumpkin. Take a look.

PUTTING IT ALL TOGETHER

Use the adaptation (page 228) of Bill Martin, Jr.'s *Brown Bear, Brown Bear, What Do You See?* (Henry Holt & Co., 1996) for the Colors big book. All you have to do is change the words from shapes to colors and add the specifics accordingly.

Additional Activities

Art/Language

Scrap Paper Collage

Have students cut or tear scrap paper and glue the pieces onto large sheets of construction paper.

Stained Glass

Use the following steps to make pictures that resemble stained glass windows.

1. Cut colored tissue paper into approximately 2" (5 cm) squares.

2. Mix two parts water with one part vinegar. Pour the mixture into a spray bottle.

3. Have students arrange the tissue pieces on sheets of white construction paper.

4. Spray the vinegar and water mixture on the tissue. Allow the pictures to dry.

5. After the pictures are dry, ask students to remove the tissue and reveal the stained glass effect.

Squeeze Bottle Painting

To do this activity you will need several squeeze bottles. These can be obtained by asking any contact lens wearer or eye care specialist for empty saline solution bottles.

Pour white glue into bowls, and mix in some water to make it runny. Make different colors by adding food coloring or tempera paint to each bowl of glue. Stir the mixtures until the desired colors are achieved. Pour each color into a separate squeeze bottle and label it. Tell the children to squeeze as they move bottles over their sheets of construction paper, making designs with the drizzled colors.

Rubber Band Painting

Set out several shallow containers of paint in a variety of colors. Wrap different widths of rubber bands around wooden blocks. To create interesting designs, have the children dip the blocks in some paint and then press them onto construction paper.

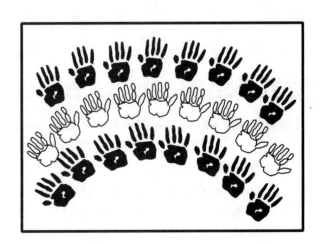

A Rainbow of Hands

This makes a great bulletin board. Use the children's handprints to create a rainbow. Group the children according to the separate colors (red, orange, yellow, green, blue, indigo, violet). Then have students place their hands in shallow containers of paint and press down on a large sheet of butcher paper to create the colorful arcs.

Additional Activities (cont.)

Math/Language

Color Bingo

Make a game using the Bingo Card (page 336) and colored sticky dots.

Color Wheels

Note: A local pizzeria or bakery may be able to donate pizza rounds or cake rounds for this game.

If you don't have pizza rounds or cake rounds, cut a large circle out of sturdy poster board or cardboard. Divide the circle into eight sections. Use crayons or paint to make each section a different color. Laminate the circle. Color eight clothespins, using the same colors as the eight sections of the circle. Have the children clip the clothespins onto sections of the circle that have the matching colors.

Science/Discovery/Language

Pudding Painting

Make colored pudding, such as pistachio (green), according to the directions on the box. If you prefer, you can add food coloring to vanilla pudding. Let the children finger-paint with the pudding.

Colored Milkshakes

Add food coloring and a little sugar or honey to milk for a nutritious treat. *Warning:* Be sure to ask parents if their children have any food allergies or dietary restrictions.

Colored Soap Crayons

Ingredients: 1 cup (225 g) powdered laundry soap that is mild, 40 drops of food coloring, water

Directions: Pour laundry soap into a bowl and add the food coloring. Stir in the water by the teaspoonful until the mixture has a liquid consistency. Place the mixture in an old, plastic ice cube tray or muffin tin. Place the tray or tin in a dry, sunny place for about two days. The crayons will become hard. Then they can be kept in the classroom at the water table or sink or sent home in plastic sandwich bags for use at bath time.

Colored Ice Painting

Fill an ice cube tray with water, cover tightly with aluminum foil, and insert craft sticks into each cube section. Freeze. Place some powdered tempera into empty seasoning/spice containers or old salt and pepper shakers. Give the children sheets of construction paper and have them sprinkle a little powdered paint onto the paper. Hand each student an ice cube. Have the children slowly rub the ice over the paint. Have students note that the paint liquefies.

Additional Activities *(cont.)*

Music/Movement/Language

Colored Kazoos

Collect enough empty toilet paper tubes for every child to have one. Set out a variety of tempera paints in small containers. Have the children paint their tubes whatever colors they like. Allow the paint to dry. Once the tubes are dry, cut a waxed paper circle that is large enough to fit over one end of a tube and secure it with a rubber band. Punch a hole in the tube near the rubber band. Play a favorite song. Have students hum the tune into the open end of the tube.

Social/Emotional/Language

I Spy

Invite the children to sit in a circle. Ask a volunteer to choose a colored object in the room and whisper its name in your ear. The volunteer then begins the game by saying, "I spy something red." Each child in turn, tries to guess what the object is. Once the object has been named, the child to the left of the spy goes next. The game continues in a clockwise fashion until everyone has had a turn or as long as there is interest.

Color Day

Have a Color Day or Color Week. Send the letter (page 45) to parents to announce this event.

Colorful Friendship Fruit Salad

Send home the note shown below asking each child to bring in one fruit. Wash all fruits thoroughly, and remove any seeds/pits. Then cut up the fruit and place it in a large bowl. A little bit of lemon juice will keep bananas from turning brown. Serve the fruit to students.

Warning: Ask parents if their children have any food allergies or dietary restrictions.

- -

Dear Parent/Guardian,

As part of our unit on colors, we are making a colorful friendship fruit salad. On _____ please send your child to school with one piece or one serving of fruit. I know this will be an enjoyable experience for our class. Thank you in advance for your snack time contribution.

Sincerely,

_____
(Teacher)

My
Book of
Colors

by _____

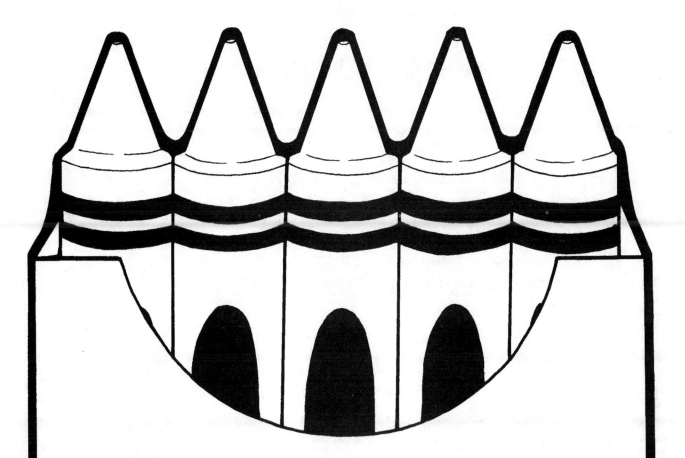

There are many
colors in this book.
Here's _____.
Take a look.

Related Resources

Books

Cousins, Lucy. *Maisy's Colors.* Candlewick Press, 1997.

Drescher, Henrik. *The Yellow Umbrella.* Broadway, 1987.

Ehlert, Lois. *Color Farm.* Lippincott, 1990.

Ehlert, Lois. *Color Zoo.* Lippincott, 1989.

Ehlert, Lois. *Planting a Rainbow.* HBJ, 1988.

Hest, Amy. *Purple Coat.* Aladdin, 1986.

Hoban, Tana. *Red, Blue, Yellow Shoe.* Greenwillow, 1986.

Imershein, Betsy. *Finding Red Finding Yellow.* HBJ, 1989.

Jackson, Ellen. *Brown Cow, Green Grass, Yellow, Mellow Sun.* Hyperion Books for Children, 1997.

Jeunesse, Galimard and Pascale de Bourgoing. *Colors.* Scholastic, 1991.

Kropa, Susan. *Sky Blue, Grass Green.* Good Apple, 1986.

Martin, Bill, Jr. *Brown Bear, Brown Bear, What Do You See?* Henry Holt & Co., 1996.

McMillan, Bruce. *Growing Colors.* Lothrop, 1988.

Tabor, Nancy Maria Grande. *We Are a Rainbow.* Charlesbridge Publishers, 1997.

Williams, Sue. *I Went Walking.* HBJ, 1990.

Music

Greg and Steve. *Playing Favorites.* "Brown Bear, Brown Bear, What Do You See?" Youngheart Records, 1991.

Greg and Steve. *We All Live Together, Vol. 5.* "Rainbow of Colors." Youngheart Records, 1994.

The Learning Station. *Where Is Thumbkin?* "Color Song." Kimbo, 1996.

Palmer, Hap. *Learning Basic Skills Through Music, Vol. 1.* "Colors." Activity Records, 1969.

Palmer, Hap. *Learning Basic Skills Through Music, Vol. 2.* "Parade of Colors." Activity Records.

Video

Barney's Shapes & Colors. (two videos about shapes and colors); 30 min. The Lyon's Group, 1997.

Software

Elmo's Preschool Deluxe. (by Sesame Street Learning Series; develops cognitive skills using shapes and colors); WIN 95 or WIN 3.1; available from Creative Wonders, ABC Electronic Arts, P.O. Box 9017, Redwood City, CA 94063-9017; 1-800-KID-XPRT.

Preschool Parade. (software that teaches colors, shapes, patterns, the alphabet, etc.); CD-ROM or disk for MAC, MPC or WIN; Forest Technologies, 514 Market Loop, Suite 103, West Dundee, IL 60118; 1-800-544-3356.

Seasons Big Book Materials

Unit Materials:

— glue

— scissors

— drawing tools: crayons, markers, chalk, colored pencils

— stapler

— construction paper: all colors

— tagboard

— paint: all colors

— scrap and collage items

Extra:

— stamps and stamp pads

— stencils

— sponge-painting shapes

Optional Materials for Additional Activities:

— cotton batting

— large pompoms

— powdered tempera paint

— spray bottles

— tissue paper or streamers

— evergreen sprigs

— acorns

— pine cones

— paper doilies

— food coloring or liquid watercolor paint

— paper towels

— play dough

— wooden blocks

— paper fasteners

— plastic cups

Seasons Big Book

Theme: My World and Me
Topics: Seasons/Weather
Duration: Long Term
Approach: Adapted Song
Combination Illustrations

This is one of the easiest big books to put together. All it takes is four pages: fall, winter, spring, and summer. The illustrations for this book can be any seasonal paperplay that you normally do throughout the year.

PAGE 1—When doing the Autumn Leaves big book (pages 64–85), have students do crayon leaf rubbings as an additional activity.

PAGE 2—In the winter, have students do a snow or snowflake activity.

PAGE 3—In the spring, do rain paintings, raindrop projects, or craft projects that include umbrellas.

PAGE 4—When doing the Families big book (pages 178–197), save leftover flower pictures.

PUTTING IT ALL TOGETHER

A sample text (pages 253–256) provided for this long-term project is an adapted version of a familiar song. However, you and your students may prefer to create your own text.

The Seasons' Song

Sing to the tune of "Did You Ever See a Lassie?"

Did you ever see a/an _____ (season), a/an _____ (season), a/an _____ (season)?

Did you ever see a/an _____ (season) with _____ just like this?

With _____ here and _____ there.

With _____ here and _____ there.

Did you ever see a/an _____ (season) with _____ just like this?

Repeat, filling in the blanks to correspond with the illustrations. Below is an example.

Did you ever see an autumn, an autumn, an autumn?

Did you ever see an autumn with leaves just like this?

With leaves here and leaves there.

With leaves here and leaves there.

Did you ever see an autumn with leaves just like this?

Additional Activities

Art/Language

Squirrel Tail or Bunny Tail Painting

You will need cotton batting or a large pompom, dry tempera paint, and spray bottles filled with water for this activity. After a discussion on squirrels or bunnies (depending on the season), draw attention to their puffy tails. If possible show a picture. Cover the art table with newspaper. Tell the children they will pretend to paint with squirrel/bunny tails and give them pompoms or wads of cotton batting. Have them dip their tails into the dry tempera and powder their papers with it. Then have them lightly spray water over the paint. Allow the paint to dry.

Wind Socks

Roll tubes from any creative paint or marker paperplay done on sheets of construction paper. Staple the tubes in keep them from unrolling. On each tube, attach colored streamers or strips of tissue paper on one end for the bottom and a handle on the other end for the top.

Painting with Evergreen Sprigs

Allow students to use evergreen sprigs in place of paintbrushes when working at the easel.

Acorn Painting

You will need a shallow container such as a cake pan or box lid, a small container of liquid tempera, large sheets of construction paper, and acorns. Line the container with a sheet of paper. Place some acorns in the small container of paint. Have a child scoop out the acorns and place them on the paper in the pan or box lid. Have the child create a design by tilting the pan/box lid and rolling the acorns over the paper. Then allow the next child to take a turn.

Pine Cone Painting

Set out shallow containers of paint and some pine cones. Have the children wet the pine cones with the paint and press them onto the paper.

Snowflake Painting

Cut a sponge into 1" (2.5 cm) strips. Lightly tape a paper doily to each sheet of black construction paper. Place some white tempera in a small container along with the cut-up sponge. Have the children sponge paint over the holes in the doilies. Promptly remove the doilies and allow the paint to dry.

Raindrop Painting

Talk about what raindrops look like. Show students an eyedropper and demonstrate how to make one drop of water fall from it. Fill some containers with liquid watercolor paint and add food coloring to small containers of water. Have the children drop the different colors one at a time onto white paper towels. These paintings can also be done on cup-type coffee filters rather than paper towels. Then they can be hung up in the windows as suncatchers.

Additional Activities *(cont.)*

Math/Language

Calendar Count

Help students use a calendar to count the number of days until winter or spring.

Seasonal Song

Ask students to be snowflakes, leaves, raindrops, and flowers when singing the following song. You may wish to allow the children to use props.

Seasons of Fun

Sing to the tune of "Battle Hymn of the Republic."

She stood outside in winter in the cold and frozen ground,
And watched the snowflakes as they fell without a single sound.
She counted all the snowflakes as they floated slowly down,
1-2-3-4-5-6 and 7 and 8-9-10. Then she started counting over again,
Beginning with one and ending with ten,
As the snow came floating down.

He stood outside in autumn in the crisp and chilly breeze,
Looking at the colors dancing all around the trees.
And as they fell around him, he counted all the leaves,
1-2-3-4-5-6 and 7 and 8-9-10. Then she started counting over again,
Beginning with one and ending with ten,
As the leaves came falling down.

She stood outside in springtime on a misty, cloudy day,
Holding an umbrella to protect her from the spray,
Counting all the raindrops as they splished and splashed her way,
1-2-3-4-5-6 and 7 and 8-9-10. Then he started counting over again,
Beginning with one and ending with ten,
As the rain came pouring down.

He stood outside in summer in the warm and shining sun,
Listening to the summer sounds and watching summer fun,
Counting all the flowers in the garden, one by one,
1-2-3-4-5-6 and 7 and 8-9-10. Then he started counting over again,
Beginning with one and ending with ten,
As the sun came shining down.

Additional Activities *(cont.)*

Music/Movement/Language

Human Wheelbarrows

Show the children pictures of wheelbarrows. These can usually be found in store flyers or catalogs. Discuss what they are and what purpose they serve. Tell the children that they will work in pairs to become human wheelbarrows. Use one pair of students to model the activity. Ask one of the children to get down on all fours. Explain that this child is going to play like he/she is a wheelbarrow. Have the other child pretend to be the gardener. He/She stands behind the "wheelbarrow" and lifts that child up by the ankles. The child that is the wheelbarrow moves along by walking on his/her hands. Remind students to make frequent stops so the children who are the wheelbarrows can rest. Allow time for the children to switch roles.

Note: This activity works well with older students as the gardeners.

Social/Emotional/Language

Flying Kites

On a windy day, take students to fly kites in an open field with no overhead obstructions.

Summer Fun

Invite students to talk about the things they are going to do to have fun during the summer. You may wish to classify these activities by letters of the alphabet.

Science/Discover/Language

Springtime Snails

Have students roll some play dough to make long ropes. Show them how to coil a rope into a circle and use the last inch (2.5 cm) to make a snail's head. Have students make their own snails. Then help them add antennae and eyes. To flatten the bottom of a snail so it will stand up, show students how to lightly press the bottom of the snail onto the table.

Sunshine Block Designs

On a hot, sunny day that isn't very windy, have each student choose two or three blocks from the Block Center. Bring these outside, along with a stack of dark blue construction paper. Give each child a sheet of paper. Ask students to place their papers on the ground in direct sunlight. Tell them to arrange their blocks in an interesting way on top of their papers. Leave these outside for a few hours. The sunlight will fade the paper, leaving the original shade of blue in the areas that were covered by the blocks.

Additional Activities *(cont.)*

Science/Discover/Language (cont.)

Windmills

After having a discussion about the wind, make windmills with the children. Trace or reproduce the Windmill Patterns (pages 258–260). Cut along the solid and dotted lines. Have students glue the windows and roof onto the windmill. Then allow them to decorate their windmills. Fold every other corner of the pinwheel and punch holes where indicated. Use a brad to attach the pinwheel to the top of the windmill.

Sailboats

Use the Sailboat Patterns (page 261) to make felt or Velcro® kits. Use the sailboats with the following song.

Five Little Sailboats

Sing to the tune of "Frere Jacques."

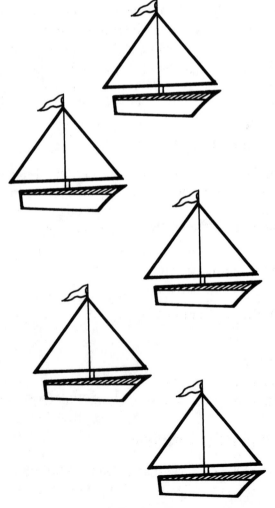

Five little sailboats, five little sailboats,
Near the shore, near the shore.
A gust of wind is blowing. Where's the sailboat going?
Now there're only four. Now there're only four.

Four little sailboats, four little sailboats,
On the sea, on the sea.
A gust of wind is blowing. Where's the sailboat going?
Now there're only three. Now there're only three.

Three little sailboats, three little sailboats,
In the ocean blue, in the ocean blue.
A gust of wind is blowing. Where's the sailboat going?
Now there're only two. Now there're only two.

Two little sailboats, two little sailboats,
Sailing in the sun, sailing in the sun.
A gust of wind is blowing. Where's the sailboat going?
Now there's only one. Now there's only one.

One little sailboat, one little sailboat,
Heading for shore, heading for shore.
The wind's about to blow. Where will it go?
I don't see any more. I don't see any more.

Additional Activities *(cont.)*

Science/Discover/Language *(cont.)*

Walnut Sailboats

Have each student put a small piece of clay in half of a walnut shell. For each boat, thread a toothpick in and out of a small triangle sail and stick one end in the clay. Allow students to have sailboat races. They make the "wind" by blowing on the sails.

Sandcastles and Mud Pies

At the sand table, mix water with dirt to make mud. Provide some plastic molds, sand shovels, plastic cups, and other toys that can be used with this medium. The children will enjoy playing with the moist, moldable mud.

Preparing for Winter

Point out that people and animals store up food to prepare for the winter ahead. In many places, it is too cold in the winter to grow food. During the warmer months, some people can and freeze vegetables and fruits from their gardens. Then they are able to enjoy these foods in the winter. Some animals also have ways to store food. Squirrels hide nuts and acorns in tree holes and under the ground so they will have food for the winter. Bears eat large amounts during the fall so they can hibernate, or sleep, during the winter. Chipmunks, groundhogs, snakes, turtles, and frogs are other animals that hibernate. Many birds migrate, or fly south, to find food in warmer climates during the winter months and return in the spring.

Spring Flowers

On the first day of spring, invite your class to celebrate by having them plant marigold seeds in recycled milk cartons, small yogurt containers, or cottage cheese cups. Be sure to punch a hole in the bottom of each container for drainage. Water the plants with diluted liquid plant food. Have students put them in the sun and watch them grow.

Nest Hunt

Take the class on a fall walk to look at abandoned bird nests. Caution students that nests should never be disturbed in the spring or summer when eggs or baby birds could be harmed.

Trees

Read Janice Udry's *A Tree Is Nice* (HarperCollins, 1956) or Shel Silverstein's *The Giving Tree* (HarperCollins, 1964). Discuss how trees change over time.

Winter Bird Feeder

Have the children spread peanut butter on pine cones. Then have them roll the pinecones in bird seed. Tie a string to the tops of the pine cones and hang them in trees on the school grounds.

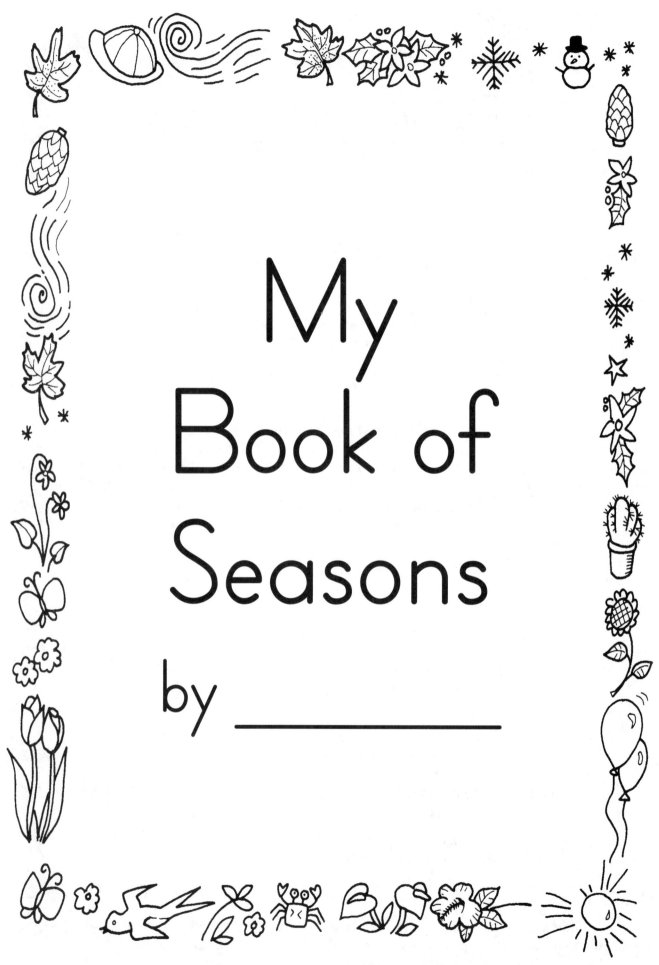

My
Book of
Seasons

by _____

Did you ever see an
autumn, an autumn,
an autumn?
Did you ever see an
autumn with _____
just like this?
With _____ here and
_____ there.
With _____ here
and _____ there.
Did you ever see an
autumn with _____ just
like this?

Did you ever see a
winter, a winter, a winter?
Did you ever see a
winter with _____
just like this?
With _____ here
and _____ there.
With _____ here
and _____ there.
Did you ever see a
winter with _____
just like this?

Did you ever see a
spring, a spring, a spring?
Did you ever see a
spring with _____
just like this?
With _____ here
and _____ there.
With _____ here
and _____ there.
Did you ever see a
spring with _____
just like this?

Did you ever see a
summer, a summer,
a summer?
Did you ever see a
summer with _____ just
like this?
With _____ here
and _____ there.
With _____ here
and _____ there.
Did you ever see a
summer with _____ just
like this?

Related Resources

Books

Barbaresi, Nina. *A Fox Jumped Up One Winter's Night.* Western, 1985.

Bedford, Annie North. *Frosty the Snowman.* Western, 1950.

Brett, Jan. *The Mitten.* Putnam, 1989.

De Coteau Orie, Sandra. *Did You Hear the Wind Sing Your Name? An Oneida Song of Spring.* Walker & Co., 1996.

Galdone, Paul. *The Three Little Kittens.* Clarion, 1986.

Gibbons, Gail. *The Reasons for Seasons.* Holiday House, 1995.

Gibbons, Gail. *The Seasons of Arnold's Apple Tree.* Harcourt Brace Children's Books, 1988.

Hartley, Deborah. *Up North in Winter.* Viking, 1986.

Keats, Ezra Jack. *The Snowy Day.* Live Oak Media, 1962.

Keller, Holly. *Will It Rain?* Greenwillow, 1984.

Lee, Huy Voun. *At the Beach.* Henry Holt & Co., 1994.

Leonard, Marcia. *Bear's Busy Year: A Book About Seasons.* Troll, 1990.

London, Jonathan. *Puddles.* Viking Children's Books, 1997.

Maestro, Betsy. *Why Do Leaves Change Colors?* HarperCollins, 1994.

Martin, Bill, Jr., and John Archambault. *Listen to the Rain.* Holt, 1988.

McCloskey, Robert. *Blueberries for Sal.* Viking Penguin, 1976.

McKee, David. *King Rollo's Spring.* Penguin Books, 1989.

McKee, David. *King Rollo's Winter.* Penguin Books, 1989.

Music

Greg and Steve. *Kids in Motions.* "The Freeze." Youngheart Records, 1987.

Greg and Steve. *Playing Favorites.* "Ain't Gonna Rain No More Rain, Rain, Go Away." Youngheart Records, 1991.

Greg and Steve. *Rockin' Down the Word.* "Snowflake." Youngheart Records, 1995.

The Learning Station. *Tony Chestnut & Fun Time Action Songs.* "Swimming Song." Kaladon Publishing, 1997.

The Learning Station. *Where Is Thumbkin?* "Raindrop Song." Kimbo, 1996.

Raffi. *Singable Songs for the Very Young.* "Mr. Sun." Shoreline Records, 1976.

Video

Frosty's Winter Wonderland and the Leprechauns' Gold. (Video); Live Home Video, 1991.

Software

Fisher-Price for School. (software for kindergarten; calendar concepts and activities for learning about seasons). CD-ROM for WIN 95, WIN 3.1 or MAC; Davidson & Assoc., Inc., Torrance, CA 90503. 1-800-545-7677.

Windmill Pattern

Place
windows
here

Place
windows
here

Windmill Pattern *(cont.)*

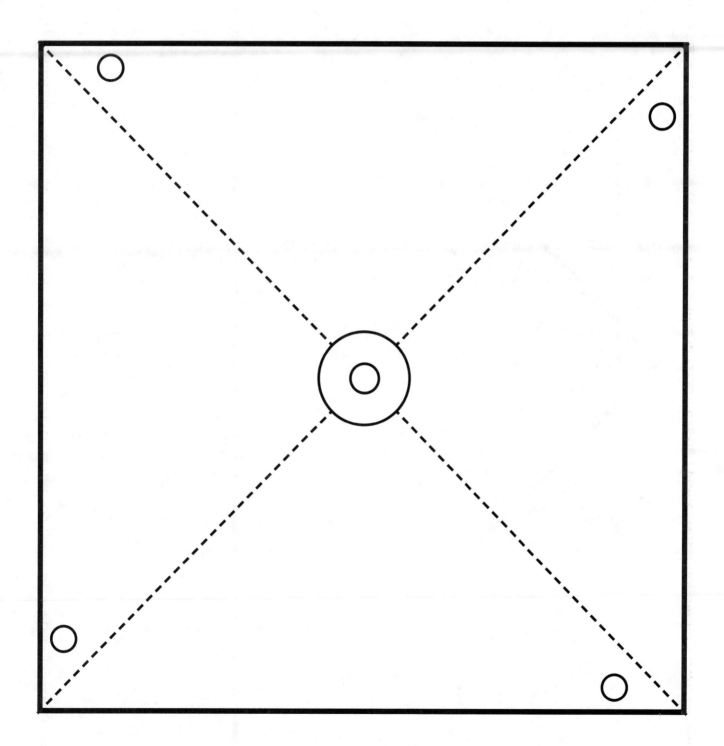

Windmill Pattern *(cont.)*

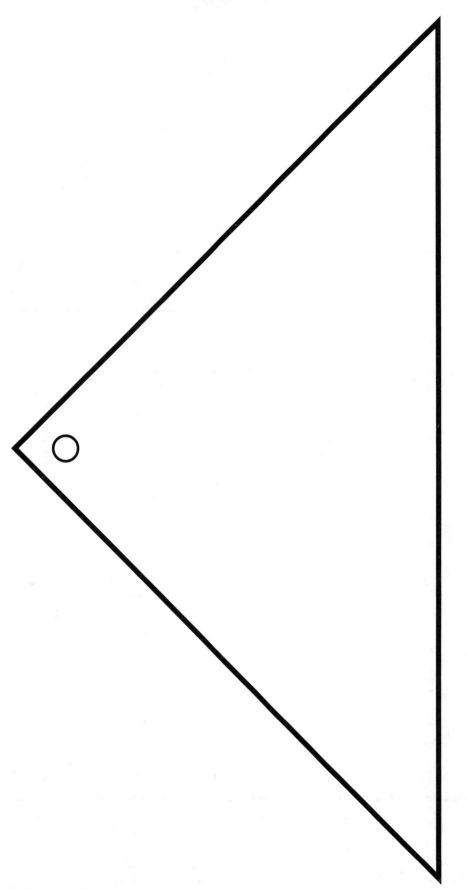

Sailboat Patterns

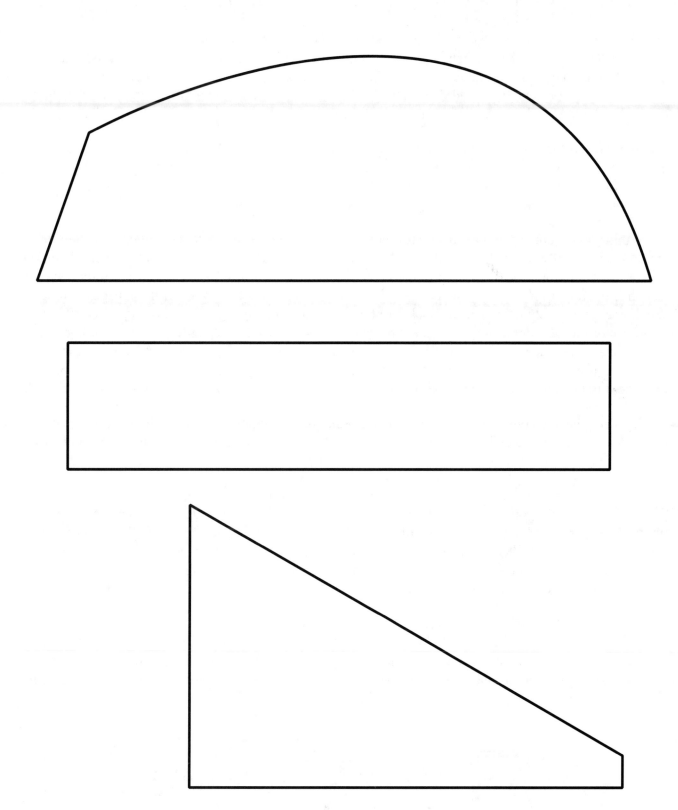

Tote Books

Another concept in child-generated big books features a book created by the class as a whole. These types of books are sometimes referred to as traveling books, shared books, or lending books. Each child contributes one page to the book, and the book is completed as a collaborative group project. Once finished, these books are then lent out to each child, library fashion, for a designated period of time. They are meant to be read and shared with the family and then returned to school for the next child to borrow. Once all the children have had an opportunity to take the book home, it can then be put in the classroom library or disassembled so the children can take their individual pages home.

These particular big books need to be transported to and from school by every child in the classroom. Since they are large, they can be awkward to carry, especially for children who ride a school bus. The easiest way for a very young child to accomplish this responsibility is to bring the book home in something sturdy and durable such as a tote bag. Hence, the term tote books.

Since this book is created cooperatively, it is completed in a fairly short period of time. Assembly of the book is basically the same as with other big books. The biggest difference is that each child needs to be responsible for only one page of text to go along with his/her illustration. After all of the children have had the opportunity to take the book home, you will need to decide whether these pages will be sent home with the children or if the book will be kept intact and placed in the classroom library. The relevance of this decision is reflected in the placement of the text. If the pages are to be sent home, the accompanying text needs to be on the same page as the illustration. If the books are to be kept for future classroom use, then the text can be placed on the pages opposite the illustrations as described for the other big books.

These tote books are consistent with the big book principle of predictability and repetition, making them easy stories for the children to remember. Students will love looking at the illustrations done by their peers and thoroughly enjoy the familiarity of the text.

Unlike the previous child-created big books, many people will handle these tote books over a long period of time. Therefore, they should be made out of something that is sturdier than construction paper. Using tagboard or poster board will give them greater durability. Laminating these books is a good idea, but doing so may not be cost effective since they have so many pages. If possible, tote books that utilize actual photographs should be laminated. The page sizes should remain the same as the other big books that are made out of large sheets of construction paper.

Since each child is contributing a page, book length depends on class size. For this reason, you may not be able to staple the pages together if you have a large class. When it is time to assemble the book, you may want to consider using a hole puncher, reinforcements, and binder rings to hold the pages together. If you do not have binder rings, you can always thread thick yarn through the holes and then tie the yarn in bows.

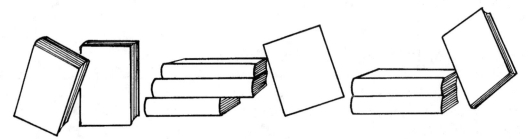

Tote Books *(cont.)*

Although completion of these tote books is quick and easy, it is important to bear in mind that it does take a while before every child in the room has an opportunity to borrow the book. All young children will want to be the first to take the book home, and it may take some time for them to understand that they'll need to wait their turn. The important thing is to reassure them that they will get their chance. It may be helpful to have a chart displayed somewhere in the classroom with every child's name on it. This will help your students know where they are in the rotation.

For very large classes, you may want to consider splitting the pages to make two books instead of one. By doing this you will cut down on the amount of time the children must wait before borrowing the book. In addition, if your class is fairly large, it is probably best to limit the loaning period to one night.

Pages 265–329 provide some tote book ideas, including book topics, guidelines, and parent letters, that will help ensure the success of a tote book program in your classroom.

Tote Bags

Four tote bags should be sufficient for the school year. There are many places that sell inexpensive tote bags. Travel agencies or grocery stores might be willing to donate them if you explain why you need them. Otherwise, you may wish to enlist the help of parent volunteers to sew the tote bags. Fabrics, such as denim or soft canvas work best because they are sturdy and durable. After the tote bags are made or obtained, use fabric paint to write something like "Room _____'s Tote Book Bag," or "Ms./Mr. _____'s Tote Book Bag" on both sides of each bag.

Tote Bag Directions

Make one pattern out of newspaper that measures 14.5" x 18" (36 cm x 46 cm).

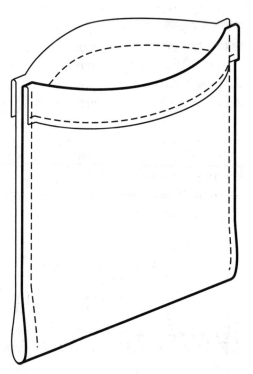

Fold the fabric with the right sides together. Lay the pattern on the fabric so that when it is placed vertically one side is flush with the fold. In other words, the bottom of the bag will be folded rather than having a seam. Pin the pattern onto the fabric and cut along the edge. Unfold the fabric and zigzag stitch all the edges to keep them from unraveling. If pinking shears are used to cut the fabric, this sewing step can be eliminated.

The piece of cloth for the bag should be unfolded and held vertically. Fold the top 2" (5 cm) towards the inside with the wrong sizes together. Sew straight across the top on each side. It may be helpful to iron the folded sections in place before sewing them.

Fold the bag in the center, right sides together, and match up the two hemmed edges. This is the top of the bag. Pin the top sides evenly together, and sew the side seams $1/4$" (0.6 cm) from the edge. Reinforce the top and bottom of each seam by tacking them with some back stitches.

Tote Books *(cont.)*

Turn the bag right side out. Cut 26" (66 cm) handles out of wide ribbon. These will be attached to the outside of the bag. On one side of the bag, pin each end of a ribbon about 1.5" (3.8 cm) from the top and sides. Sew a 1" (2.5 cm) square on each end of the ribbon. Then sew a reinforcement X in the square, from corner to corner. Follow the same procedure for the other side of the bag.

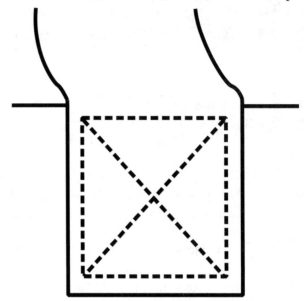

The Log Sheet (page 268) can be duplicated for the purpose of keeping track of whose turn it is to bring the tote book(s) home.

Since the success of this lending program is contingent upon parental cooperation, there is also a reproducible letter (page 265) explaining what the tote book program is all about, as well as providing information about the importance of returning the books on time. Included in the letter is a request for parent volunteers to sew tote bags. Letters should be sent home approximately two weeks before implementing the tote book program. Reproduce the note on page 266 and glue a copy of it to the inside cover of each tote book. This will serve as a reminder to parents about the proper handling and prompt return of these books.

Send the Comment Sheet (page 267) home with each tote book. It is great fun for the children to find out what parents thought of their books. Every day be sure to pull out the returned books and check for notes on the Comment Sheets. Read these aloud to your class.

Below is a sample name chart that can be made out of poster board and laminated. Self-adhesive Velcro can be placed near every child's name. A laminated arrow made out of different-colored poster board can be attached by Velcro daily, indicating whose turn it is to bring a particular tote book home. This chart has a multitude of purposes and can also be used for designating the line leader, helper of the day, etc.

Name Chart
☐ 1. Bobby Klein
➤ ☐ 2. Kisha Comares
☐ 3. Martin Bevins

Tote Book Information

_____

(Date)

Dear Parent/Guardian,

We are happy to inform you that we will soon begin our tote book program. All of the children will work together to compile a book that can be taken home and shared with their families.

Each child will have the chance to bring the book home overnight. Your child is looking forward to sharing some reading time with you. Please take this opportunity to review what we've been doing in class. These books are fun, fast, and easy to read.

The children are interested to know what you think of their books. For this reason, there will be a Comment Sheet attached to the back cover of every tote book. Please take a few moments to let us know what you think of each book.

The children will be anxiously waiting for their turn to take these books home, so please remember to return each tote book the following school day.

If you are interested in volunteering to sew some tote bags for the children to use when carrying these books, please let me know.

Thank you for your time and cooperation. Our class looks forward to hearing from you.

Sincerely,

_____

(Teacher)

_____

(School)

_____

(Phone)

Tote Book Note

_____

(Date)

Dear Parent/Guardian,

Thank you for helping your child take special care of this tote book. Please take some time to read it with your child and discuss what your child is learning at school. When you are finished reading the book, our class would appreciate your taking a few moments to write your thoughts about it on the Comment Sheet. We are looking forward to reading your comments in class tomorrow.

Sincerely,

_____

(Teacher)

_____

(School)

_____

(Phone)

266   © Teacher Created Materials, Inc.

Comment Sheet

Please take a few moments to let us know what you think of this tote book by writing a line or two in the comments section. Please remember to sign your name in the space provided.

Thank you!

Child's Name	Comments	Parent/Guardian Signature

Log Sheet

Tote Book Title: _____

Date	Name of Student

School Time Tote Book Materials

Unit Materials:

— camera and film
— glue
— scissors
— drawing tools: crayons, markers, chalk, colored pencils
— stapler
— tagboard

Extra:

— laminator with laminating film

Optional Materials for Additional Activities:

— small or medium-sized blank index cards
— craft sticks
— yellow and black paint
— miniature toy cars, trucks, and other wheeled vehicles
— butcher paper
— felt
— fabric paint
— acetate sheets or overhead transparencies
— magnifying glasses with handles
— large cardboard box

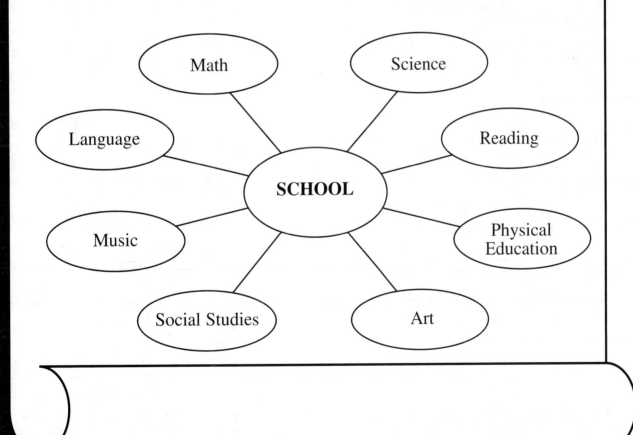

School Time Tote Book

Theme: My Friends and Me
Topics: School Experiences/School Days
Duration: Short Term
Approach: Original Story
Photography

A good introductory tote book is a big book illustrating the entire school day. Although the children do not actually create the illustrations themselves for this particular book, they will, however, be the models in the photographs.

This is a good beginning tote book because it acquaints the children and their parents with the concept of borrowing books that need to be returned the next school day. In addition, it gives parents a good idea of what their children are doing in school. Because it is based on the children's own school experiences and not on a fingerplay, song, or story, there is no text to learn. For this reason, the School Time big book can easily be created right at the beginning of the school year to introduce and implement the tote book program. Sample text for this book is provided (page 276–283), but it is not necessary to use it. The text is mostly for the benefit of parents or other family members with whom the children might share the book. It also serves the purpose of helping the children remember the names of people who are in the photographs. However, the photographs alone lend themselves nicely to building language skills, and the children like to tell their own stories about the school day. Including pictures of school faculty members, such as the principal, secretaries, custodians, and kitchen/cafeteria workers, is also a good idea. It helps the children and their families get to know who's who at the school.

This big book is a favorite among children. They absolutely love looking at photographs of their schoolmates and friends that were taken in familiar and comfortable surroundings. They will be anxious to take this book home and share information about their daily routine with their families. Once all the children have had a turn to take the book home, it will make a great addition to the classroom library. In fact, this book will most likely be handled so often by so many children that it is highly recommended that you laminate it before students start taking it home.

The concept of time is a very difficult one for young children. Displaying pictures of clocks showing the specific times for certain activities helps very young children make the connection that clocks and watches help us know when to do things. The exact time is not important and need not be stressed. Simply having a clock on the same page as the activity being shown in the photograph gives the subtle message that clocks play an important part in the scheduling of the school day.

Making the Book

COVER PAGE

An obvious choice for the cover is to have a photograph of the outside of your school building. This can be a photo of the school by itself or one with the children standing in front of the building. An alternative cover page could be a collage of photographs that were taken for this particular tote book but were not used to tell the story.

What makes these books so special is the feeling of ownership each child shares. Since this tote book is a very personal one for the children, you may want to ask them what they would like the title to be. Let them brainstorm and vote on their favorite title. They may come up with something entirely different from School Time. The chosen title can either be hand printed onto the cover, or it can be printed out on a computer and then glued onto the cover.

PAGES 1–?

Page 1 should begin with the children's arrival at school. You may wish to consider taking a series of photos showing the children getting off the bus, getting out of their family cars, and walkers coming in with their parents.

Depending on the size of your photographs, you will most likely be able to fit more than one per page.

The details and the number of photographs you take are up to you. If you wish, you can include pictures of the children hanging up their coats after they enter the classroom or washing their hands before lunch. Both of these activities are part of the school day. It really depends on how much film you want to use and how many pages you wish to include in this big book. Cost is an important factor also. If you are paying for all these expenses out of your own pocket and have both morning and afternoon sessions consisting of twenty children, the number of photographs will not be the same as someone who has a class of twelve students for the entire day. Some schools have money in their budgets to pay for film and film development, but more often than not, teachers find themselves paying for these. The thickness of this book is not relevant. The important thing to remember is that you have at least one photograph of every student in your class. Try to take photographs that include fewer than four children. Keep in mind that this is a book about the entire school day, so you'll need to represent all aspects of the day, including lunch and outside activities. If there are other adults such as teaching assistants, foster grandparents, specialists, or parent volunteers that help out in the classroom, make sure to include them in the photographs too.

Note: If you are the photographer for this book, make sure you have someone take pictures of you as well. Remember, you are an important part of the children's school experiences, and you should be in several of the photographs.

Making the Book *(cont.)*

PUTTING IT ALL TOGETHER

Once the pictures have been developed, the children will be excited to see them. This can be done during Circle Time or any time you think is the best for students to view them. Teach a sequencing lesson by asking the children to help you organize the photographs according to the sequence of events during the school day. Have the children help place and glue the photographs onto the big book pages.

Since using photographs is a personal way of illustrating this book and every teacher's pictures will be different, you and your students may opt to write your own story. However, you may choose to use the generic text provided (pages 277–283). Below are some additional ideas.

Possible Text for PAGE 1:

It's 8:00 A.M. and time for school to begin.

Vanessa and Sara take the bus to school.

Paulo walks to school every day.

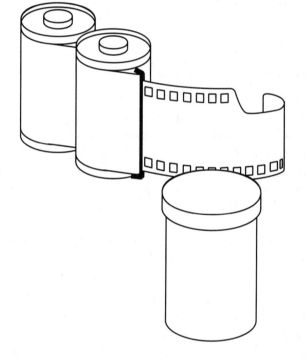

Possible Text for PAGE 2:

Felicia is hanging up her coat.

It's time for breakfast. Michael loves French toast sticks.

It's Circle Time. Sean and Kimberly are singing the "Good Morning Song."

Possible Text for PAGE 3:

It's Learning Center time.

Kelvin is painting a dinosaur at the easel.

Sofia, Eric, and Chris like playing in the Home Center.

Duarte is building a castle with blocks.

The remainder of the book follows the same principle. Simply state the name of the children and tell what they are doing in the photos. Invite the children to help you decide what the text should say. When writing about the adults in the photographs, be sure to include their titles with their names. Examples: Mrs. Camara, our teaching assistant, is playing bingo. Ms. Kay, the principal, is sitting at her desk. Grandpa Lou, our foster grandfather, is at the sand table. Mr. Mendes, the secretary, is waving hello.

Note: This particular book should be laminated prior to lending to be sure that the photographs stay clean and do not fall off the big book pages. Don't forget to place the note (page 266) on the inside front cover of this tote book and the Comment Sheet (page 267) on the back cover.

Additional Activities

Art/Language

Flags

Tell the children that they can design their own school flags. Give each child a blank index card and a craft stick. The children can use markers, crayons, and colored pencils to decorate the cards. Then have them glue their cards onto the craft sticks to make flags. Mold some modeling clay into small mounds, insert the craft sticks into the clay, and display the flags on windowsills or bookshelves.

School Bus Colors

If any students ride on yellow school buses, set up that paint color at the easel.

Wheels

After singing the song "The Wheels on the Bus," talk about wheels. Discuss the shape of wheels. Set up at the Art Center a variety of items that the children can use to print out circle shapes.

In addition, place some miniature cars, trucks, and buses in a shallow pan of paint. Let the children roll the wheels of the toy vehicles in the paint. Then have them roll the painted wheels on sheets of large construction paper.

Bulletin Board: Children are fascinated by monster trucks. This activity could be extended by stretching out long sheets of butcher paper. Have students make tracks using plastic monster trucks. Black on white gives a nice effect and looks great as a bulletin board background. If you have a favorite truck, car, or bus pattern, the children can make these vehicles out of a variety of colors. After the painted tracks are dry, cut the butcher paper to fit the bulletin board. Add a border, and then staple the vehicles on top of the butcher paper. Display a banner with a caption of your choice. See the example suggested below. Suggested shapes for a truck are one rectangle, one square, and four circles.

Keep on Truckin'

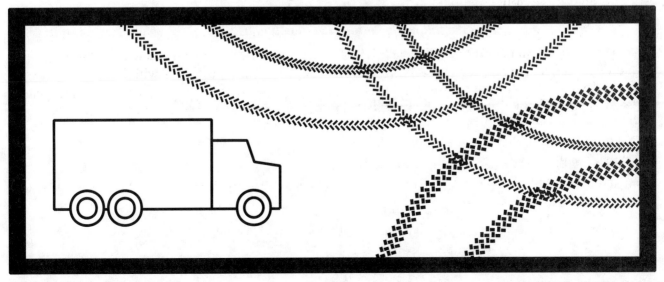

Additional Activities *(cont.)*

Math/Language

The Way to School

Reproduce the patterns (pages 286 and 287). Color, cut, and laminate the children and the school. Mount the children and the school some distance away from each other but at the same level on a wall or bulletin board. Put loops of tape or Velcro® on the backs of several blank index cards. Place the index cards on the wall/bulletin board, end-to-end, going from the school to the children. Use a wide-tipped marker to draw a squiggly line from the card closest to the children to the card closest to the school. Take the cards off the wall/bulletin board. Tell students that they will need to show how the children on the wall/bulletin board get to school. Have the children attach the cards to the wall in the appropriate order by connecting the line that represents the path to school.

School Bus Math

Using the patterns (pages 285 and 287), make felt or Velcro® kits by tracing and cutting out five school buses and one school.

Note: You may wish to add other felt pieces such as a flag, trees, flowers, clouds, and children.

Going to School

Sing to the tune of "Mary Had a Little Lamb."

One bus going down the road, down the road, down the road.

One bus going down the road—on its way to school.

Two buses going down the road, down the road, down the road.

Two buses going down the road—on their way to school.

(Continue as above with three, four, and five buses.)

The first bus parked to the right of the school, the right of the school, the right of the school.

The first bus parked to the right of the school—waiting to go home.

(Continue by substituting the following words: The second bus...left of the school...; The third bus...in front of the school...; The fourth bus...away from the school...; The fifth bus...near another bus....)

Note: You can make up different or additional verses according to the children's interest and ability levels. Students can also come up with their own verses. They may choose to be silly and place the bus on top of or over the school. Adding silly lyrics gives you the opportunity to discuss fantasy and reality with your students.

Block Building

Encourage children to design and build their own schools and classrooms in the Block Center.

Additional Activities *(cont.)*

Science/Discovery/Language

Inclines

Set up some inclines in the Block Center and tell students to experiment with rolling some miniature vehicles down the ramps.

Transparencies

Show the children some transparencies and explain what they are. Demonstrate how you can see objects through the transparencies. Give each child a transparency and an overhead marker. Encourage students to draw designs on the transparencies. When they are done drawing, place the transparencies, one at a time, on an overhead projector. Display them on a wall or screen. Talk about how an overhead projector works. Describe how the image is projected on the wall by using the light and magnification mirror in the overhead projector.

Magnification

After doing the above activity, give small, hand-held magnifying glasses to students. Have the children use these tools to examine different objects in the classroom. Discuss their findings.

Music/Movement/Language

On the Bus

Sing and act out "The Wheels on the Bus." Arrange chairs to look like seats on a bus. Have the children take turns being the driver and different characters on the bus. Change the words to the song by asking the children to substitute animals and their sounds or actions. For example, "The cat on the bus went meow, meow, meow…."

Getting Ready for School

Using the tune of "Here We Go 'Round the Mulberry Bush," make up words about school or school bus safety. For example, "This is the way we dress for school...so early in the morning."

Social/Emotional/Language

Tour of the School

During the first week of school, take your students on a tour of the building. If possible, introduce them to school personnel such as the principal/director, secretaries, custodians, kitchen workers, and librarian. Bring your camera along and take photos of the children meeting some of these people. Save the photos for the School Time tote book.

Cardboard School Bus

Make a large cardboard box into a school bus. Draw windows, doors, and wheels on the box. Ask the children to paint it. After the paint dries, the box can be used for dramatic play.

School Time

by _____

This is our school.

- Cut -

This is where we keep our

_____ .

It's time to start our school day. Yippee!

page 3

- Cut -

These are some of our favorite centers.

page 4

This is _____.
He works at our school. He is the _____.

This is _____.
She works at our school. She is the _____.

_____ is one of

our

quiet-time

activities.

page 7

- Cut -

_____ is one

of our noisy

activities.

page 8

It's lunchtime!

page 9

- Cut -

It's time for

_____.

page 10

These are some of our outside activities.

- Cut -

These are some of our indoor activities.

This is our

_____ .

page 13

- Cut -

We like to

_____ here.

page 14

- Cut -

Now it's time to go home. Awww!

page 15

Related Resources

Books

Arnold, Caroline. *Where Do You Go to School?* Watts, 1982.

Baer, Edith. *This Is the Way We Go to School.* Scholastic, 1990.

Brown, Marc. *Arthur Goes to School.* Random House Publishers, 1995.

Cole, Joanna. *The Magic School Bus Lost in the Solar System.* Scholastic, 1990.

Cole, Joanna. *The Magic School Bus on the Ocean Floor.* Scholastic, 1992.

Crews, Donald. *School Bus.* Scholastic, 1990.

Delacre, Lulu. *Time for School, Nathan!* Scholastic, 1989.

Gibbons, Gail. *Check It Out! The Book About Libraries.* Harcourt Brace Jovanovich, 1985.

Johnson, Dolores. *What Will Mommy Do When I'm at School?* Aladdin Paperbacks, 1998.

Kimmel, Eric. *I Took My Frog to the Library.* Viking, 1990.

Mayer, Mercer. *A Monster Followed Me to School.* Western, 1991.

Murphy, Stuart J. *Get Up and Go.* HarperCollins Publishers, 1996.

Penn, Audrey. *The Kissing Hand.* Child Welfare League of America, 1993.

Radlauer, Ruth Shaw. *Molly at the Library.* Simon & Schuster, 1988.

Simeon, Lorrain. *Marcellus.* Writers & Readers, 1995.

Tompert, Ann. *Will You Come Back for Me?* Albert Whitman & Co., 1988.

Watanabe, Shigeo. *What a Good Lunch!* Putnam, 1988.

Music

CJ Fundamentals. "Wheels on the Bus." Handy Music Inc., 1995.

Hallum, Rosemary, Ph.D. & Henry "Buzz" Glass. *Fingerplays and Footplays for Fun and Learning.* "The Wheels On The Bus." Activity Records, Inc., 1987.

Jenkins, Ella. *And One And Two.* "I'm Going To School Today." Folkways Records & Service Corp., 1971.

Palmer, Hap. *Learning Basic Skills Through Music, Vol. 1.* "This Is the Way We Get Up in the Morning." Activity Records, 1969.

Software

All-Star Kid's Pack. (Software that reinforces numbers, colors and shapes); CD-ROM for MAC or WIN; Forest Technologies. 514 Market Loop, Suite 103, West Dundee, IL 60118. 1-800-544-3356.

Preschool Parade. (software that builds math, music, and language skills; includes verbal directions and on-screen feedback); CD-ROM or disk for MAC, MPC or WIN; Forest Technologies, 514 Market Loop, Suite 103, West Dundee, IL 60118. 1-800-544-3356.

School Bus Pattern

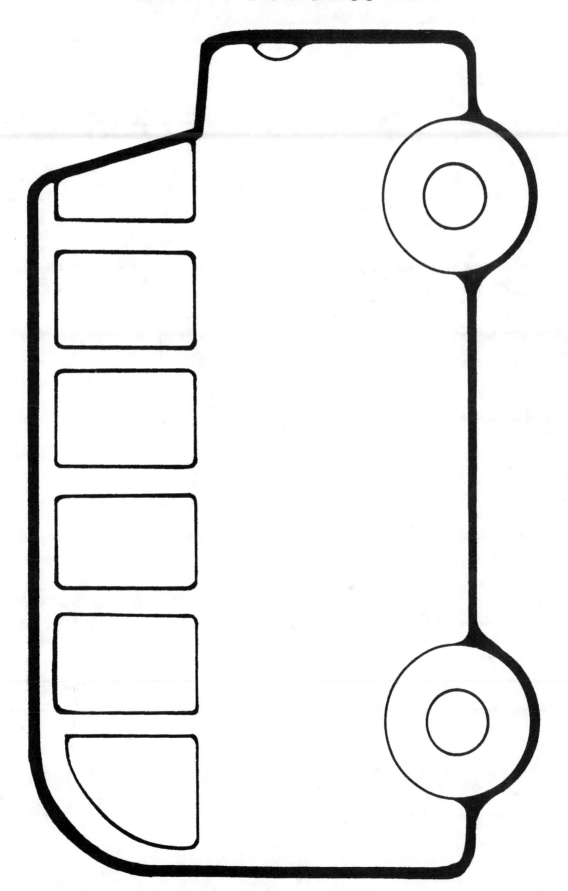

Children Patterns

School Pattern

Mittens Tote Book Materials

Unit Materials:

— glue

— scissors

— drawing tools: crayons, markers, chalk, colored pencils

— stapler

— tagboard

— construction paper: any color

— paints: any color

— magazines, outdated catalogs, store flyers, and advertisements

— plastic spoons

— small paint containers

Extra:

— laminating machine/laminating film

Optional Materials for Additional Activities:

— spring-type clothespins

— poster board

— gift wrap or wallpaper

— familiar school-related items: crayon, block, ball, button, glue bottle, glue stick, toy car, etc.

Mittens Tote Book

Theme: Me
Topic: Hands/Mittens
Duration: Short Term, Week
Approach: Adapted Story
Combination

The Ukrainian folk tale entitled *The Mitten* is always a favorite among young children. The adapted version by Jan Brett (Putnam, 1989) is a wonderful way to introduce this tote book project.

After reading the story with the children, ask them if they've ever lost gloves or mittens. Explain that they will be working together to create a tote book by making mittens that will become the illustrations for the book.

Mitten Patterns

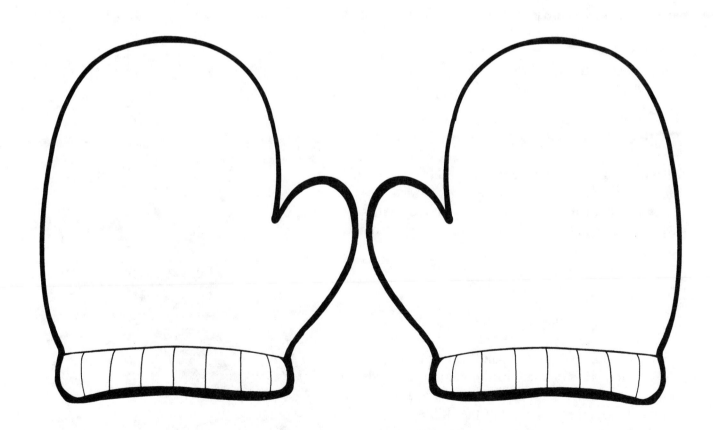

Making the Book

COVER PAGE

Reproduce the pattern (page 289). The cover page can consist of a couple of mittens that have been decorated and then cut out and glued onto the cover page. The mittens for the cover page can be made at the same time that the children make theirs. Just ask a volunteer to make an extra pair.

Text: Reproduce the title (page 295) and text (page 296). Glue these onto the big book pages.

> There's something in _____ 's (child's name) mitten.
>
> I wonder what's inside.
>
> Oh, boy! It's a toy.
>
> A _____ (name of toy cut out of magazine) has been spied.
>
> It's a day for lots of play.
>
> There's no need to hide.

Activities: Have students choose from blot-painting or any other creative art activity or cutting pictures of toys from catalogs, magazine, and/or newspaper advertisements.

Setup: Sequentially, the first thing that should be done is the mitten activity. Before beginning, enlarge the Mitten Patterns (page 289) and trace them onto large sheets of construction paper. Precut the patterns unless you are planning to have students cut out their own mittens. Be sure you have a right and a left mitten for each student.

Collect magazines, catalogs, and store flyers containing pictures of toys. Place these on the table along with some scissors and glue.

For blot-painting, you will need to set up a variety of differently colored paints in small containers along with some small plastic spoons.

Introduction: After reading the story *The Mitten,* ask the children to think about what they would like to find hiding in their mittens. Explain that they will each be decorating a mitten to illustrate the tote book. Tell them that there will also be a Cutting Center set up where they will be able to look at and cut out pictures of toys to put inside their mittens.

Directions: Have students fold their mittens in half. Then tell them to open up the mittens. Show them how to spoon a few blobs of paint onto a mitten, refold it, and press on the folded mitten to squish the paint around. Have students follow your example with both of their mittens. After the children are done, open up the mittens to allow the paint to dry.

Making the Book *(cont.)*

Note: If the children enjoy this activity and would like to make more than one pair of mittens, let them. Extra mittens can be saved, laminated, and used for activities like Matching Mittens or Graphic Organizer (page 292).

Talk about right and left. Ask the children to decide which of their mittens (left or right) they want to place in the tote book. The other mittens can be used as decorations for the classroom or taken home. The mittens placed in the big book should be glued onto a sheet of tagboard with the fingers pointing down. The child's name and the date should be used as labels for each mitten.

At the Cutting Center, let the children look through the catalogs, magazines, and newspaper advertisements from toy stores. This center is a great opportunity for language building as well as fine-motor skills. Children love to create a toy wish list and will undoubtedly provide you with lots of topics for conversation.

Have each child choose and cut out a picture of a toy. Then have students glue their chosen pictures so the toys are placed on the wrist part of their mittens.

Note: It is necessary to consider the size of the picture when doing this activity. Remember that it should not be so small that it is difficult to see. However, it also can't be too large, or it won't fit on the mitten.

PUTTING IT ALL TOGETHER

Organize all the mitten pages and staple them together. Reproduce enough sheets of the corresponding text (page 296) so that you'll have one sheet for each page in the book. If there are too many pages for the book to be stapled, you may have to consider punching holes and binding the book with rings or yarn. If you punch holes, it may be necessary to reinforce them for added durability.

Beginning with page 1, ask the child who created it to help you fill in the blanks. Fill in the first blank with that child's name. Then let him/her tell you the name of the toy that should appear in the second blank. After filling in the blanks, let the child glue the text onto the big book page.

Note: If you plan to keep the book after all the children have taken it home, the text can go on the opposite page. However, if you plan to send the individual pages home, the text needs to be placed directly on the page with the appropriate illustration.

Once the tote book is completed but before students start taking it home, read through it a few times to familiarize the children with the text. Don't forget to read the comments that parents make when the book is returned each day.

Additional Activities

Art/Language

Hand Prints

Handprint activities are a perfect addition to this unit. Use any of the various art and craft activities that use hand prints.

Math/Language

Graphic Organizer

For this activity, you will need two overlapping hoops/circles to create a Venn diagram. Once the hoops are in place, trace your right and left hand onto of construction paper. Tape the right hand on the far right section of the Venn diagram and the left hand on the opposite side. Then, using the patterns (page 289), cut 10–15 matching pairs of mittens out of different patterns of wallpaper or scrap paper.

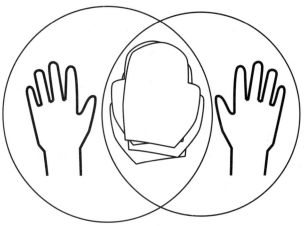

Place all the mittens in the center section. Working with small groups, have a volunteer take a mitten from the center, tell on which hand the mitten belongs, and place it on the appropriate side of the diagram.

Matching Mittens

The mittens used for the above activity can also be used for a matching activity. Provide enough spring-type clothespins for each pair of mittens. Have the children match and clip the matching pairs together.

One Size Does Not Fit All

To make this game, you will need to cut a piece of poster board in half. Draw three hands on the board—one small, one medium, one large. Outline the hands with black marker and color inside the outlines.

Laminate the poster board. At the same time, laminate some printed paper such as gift wrap or wallpaper. Copy the patterns (page 289) as they are, reduced, and enlarged to make the sizes small, medium, and large. Trace the different sizes onto the printed paper, making matching pairs of mittens. Cut out the mittens. Then shuffle them for students. Encourage the children to match the pairs according to size.

Additional Activities *(cont.)*

Science/Discovery/Language

Fittin' in a Mitten

After reading the story *The Mitten,* find out what can really fit in a mitten. Divide the class into groups, and have each group go to a different area of the room. Ask the children to work together to collect things and put them inside a mitten. At Circle Time, take the items out of the mittens and discuss students' findings.

White on White

Ask the children why the mitten in the story *The Mitten* was so difficult to see in the snow. Have them determine why the mitten wasn't spotted right away. While the children are suggesting answers, start cutting a mitten out of white paper. After you have cut it out, place it on top of another sheet of white paper. Discuss how this is like the mitten in the story.

What's in the Mitten?

Place a familiar school object inside a mitten and hold the top closed. Have the children take turns feeling the mitten and guessing what's inside. Some item suggestions include a crayon, marker, pair of blunt scissors, block, spoon, ball, clothespin, large ball of cotton, small glue bottle, and toy car or truck. If the children are having difficulty guessing, provide them with some clues such as, "It's something we use for cutting." After a student has guessed the correct answer, take the object out of the mitten to show the class.

Music/Movement/Language

Musical Hands

Allow the children to explore the many ways they can make music with their hands. Suggestions include clapping, snapping fingers, rubbing hands together, and patting.

Copycat Clap

Create a series of clapping sequences, beginning with two claps at a time. Then increase the number of claps and the speed in each sequence. Have the children watch and listen as you present the pattern. Then ask them to repeat the sequence.

> **Example:**
> Clap twice slowly.
> Clap twice quickly.
> Clap once. Pause. Then clap twice quickly.
> Clap twice quickly. Pause. Then clap twice quickly again.
> *(Continue the pattern until the children can repeat it.)*

Additional Activities *(cont.)*

Social/Emotional/Language

Five Fingers Fingerplay

The following fingerplay can be done as a poem or a song.

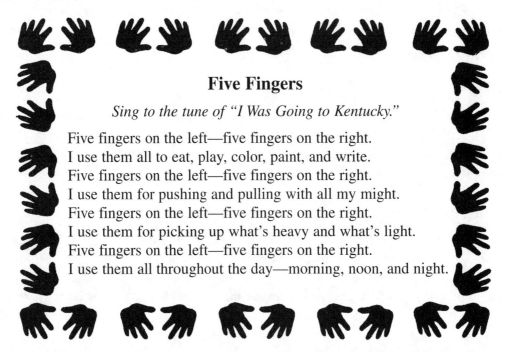

Five Fingers

Sing to the tune of "I Was Going to Kentucky."

Five fingers on the left—five fingers on the right.
I use them all to eat, play, color, paint, and write.
Five fingers on the left—five fingers on the right.
I use them for pushing and pulling with all my might.
Five fingers on the left—five fingers on the right.
I use them for picking up what's heavy and what's light.
Five fingers on the left—five fingers on the right.
I use them all throughout the day—morning, noon, and night.

After doing this activity, review the second line and discuss other uses of hands/fingers. Draw attention to the fourth line. Ask what kinds of things are pushed, what kinds of things are pulled, and what the difference is between pushing and pulling. Have students think about the sixth line, and ask them to name things that are heavy or light. Focusing on the last line, have the children talk about specific activities they use their hands/fingers for in the morning, at noon, and during the night.

Mittens and Gloves

Let children examine a pair of mittens or gloves. Have them compare/contrast the two.

Mitten Relay

You'll need a kitchen timer to play this game. Set the timer for an amount of time that you feel is appropriate for the developmental level of your students.

Note: The idea is for the children to cooperatively race against the clock, not against each other. Everyone who beats the clock wins.

Divide the class into two groups. Line up the groups parallel to each other. Hand the first child in each group a left or right mitten. These two children must put on the mittens, "high five" each other, take off the mittens, and pass them to the next players in their lines. The students who have already gone can help the next children put on and take off the mittens. This continues until everyone has had a turn. The object of the game is to complete the cycle before the timer rings.

Note: Some children may require adult help putting on and taking off the mittens.

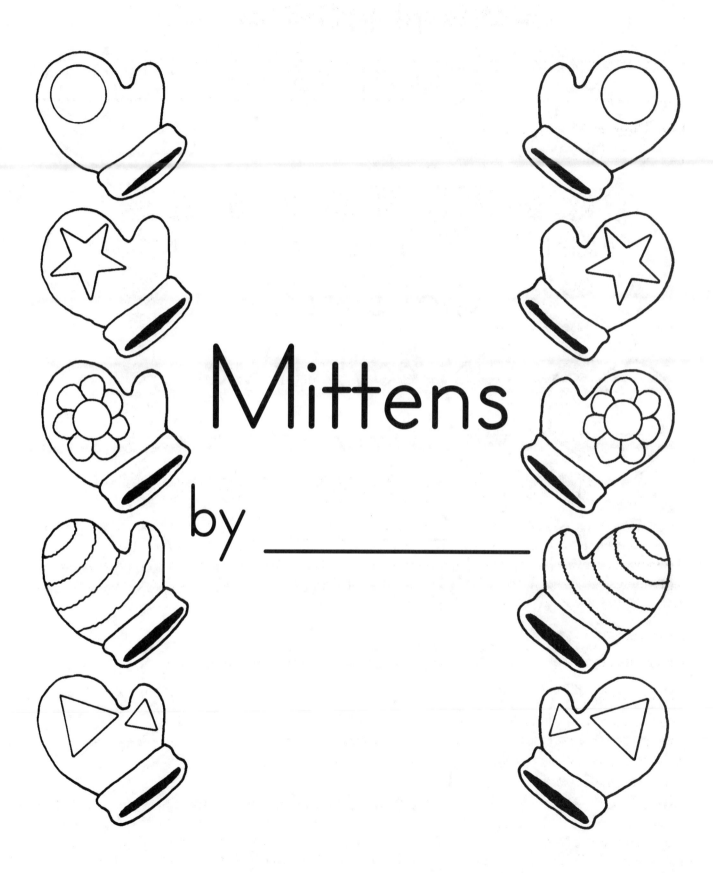

Mittens

by _____

There's something in _____'s mitten. I wonder what's inside. Oh, boy! It's a toy! A _____ has been spied. It's a day for lots of play. There's no need to hide.

Related Resources

Books

Aliki. *My Hands.* HarperCollins, 1990.

Andersen, Hans Christian. *The Emperor's New Clothes.* Troll, 1979.

Andersen, Hans Christian. *Thumbelina.* Troll, 1979.

Borden, Louise. *Caps, Hats, Socks and Mittens.* Scholastic, 1992.

Brett, Jan. *The Mitten.* Putnam, 1989.

Brown, Marc. *Hand Rhymes.* Puffin Books, 1993.

Calstrom, Nancy White. *Jesse Bear, What Will You Wear?* Macmillan, 1986.

Cutts, David. *Tom Thumb.* Troll, 1988.

dePaola, Tomie. *Charlie Needs a Cloak.* Simon & Schuster, 1973.

Dorling Kindersley Editors. *My First Look at Clothes.* Random House, 1991.

Martin, Bill & John Archambault. *Here Are My Hands.* Henry Holt & Co., 1989.

Monsell, Mary Elise. *Underwear!* Albert Whitman & Company, 1988.

Morris, Ann. *Hats, Hats, Hats.* Lothrop, 1989.

Munsch, Robert. *Thomas' Snowsuit.* Annick Press, 1985.

Penn, Audrey. *The Kissing Hand.* Child Welfare League of America, 1993.

Pulver, Robin. *Mrs. Toggle's Beautiful Blue Shoe.* Four Winds, 1994.

Pulver, Robin. *Mrs. Toggle's Zipper.* Macmillan, 1990.

Rohmer, Harriet and Rosalma Zubizarreta. *Uncle Nacho's Hat.* Childrens Press, 1989.

Seuss, Dr. *The Cat in the Hat.* Random House, 1987.

Seuss, Dr. *The 500 Hats of Bartholomew Cubbins.* Random House, 1989.

Sonnenschein, Harriet. *Harold's Hideaway Thumb.* Simon & Schuster, 1993.

Weil, Lisl. *New Clothes: What People Wore—from Cavemen to Astronauts.* Macmillan, 1988.

Ziefert, Harriet. *A New Coat for Anna.* Alfred A. Knopf, 1986.

Ziefert, Harriet. *Zippity Zap! A Book About Dressing.* Penguin, 1984.

Music

Greg and Steve. *We All Live Together, Vol. 4.* "Hand Jive." Youngheart Records, 1980.

Hallum, Rosemary, Ph.D. & Henry "Buzz" Glass. *Fingerplays and Footplays for Fun and Learning.* "I Have Ten Little Fingers." Activity Records, Inc., 1987.

Palmer, Hap. *Learning Basic Skills Through Music, Vol. 1.* "Put Your Hands Up In The Air." Activity Records, 1969.

The Learning Station. *Where Is Thumbkin?* "Open, Shut Them." Kimbo, 1996.

The Learning Station. *Where Is Thumbkin?* "Where Is Thumbkin?" Kimbo, 1996.

Tickle Tune Typhoon. *Circle Around.* "Clap Your Hands." Tickle Tune Typhoon Records, 1983.

Textured Bears Tote Book Materials

Unit Materials:

— glue
— scissors
— drawing tools: crayons, markers, chalk, colored pencils
— stapler
— tagboard
— construction paper: any color
— paints: any color
— large and small paint containers
— textured scrap materials: corrugated cardboard, cotton balls, pompoms, felt, vellux, chenille pipe cleaners, yarn, fleece, sandpaper, burlap, contact paper, sponge, feathers, bubble wrap, wool, craft fur, Velcro, aluminum foil, twist-type craft paper, craft sticks, velvet, rubber bands, spandex, lace, vinyl, leather
— wallpaper
— hole puncher
— yarn or thin macramé cord
— masking tape
— 3" x 5" (8 cm x 13 cm) index cards

Extra:

— bear stencil (sized for the easel)
— glue gun or glue sticks

Optional Materials for Additional Activities:

— 9" (23 cm) white paper plates
— black construction paper
— small, bathroom-size, paper cups
— butcher paper: any color
— fly swatters
— streamers or ribbons
— instant oatmeal or creamed wheat
— small, medium, and large containers
— paper grocery bag
— craft sticks
— poster board
— parachute, large sheet, or blanket
— margarine tubs
— brown sugar or cinnamon

Textured Bears Tote Book

Theme: My Friends and Me
Topics: Bears/Senses
Duration: Short Term
Approach: Original
        Teacher-Directed Activities

Most children love stuffed animals. Many of them sleep with these buddies. Teddy bears are usually a favorite among children as well as adults. This unit can be done at any time, but you may want to consider implementing it at the beginning of the school year when the children are in the process of getting acclimated. Young children experiencing some initial separation anxiety will appreciate the comfort connected with carrying their favorite teddy bears.

Be sure to send home the parent letter (page 313) before beginning this unit. The letter requests that parents send their children to school with a favorite teddy bear, doll, or stuffed animal. You may also want to keep some extra teddy bears, dolls, or stuffed animals on hand in case some children don't have any or forget theirs at home. Parents whose children have outgrown some of their stuffed toys may be willing to donate them to your class. Teddy bears can also be purchased at yard/garage sales at bargain prices. Teddy bears and other donated stuffed animals can be recycled after this unit by placing them in the classroom library. Children can take them out and read to them throughout the day.

Making the Book

COVER PAGE

Setup: Set out a stack of construction paper and bear-shaped cookie cutters. Place any color of paint in a shallow pan.

Introduction: Ask the children to share their stuffed animals during Show and Tell. Read *A Pocket for Corduroy* by Don Freeman (Viking, 1978). Explain that bears will be the topic of discussion for the next few days. Tell students that they will be working on a tote book about bears. Point out that the cover page will be designed out of cookie-cutter prints. Using the cover sheet as an example, show the children how to dip the cookie cutters into the paint and use the cutting edge to make a bear print. Set this sheet aside for the book. Then direct their attention to the creative art table. Allow the children to experiment with the cookie cutters.

Making the Book (cont.)

PAGES 1–?

Text: Tell me, Bear. What do you hide?

There's something _____ tucked inside.

The text is the same for every page except for the texture words that are written in the blanks. The textures chosen are contingent upon what you have available in your classroom and what you can easily obtain. The number of textures needed depends on how many children there are in your classroom. Since every child will contribute one page, you will need a texture for each. Ideally, each texture should be different. However, if you have a large class and it is impossible to compile a great assortment of textured materials, just repeat some throughout the book. You can also use the same descriptive word with different items.

Following are some text examples.

Tell me, Bear. What do you hide?

There's something *wrinkly* tucked inside. (corrugated cardboard or bulletin board border)

Tell me, Bear. What do you hide?

There's something *fluffy* tucked inside. (cosmetic puffs, cotton balls, or pompoms)

Other suggested textures:

fuzzy—felt, vellum, thick chenille pipe cleaners, yarn, fleece

rough—sandpaper or burlap

smooth—contact paper on an index card

puffy—an old shoulder pad

tickly—feather

bumpy—glue drizzled and hardened on an index card

soft—bubble wrap, velvet, cotton, sponge

itchy—wool or burlap

sticky—self-adhesive labels (glued onto an index card right side down and covered with wax paper) or tape with the sticky side out

furry—craft fur

bristly—the looped part of Velcro® glued onto an index card

crinkly—foil or twist-type craft paper

hard—craft stick, wooden spoon, or parquetry block

rubbery—flat, jar opener or a rubber band

stretchy—a piece of wide waistband elastic; a remnant of spandex cloth; or the wrist portion of an old, long sleeved shirt

In addition to the suggestions provided above, you can also add fabric items to go along with the following textures: velvety, lacy, leathery, satiny, cottony.

Making the Book *(cont.)*

Activity 1—Stencil Painting

Setup: Use a large, easel-sized bear stencil if you have one. If you don't already have a stencil, you can easily make one by enlarging the pattern (page 314), tracing it onto a sheet of tagboard, laminating it, and then cutting out the bear shape.

Note: If you have older children and prefer to give them cutting practice, you can skip the painting activity and just have them cut and paste the bears onto sheets of tagboard. Then ask them to add eyes, noses, and mouths to their bears.

Introduction: Review the story *A Pocket for Corduroy,* and explain that each page of the next big book will consist of a bear with a front pocket. Show them the bear stencil and let them know that they will be using it to create their tote book illustrations. Have the children use regular or sponge paintbrushes to paint the bear onto big book-sized sheets of tagboard. After the paint has dried, allow the children to add facial features with markers, paint, or crayons.

Activity 2—Lacing Pockets

Setup: Precut wallpaper samples into 5" (13 cm) squares. You'll need two identical squares per child. With the front sides facing out, clip each pair together and punch holes along three sides.

Cut yarn or thin macramé cord into 36" (91 cm) strands. Tightly wrap some masking tape around one end of each piece of yarn or cord. The children will use this end like a sewing needle.

Introduction: After reviewing *A Pocket for Corduroy,* let the children know that they will be sewing some pockets for their stencil bears. Point out that these pockets are a very important part of their tote books because each page will show a bear tucking something in its pocket.

Directions: Show students how to hold the wallpaper squares so that the side without holes is at the top. Then demonstrate how to thread the untaped end of yarn/cord through the first hole on the left side and knot it securely onto the square. Then model how to use the taped end of the yarn/cord to lace up the square.

Give each child a wallpaper square to lace. Once the lacing is completed, leave about 8" (20 cm) of yarn or cord extending from the right-hand side of each pocket. Use clear tape to secure the loose end of the yarn/cord to the bottom center of a 3" x 5" (8 cm x 13 cm) index card. If you prefer, you can punch a hole in the bottom center of the card and tie the end of the lacing yarn to it. Later, all the textures will be taped or glued directly onto these cards.

Making the Book (cont.)

Activity 3—Comparing Textures

Setup: Place all of the items that students will be using for the tote book on the science/discovery table. Let the children touch, compare/contrast, and talk about them. Allow the children to direct the conversations. Your role is to act as a facilitator, interjecting only if their descriptions are inaccurate or if the conversation needs to be stimulated.

Introduction: No introduction is necessary for this particular activity. Let children notice the table by themselves and inform the others without directions from you. The children's curiosity should be enough to motivate them to approach this center.

Directions: Observe and take notes while the children interact at the science/discovery table.

Activity 4—Describing Textures and Making Choices

Setup: Bring out the stenciled bears and the laced pockets. Staple or bind all the pages together to form the tote book. If the text (page 311) will be attached to each bear page, you will need to reduce it to fit. If the text will be glued onto the pages opposite the bears, then you can reproduce it as is. Make one copy of the text per child. You will also need to provide some glue, clear tape, and all the textured items that will be used for the book.

Introduction: Bring out the notes that you took during Activity 3 (above). Review the activity and discuss some of the comments that the children made during the discovery process. Inform students that you will be working with them on an individual basis to complete the tote book. Explain that you will be asking them to choose and describe one type of texture that they found particularly interesting.

Directions: Call the children up one at a time and have them glue their pockets directly onto their bears. Reread the text to the class, and have each child choose one item from the textured options. Glue or tape the desired items onto the attached cards. Then write the corresponding adjective in the blank provided (page 311) and glue the text onto the appropriate big book page.

PUTTING IT ALL TOGETHER

A suggested title and text for this book are provided (pages 310 and 311). Unlike most other big books, this interactional copy has raised surfaces due to the sensory nature of the topic. As a result it will be frequently touched. Review proper handling of this book with the children prior to sending it home.

Additional Activities

Art/Language

Paper Plate Pandas

For this activity, you will need black construction paper, white paper plates, white sticky dots, and bathroom-size disposable cups. Use the rim of the cups to trace circles onto the black construction paper. Cut out enough circles so that each child will have two. These will be the pandas' ears. The children will use black paint and paintbrushes or dab bottles to make the eye markings. Help students place glue around the rim of the cups and glue each cup to the middle of a plate. Have them use markers or dab bottles to add on the mouth. Wait until the markings are dry. Give each student two sticky dots. Have them use black markers to draw small circles in the center of the dots. Then tell them to place the dots in the middle of the eye markings. If you do not have sticky dots, glue on white circles cut out of copier paper instead.

Note: Make an extra panda for the Feed the Panda activity (page 307).

Bulletin Board: These paper plate pandas make a great bulletin board as well. You may wish to have the bulletin board pandas peeking out from behind leaves. Set out some white or light-blue butcher paper. Let the children creatively print on it by placing fly swatters in small amounts of green paint then lightly slapping them on the paper. Ask them to make repeated prints until the paper is covered. Measure the butcher paper and cut it to fit your bulletin board. Attach the paper plate pandas to the background. Then add a cute caption such as "Panda-monium" or "Have a BEARY good day."

Note: This activity can be quite messy. Protective paint shirts or smocks and an outside setup are recommended.

Alternative: If you do not wish to have the children create the background for the pandas, cover the bulletin board with red paper butcher paper. The black, white, and red make a striking combination.

Teddy Bear Shakers

Have each child paint the bottom side of one paper plate. Allow the paint to dry. Use the bears from the above activity. Glue the back of the child's bear plate onto the back of a painted paper plate. Turn the plates over. Tell the child to place two or three large beads, lima beans, milk caps, or any other appropriate item that will make a noise in the plate. Cover the noisemakers by placing the second plate facedown on top of them. Staple the rims of the painted plates together. Follow this same procedure for each child.

Optional: Before stapling the plates together, add 6" (15 cm) streamers or ribbons for decoration.

Additional Activities *(cont.)*

Art/Language *(cont.)*

Beautiful Bears

Using the pattern (page 314), trace and cut the bears in a variety of colors. Let the children add facial features and decorate the bears by gluing on their choice of collage and craft items.

Paw Prints

Cut out circle shapes from sponges. Cut one large circle, approximately 2.5" (6.3 cm) in diameter and five smaller circles, approximately 0.5–0.75" (1.3–1.9 cm) in diameter. Use a hot glue gun to attach the circles to a wooden block. Have students use the block to make paw prints by dipping it into a container of paint, and then pressing it onto sheets of construction paper.

Note: This activity can be extended to include math by reviewing the circle shape, small and large sizes, and counting the number of toes. You can also reinforce the concept of right and left by having the children switch hands while printing. Draw a line down the center of the paper or have students fold the paper in half. Have them use their right hands to print on the right side of the paper and their left hands to print on the left side. Ask which side was easier to do.

Math/Language

Sorting Bears

Using the bears and stuffed animals brought in by the children, work with the class to sort and characterize the toys according to size, color, type, clothing, etc.

Science/Discovery/Language

Bear Caves

Encourage the children to make caves out of wet sand by using margarine containers as molds.

Porridge

Read *Goldilocks and the Three Bears*. Make some porridge by mixing some instant oatmeal or creamed wheat according to directions, and then sprinkling a little brown sugar and cinnamon over the top. Serve in small, medium, and large containers.

What Do You Hear?

Read aloud *Polar Bear, Polar Bear, What Do You Hear?* by Bill Martin, Jr. (Henry Holt & Co., 1996). Choose one student to be the bear. Place a blindfold on that child or simply have the child turn around. Say to the child, "Polar bear, polar bear, what do you hear?" Then, using common objects, make a noise. The child must guess what is making the sound.

Additional Activities (cont.)

Social/Emotional/Language

Going on a Bear Hunt

For this activity, have the children sit in a circle with their legs crossed. Tell them that you are going to take them on a bear hunt. To go on this trip they will need to pack some imagination, giggles, and fun. Pretend to pack these things into a make-believe backpack and then put the backpack on your back.

Inform the children that they will need to provide the sound effects for this trip. Let the children know that to do this activity, they will need to listen carefully and repeat each sentence after you say it. To begin, they must make a sound effect for people walking by alternately tapping their hands on their knees or the floor. This will make the sound of footsteps. Tell students that they will be making the walking sound effect for the duration of the trip unless otherwise specified.

Then say the following chant, allowing time for the children to repeat each line.

Going on a bear hunt.

Want to come along?

Okay.

All right.

Let's go.

Open the gate. (Clap.)

Close the gate. (Clap.)

Coming to a field.

Can't go over it. (Shake head.)

Can't go under it.

We'll have to go across.

Okay. (Shrug shoulders.)

All right.

Let's go. (Rub hands together briskly while making a TCH, TCH, TCH sound with mouth.)

Coming to a bridge.

Can't go over it. (Shake head.)

Can't go under it.

We'll have to go across.

Okay. (Shrug shoulders.)

All right.

Let's go. (Use tongue to make a clicking noise while snapping fingers.)

Tote Books   Textured Bears Tote Book

Additional Activities *(cont.)*

Going on a Bear Hunt *(cont.)*

Coming to a swamp.

Can't go over it. *(Shake head.)*

Can't go under it.

We'll have to go across.

Okay. *(Shrug shoulders)*

All right.

Let's go. *(Fill cheeks with air and then force air out through lips by pressing palms against cheeks.)*

Coming to a lake.

Can't go over it. *(Shake head.)*

Can't go under it.

We'll have to go across.

Okay. *(Shrug shoulders.)*

All right.

Let's go. *(Make swimming motions while saying, "Splish, splash," etc.)*

Coming to a cave. *(Slow down and say next lines as if telling a spooky story.)*

Can't go over it.

Can't go under it.

We'll have to go inside. *(Whisper.)*

Okay.

All right.

Let's go. *(Close eyes and extend arms and hands as if feeling around in darkness.)*

Oooohhhh!

It's dark in here.

I feel something furry.

I see two big eyes.

I feel a wet nose.

IT'S A BEAR! RUN!

(Speed up all motions and sound effects. From this point on, the children need not repeat any lines if they are wrapped up in the excitement of following the motions and running away from the bear.)

Let's go across the lake. *(Splish, splash.)*

Let's go across the swamp. *(Fill cheeks with air and then force air out through lips by pressing palms against cheeks.)*

Let's go across the bridge. *(Use tongue to make a clicking noise while snapping fingers.)*

Let's go across the field. *(Rub hands together, back and forth briskly while making a TCH, TCH, TCH, sound with mouth.)*

Open the gate. *(Clap.)* Close the gate. *(Clap.)*

Whew! We're home. *(Run back of hand over forehead)*

#2311 A Year Full of Themes   306   © Teacher Created Materials, Inc.

Additional Activities *(cont.)*

Music/Movement/Language

Teddy Bear Picnic

For this activity, you will need to make a sun and some raindrops out of poster board or large sheets of construction paper. Place a parachute or large bed sheet on the floor. Seat the children around the edge with their bears on their laps. Tell them to hold the edge of the parachute or sheet with fingers over it and their thumbs under it. Have the children keep the parachute or sheet on the floor. Choose two children to stand up and be in charge of props. These children take turns holding the sun and raindrops according to the following song.

Picnic Song

Sing to the tune of "For He's a Jolly Good Fellow."

(Child with sun prop holds it up while everyone sings.)

We're going to a picnic. We're going to a picnic. We're going to a picnic.

(spoken in a loud voice) Uh-oh, rain.

(The sun prop is lowered and the rain prop is held up.)

Down comes the rain. Down comes the rain. *(Lift parachute/sheet high overhead.)*

We need to take cover. We need to take cover. We need to take cover,

'Til the sun comes out again. *(Let parachute fall back down.)*

(Choose two more children to hold the sun and raindrops.)

Feed the Panda

Attach a paper plate panda (page 303) to the side of a paper grocery bag. Explain that pandas love bamboo. If possible, show them what real bamboo looks like. Tell them that the object of this game is to feed the panda some bamboo. Place a masking tape strip on the floor a certain distance away from the bag. For very young children, about a yard (91 cm) is sufficient. Instruct the children to stand behind the tape. To play this game so there are no winners or losers, praise all the children for the total amount of bamboo that was tossed into the bag.

Hand each child some craft sticks and let them toss the sticks into the bag while reciting the following chant.

Little panda is calling you.

He is hungry for bamboo.

Toss some in and feed him quick.

But not too much, or he'll get sick.

Additional Activities *(cont.)*

Music/Movement/Language *(cont.)*

Teddy Bear Color Game

For this activity, you will need red, blue, and yellow colored yarn, macramé cord, or ribbon. Have children hold their Teddy bears on their laps. Tie a bow around the neck of each child's stuffed animal. Use these to act out the following song.

Dancing Bears

Sing to the tune of "Hokey Pokey."

Before we go, take a look at your bow,

Remember the color so you will know,

When it's your turn to get up from your seat,

To follow directions and move to the beat.

If your bear is wearing red,

Rub your tummy and shake your head.

Jump up and turn around,

Stamp your feet, then sit back down.

If your bear is wearing blue,

Reach up high, then touch your shoe.

Jump and turn around,

Stamp your feet, then sit back down.

If your bear is wearing yellow,

Make your body jiggle like Jell-O®.

Jump up and turn around,

Stamp your feet, then sit back down.

Red, blue, yellow, stand up, please.

Shrug your shoulders, and knock your knees.

Jump up and turn around,

Stamp your feet, but don't sit down.

Shake your hips without a sound.

Shake them up. Shake them down.

(Whisper next line, then pause for a short while.)

Down is where you need to stay.

(Raise voice.) Now, jump up and shout, "Hooray!"

Note: For older children, you can tie more than one color around the bear. Children can also trade bears, thus trading colors.

Additional Activities (cont.)

Music/Movement/Language (cont.)

Follow the Bear

The children hold their bears and form a circle for this variation of Follow the Leader. Play some music and let the children take turns leading the group by moving their bears while marching or dancing to the music. As the leader moves her/his bear up, down, around, etc., the rest of the group follows by imitating the leader's actions.

Teddy Bear Parade

Give the children an instrument that they can play with one hand, such as bells, jingle togs, tambourine, a maraca, shaker, or hand castanets. Play some marching music and have them carry their stuffed animals in one hand while playing their musical instruments with the other hand.

Missing Bears

Choosing from the bears the children brought in, pick out four or five that have very distinct features and characteristics. Take into consideration, color, shape, size, articles of clothing, etc. Set them up side by side. If you have a portable bulletin board or a flannelboard with a stand, you can lean the bears against it. If not, the bears can be placed against the wall. Lead a discussion about what makes each bear different.

Choose one child to be the zookeeper and another child to be the one who hides a bear. The zookeeper must take a good look at all the bears and then turn around and cover her/his eyes.

Then the other child takes one of the bears and hides it. If you are using a portable board, the bear can be placed behind it. Otherwise, the child can hide the bear behind a nearby shelf or put it into a box, bag, closet, etc. After the bear has been hidden, the zookeeper turns around and guesses which bear is missing.

Different children are then chosen to hide and guess. The game can proceed according to interest and active participation.

Care Bear

During Circle Time, with the bears sitting on the children's laps, go around and ask each child how her/his bear feels that day. Once children respond, ask why the bear feels that way. This activity may give you some insight as to how your students are feeling. If the children are not responding, you can ask leading questions like, "What makes your bear happy? What does your bear like to do when she/he is not at school? What kinds of things surprise your bear? What makes your bear feel scared? What makes your bear feel bored?"

The
Textured
Bear

by _____

Tell
me, Bear.
What do
you hide?
There's something

_____

tucked inside.

 #2311 A Year Full of Themes

Related Resources

Books

Berenstain, Stan and Jan. *The Berenstain Bears and Too Much TV.* Random House, 1984.

Brett, Jan. *Goldilocks and the Three Bears.* Putnam, 1987.

Carlstrom, Nancy White. *It's About Time, Jesse Bear, and Other Rhymes.* Scholastic, 1990.

Carlstrom, Nancy. *Jesse Bear, What Will You Wear?* Macmillan, 1986.

Cosgrove, Stephen. *Jingle Bear.* Price, Stern, Sloan, 1985.

DuBois, William Pene. *Bear Party.* Puffin, 1987.

Fowler, Allan. *Please Don't Feed the Bears.* Childrens Press, 1991.

Gretz, Suzanna. *Teddy Bears 1 to 10.* Macmillan, 1986.

Hague, Kathleen. *Alphabears: An ABC Book.* Holt, Rinehart, and Winston, 1984.

Katz, Bobbie. *Month By Month : A Care Bear Book of Poems.* Random House, 1984.

Leach, Michael. *Bears.* Mallard, 1990.

Leonard, Marcia. *Bear's Busy Year: A Book About Seasons.* Troll, 1990.

Martin, Bill, Jr. *Brown Bear, Brown Bear, What Do You See?* Henry Holt & Co., 1996.

Martin, Bill, Jr. *Polar Bear, Polar Bear, What Do You Hear?* Henry Holt & Co., 1996.

Milne, A. A. *Winnie the Pooh and the House at Pooh Corner.* Dell, 1970.

Mole, Karen Bryant. *Texture.* Silver Burdett Press, 1996.

Nentl, Jerolyn. *The Grizzly.* Crestwood, 1984.

Rosen, Michael. *We're Going on a Bear Hunt.* Margaret K. McEldeny Books, 1989.

Ryder, Joanne. *White Bear, Ice Bear.* Morrow, 1989.

Slier, Avery. *The Day Teddy Bear Got Lost.* Random House, 1986.

Waddell, Martin. *Can't You Sleep, Little Bear?* Candlewick, 1988.

Waddell, Martin. *When the Teddy Bears Came.* Candlewick Press, 1988.

Ward, Lynd. *The Biggest Bear.* Houghton Mifflin, 1992.

Weiss, Nicki. *Where Does the Brown Bear Go?* Greenwillow, 1989.

Music

Greg and Steve. *Playing Favorites.* "Brown Bear, Brown Bear, What Do You See?" Youngheart Records, 1991.

Raffi. *Everything Grows.* "Teddy Bear Hug." A&M Records

Tickle Tune Typhoon. *Circle Around.* "Bear Hunt." Tickle Tune Typhoon Records, 1983.

Video

Bears. (Video); 8 min. Troll Associates, Catalog Sales Dept., 100 Corporate Dr., Mahwah, NJ 07498. 1-800-929-8765.

Birthday Buddies. (video about a bear's special birthday present for his grandfather); 8 min. Troll Associates, Catalog Sales Dept., 100 Corporate Dr., Mahwah, NJ 07498. 1-800-929-8765.

Corduroy. (Video); Wood Knapp Video, 1993.

A Pocket for Corduroy. (Video); Good Times Entertainment, 1996.

Letter

_____

(Date)

Dear_____,

On_____, we will begin a unit on bears. Our art, math, science, music, social studies, and language lessons will revolve around these soft and cuddly friends. Your child's very own teddy bear is invited to join us for these activities. If the bears are needed at home, the children are free to bring them back and forth. However, all bears are certainly welcome to stay at school for the week. Please label the bear with your child's name, making sure the tag or label is clearly visible and secure.

If your child does not have a teddy bear, another stuffed animal can be substituted, or I can let him/her borrow one.

If you or anyone you know would like to donate teddy bears to the school, please let me know.

Sincerely,

_____

(Teacher)

_____

(School)

_____

(Phone)

- -

Please fill out the following section, cut on the dotted line, and return it to school by_____.

❑ My child can bring a stuffed bear to school for the week_____.

❑ My child will not be able to bring a stuffed bear to school.

❑ I can donate extra teddy bears to the school.

_____

Child's Name

_____

Parent/Guardian Signature

Teddy Bear Pattern

The Cloth Moth Tote Book Materials

Unit Materials:

— glue
— scissors
— drawing tools: crayons, markers, chalk, colored pencils
— stapler
— tagboard
— construction paper: white or light colors
— a variety of fabric scraps or remnants
— circle sponges
— two wooden blocks
— paint: any colors
— large, shallow paint containers
— thick yarn: any colors
— wooden craft spoons or craft sticks
— wax paper or white paper towels
— pipe cleaners

Extra:

— pinking shears
— food pictures
— Velcro®
— paper cutter

Optional Materials for Additional Activities:

— stamps/stamp pads
— watercolor paints
— bingo markers
— stickers
— pompoms
— beads
— small wiggle eyes
— gems, sequins, glitter pens
— index cards

— spring-type clothespins
— licorice strings
— o-shaped cereal
— black construction paper
— plastic darning needle
— 8" x 10" (20 cm x 25 cm) Styrofoam sheets (like the kind used for packing or insulation purposes)

The Cloth Moth Tote Book

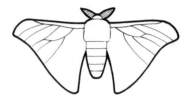

Theme: My World and Me
Topics: Caterpillars/Moths
Duration: Short Term
Approach: Original Poem
          Cut and Paste Activity

This tote book which is also an adaptation of Eric Carle's *The Very Hungry Caterpillar,* can easily piggyback The Very Hungry _____ unit (pages 86–105). In this version, the caterpillar becomes a moth instead of a butterfly and nibbles through fabric instead of eating food. For this unit, you will need to send parents a letter requesting small, cloth remnants (page 327). The children use a pompom caterpillar to insert through moth holes as the book is read. Because this book gets the children actively involved, it's sure to be a favorite, especially with the tactile/kinesthetic learners in your classroom.

Following are some moth facts that may be helpful when doing this unit.

- When making butterfly crafts, it is customary to add antennae with little knobs at the end. However, unlike butterflies, moths do not have these little knobs.
- Many moth caterpillars are mistaken for worms.
- Moth caterpillars eat food plants and fruit in addition to cloth and clothing.
- Clothes moths either spin a shelter case of silk and bits of the fabric on which have fed, or they spin webs as they move over a piece of cloth.
- Unlike the butterfly, a moth caterpillar does not form a chrysalis. It forms a cocoon or simply burrows in the ground, taking shelter under a stone or leaf.
- Butterflies fly and feed in the daytime. Most moths fly and feed at night.
- Butterflies rest with their wings upright over their backs. Most moths rest with their wings spread out.
- Not all moths are white. Some are beautifully colored and mistaken for butterflies.

The Cloth Moth

Once there was a hungry little caterpillar that looked like a worm.

There were many good things to eat, but Katy's favorite food was cloth.

On Sunday, she ate through _____ 's _____.

On Monday, she ate through _____ 's _____.

On Tuesday, she ate through _____ 's _____.

On Wednesday, she ate through_____ 's _____.

On Thursday, she ate through _____ 's _____.

On Friday, she ate through_____ 's _____.

On Saturday, she ate through_____ 's _____.

One day, she spun a little house called a cocoon and stayed there a while.

When she finally came out, she was no longer a caterpillar. She was a moth.

Making the Book

COVER PAGE

Activity: Make a fabric collage.

Setup: Make sure the title (page 322) is attached to the big book cover before beginning this activity. Cut small bits and pieces from all the cloth remnants that were brought in and place them in a basket or box. Place the basket/box on a table with some glue and the cover page.

Introduction: Read/Review Eric Carle's *The Very Hungry Caterpillar.* Explain that the next tote book will be about a caterpillar. Provide some facts by telling them that this caterpillar looks like a worm and turns into a moth. Talk about some of the similarities and differences between moths and butterflies.

Directions: Have the children glue tiny pieces of fabric onto the cover page surrounding the title.

PAGE 1

Text: Once there was a hungry little caterpillar that looked like a worm.

Activity: Make a pattern circle caterpillar.

Setup: You will need two sponges, two wooden blocks, shallow containers of two different-colored paints, and tagboard. Glue the sponges onto appropriately sized wooden blocks.

Introduction: Explain that many moth caterpillars are mistaken for worms. If possible, show the children a picture of some. Tell them that they will be creating a caterpillar by alternating sponge prints.

Directions: Have students alternate the two colors of paint as they make sponge-print circles in a line across the entire page.

PAGE 2

Text: There were many good things to eat, but Katy's favorite food was cloth.

Activity: Draw and color favorite foods.

Setup: At a table, set out crayons, colored pencils, and markers. Use a white or light-colored sheet of paper for this page.

Note: You may wish to provide books with pictures of food for students. You can also use these book to build additional language skills by discussing colors, shapes, sizes, food categories, etc., while the children are browsing through the pages.

Making the Book *(cont.)*

Introduction: Read the text for this page. Direct students' attention to the line, "There were many good things to eat…." Ask the class what they think some of those good things might have been. Tell them that they must choose different foods to draw.

Directions: On this big book page, have the children draw and color as many foods as they like. Beside each illustration, write the child's name and the name of the food. Additional pages can be made if the children want to illustrate more foods.

PAGES 3–?

Text: On _____ (day of the week), she ate through _____' s (person's name)

_____ (piece of clothing).

Activity: Compare and discuss fabrics.

Setup: Reproduce the story (pages 323–325), making as many copies of the text shown above as needed. Use pinking shears to precut all the remnants, making sure they are no smaller than 6" (15 cm) squares. Trace and cut a 2–3" (5–8 cm) circle in the center of each piece of fabric. Using the same circle pattern on the tagboard sheets, trace and cut one circle per child. Each hole should be situated in the same spot so that when all the pages are closed together, you can poke your finger through every sheet at the same time. Place bottles of glue on the table.

Introduction: In small groups at the bookmaking table, review the story. Compare/contrast the various types of cloth. Discuss textures, colors, patterns, and uses for the cloth.

Directions: Have the children rummage through the cloth scraps and choose one to glue onto the page. Ask the children to think about where the cloth might have come from or what it could be used to make. Write the day of the week in the first blank, the student's name in the second blank, and the article of clothing suggested by the child in the third blank. Use each day of the week consecutively, utilizing as many days as necessary.

Have the child place glue around the perimeter of the opening in the tagboard. Then have him/her place the cloth over the tagboard, matching the holes. Once this is done, the rest of the cloth can be glued onto the big book page. Allow the glue to dry. Then attach the text.

NEXT TO THE LAST PAGE

Text: One day, she spun a little house called a cocoon and stayed there for a while.

Activity: Reproduce a pattern.

Setup: Reproduce the pattern (page 328) on two sheets of white paper and color one with a striped pattern. Provide thick yarn matching the colors used on the pattern, glue, and scissors.

Making the Book *(cont.)*

Introduction: If possible, show the children a picture of a real moth cocoon. Discuss the color, shape, and size. Explain that the story requires a page that shows a picture of a cocoon.

Directions: The children will measure the yarn, cut it, and glue it onto the second pattern sheet (the one that was not colored) to reproduce the design. Once the pattern is completed, allow it to dry. When it is dry, cut it into an oval shape and glue it onto a big book page.

Note: With very young children, the yarn can be precut.

LAST PAGE

Text: When she finally came out, she was no longer a caterpillar. She was a moth.

Activity: Make a kitchen paper moth.

Setup: Materials for this activity include craft sticks, wax paper or white paper towels, glue, markers, and pipe cleaners that have been cut into 1" (2.5 cm) lengths or tiny feathers. Don't forget to make an extra moth for the tote book and to use as a model.

Introduction: Review all the moth, butterfly, and caterpillar facts. Show them the sample moth. Explain that there will be a craft table set up for making moths if they choose to do so.

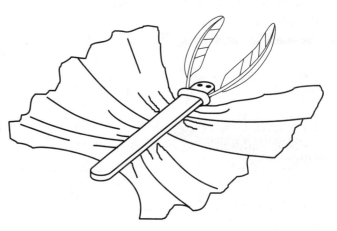

Directions: Tear off a sheet of the kitchen paper of your choice and have the children wrinkle it. Glue the gathered middle section onto a craft stick. Hold it in place to set. Carefully spread out the wings. Use a marker to add facial features to the stick and glue or tape the pipe cleaner or feather antennae onto the wood and curve towards the face. The moth can be sent home, pinned onto the classroom window curtains, or used for a bulletin board.

Bulletin Board: Instead of butcher paper, use an old curtain or a few yards of fabric for the background. Another idea is to staple an old sweatshirt, blouse, etc., onto the bulletin board with the moths flying around it. Arrange and staple all the moths as desired. Add a banner of your choice. Some ideas for banners include Cloths-ing in on Math Skills and School Is a "Hole" Lot of Fun. If gingham or checkered cloth is used, try the caption: "Check" This Out.

PUTTING IT ALL TOGETHER

Unlike the other big books in which the text is placed in the center of the pages opposite the illustrations, this book cannot be assembled that way because of the moth holes. Subsequently, the text must be placed on the page with the illustration, above and/or below the circular cutouts. The title and text for this big book can be found on pages 322–325.

Additional Activities

Art/Language

Tote Book Caterpillar

If you choose to make pompom caterpillars (below) as an additional activity, the tote book caterpillar can be made at that time. If not, you will need to make some to go along with this book. It is best to make the tote book caterpillars on craft spoons or craft sticks. The caterpillar can be stored by attaching one side of self-adhesive Velcro® to each craft stick and the other side to the cover of the big book, making it easy and convenient to remove and replace.

Quilt Samples

Throughout this unit, set up a variety of creative art activities. Any creative paperplay will do. Make sure these are done on tagboard. When completed, cut them in half. Send half home and save the remaining portion for a friendship quilt (page 321). Some ideas for creative art projects include the following: textured crayon rubbings, stamp art, watercolor paintings, bingo marker art, drawings with chalk, sticker art, fingerpainting, felt-pen drawings, or any tempera painting activity such as marble painting, blow painting, string painting, splatter painting, sponge painting, and easel painting.

Pompom Caterpillars

Have each student glue pompoms side by side on a piece of green tagboard that has been cut into the shape of a leaf or on craft sticks or spoons. Have the children use tiny pompoms, wiggle eyes, beads, gems, sequins, or fabric paint to add the eyes. Antennae can be made out of pipe cleaners. If these are made on spring-type clothespins, a strip of magnetic tape can be attached to the backside to create a refrigerator magnet.

Math/Language

Cloth Matching Cards

Using the fabric remnants brought in by students, make some matching cards by gluing two identical cloth squares onto index cards. Include a variety of colors and textures. Have the children mix the cards in a pile and then match the pairs together.

Edible Caterpillar Necklaces

Use the thin, string-type licorice to thread a few inches of O-shaped cereal. Reinforce math skills by having the children count out pieces of cereal and place them in sets. If colored O's are used, you can create a pattern for students to copy. Once the pattern is finished, help the children tie the licorice ends together. Tell students they can wear the necklaces.

Additional Activities *(cont.)*

Science/Discovery/Language

Light Designs

Moths are attracted to light. This paperplay allows the child to have some fun with light. Lay a piece of black paper on a sheet of Styrofoam or a carpet mat. Reproduce the design (page 329). Place this paper on top of the black sheet and clip it in place. Supervise the children as they use the point of a pencil to poke holes through the paper, following the pattern.

Note: This activity can be done without a pattern by having the children randomly poke holes in the paper.

Music/Movement/Language

Snacking Caterpillar

Have the children hold hands and move in a circle. One child is chosen to be the moth caterpillar and stands in the center of the circle. As everyone recites the poem below, the caterpillar acts out the movements that are described. You should fill in the blank with a student's name. The caterpillar and the person whose name was called change places. Continue in this manner until everyone has had a turn.

> One day, I saw a caterpillar wriggling in the dirt.
>
> He said, "I just had dinner, and now I want dessert."
>
> He looked all around him and warned, "Be alert!"
>
> Then he started nibbling on _____ 's shirt/skirt.

Note: The word *skirt* can be substituted for *shirt* when applicable.

Social/Emotional/Language

Friendship Quilt

Explain that a wonderful way to recycle fabric scraps, like the ones used to make *The Cloth Moth* tote book, is to sew them together to make a quilt. If possible, show the children an actual quilt and explain that lots of small fabric pieces that might otherwise have been discarded were sewn together to make something useful and durable. Tell the children that scraps taken from their artwork will be used to make a fingerplay friendship quilt. The 6" x 6" (15 cm x 15 cm) quilt squares can be cut by using the paper cutter. Then glue them onto large sheets of construction paper. The children can individually glue on their six squares, making a small quilt of their own.

Bulletin Board: All of these mini-quilts can then be assembled and stapled onto a bulletin board to create a class quilt.

The Cloth Moth

by _____

Once there was a hungry little caterpillar that looked like a worm.

There were many good things to eat, but Katy's favorite food was cloth.

On _____ , she
ate through
_____ 's _____ .

One day, she spun a
little house called a cocoon
and stayed there for a while.

When she finally came out,
she was no longer a
caterpillar.
She was a moth.

page 5

Related Resources

Books

Andersen, Hans Christian. *The Emperor's New Clothes.* Troll, 1979.

Carlstrom, Nancy. *Jesse Bear, What Will You Wear?* Macmillan, 1986.

Castaneda, Omar S. *Abuela's Weave.* Lee & Row Books, 1993.

Chocolate, Debbi. *Kente Colors.* Walker & Co., 1997.

Coerr, Eleanor. *The Josefina Story Quilt.* Harper & Row, 1986.

Dorling Kindersley Editors. *My First Look at Clothes.* Random House, 1991.

Farrand, John, Jr. *Butterflies.* W. H. Smith, 1990.

Flournoy, Valerie. *The Patchwork Quilt.* E. P. Dutton, 1985.

Gibbons, Gail. *Monarch Butterfly.* Holiday House, 1989.

Howe, James. *I Wish I Were a Butterfly.* Gulliver, 1987.

Johnston, Tony and Tomie dePaola. *The Quilt Story.* Putnam, 1985.

Jonas, Ann. *The Quilt.* Greenwillow, 1985.

Katz, Bobbi. *The Creepy Crawly Book.* Random House, 1989.

Low, Alice. *The Quilted Elephant and the Green Velvet Dragon.* Simon and Schuster, 1991.

Merrill, Jean. *The Girl Who Loved Caterpillars.* Philomel Books, 1992.

Monsell, Mary Elise. *Underwear!* Albert Whitman & Company, 1988.

Munsch, Robert. *Thomas' Snowsuit.* Annick Press, 1985.

Oberman, Sheldon. *The Always Prayer Shawl.* Boyds Mills, 1994.

Pulver, Robin. *Mrs. Toggle's Beautiful Blue Shoe.* Four Winds, 1994.

Polacco, Patricia. *The Keeping Quilt.* Simon & Schuster Books, 1994.

Seuss, Dr. *The Cat in the Hat.* Random House, 1987.

Seuss, Dr. *The 500 Hats of Bartholomew Cubbins.* Random House, 1989.

Slobodkina, Esphyr, told by. *Caps for Sale: A Tale of a Peddler, Some Monkeys and Their Monkey Business.* Young Scott Books, 1968.

Still, John. *Amazing Butterflies and Moths.* Knopf, 1991.

Ziefert, Harriet. *A New Coat for Anna.* Alfred A. Knopf, 1986.

Music

Grammer, Red. *Sing Along Songs.* "Guy With The Polka Dotted Tie." Red Note Records, 1993.

Palmer, Hap. *Learning Basic Skills Through Music, Volume 1.* "What Are You Wearing?" Activity Records, 1969.

Raffi. *The Corner Grocery Store.* "Pick a Bale o' Cotton." Troubadour Records Ltd., 1979.

Raffi. *Singable Songs for the Very Young.* "Baa, Baa Black Sheep." Shoreline Records, 1976.

Video

The Keeping Quilt. (Video); 11 min. Pied Piper/AIMS Multimedia, 9710 De Soto Ave., Chatsworth, CA 91311. 1-800-367-2567.

Request Letter

_____

(Date)

Dear Parent/Guardian,

We will soon be working on our next tote book that will be entitled
The Cloth Moth. In order to complete this big book, we will need
cloth remnants. We are hoping to get a variety of colors and textures.
These fabric scraps can be any type of material: cotton, wool, nylon,
polyester, acrylic, rayon, fleece, flannel, mesh, silk, satin, terrycloth,
denim, spandex, or anything else you may have. Any fabric will do,
and it does not have to be new or in perfect condition. Old clothes can
be cut into pieces so the material can be used for a variety of activities.

Please send fabric donations to school by _____.
We look forward to sharing our latest book with you. Thank you for
your help.

Sincerely,

_____

(Teacher)

_____

(School)

_____

(Phone)

Cocoon Pattern

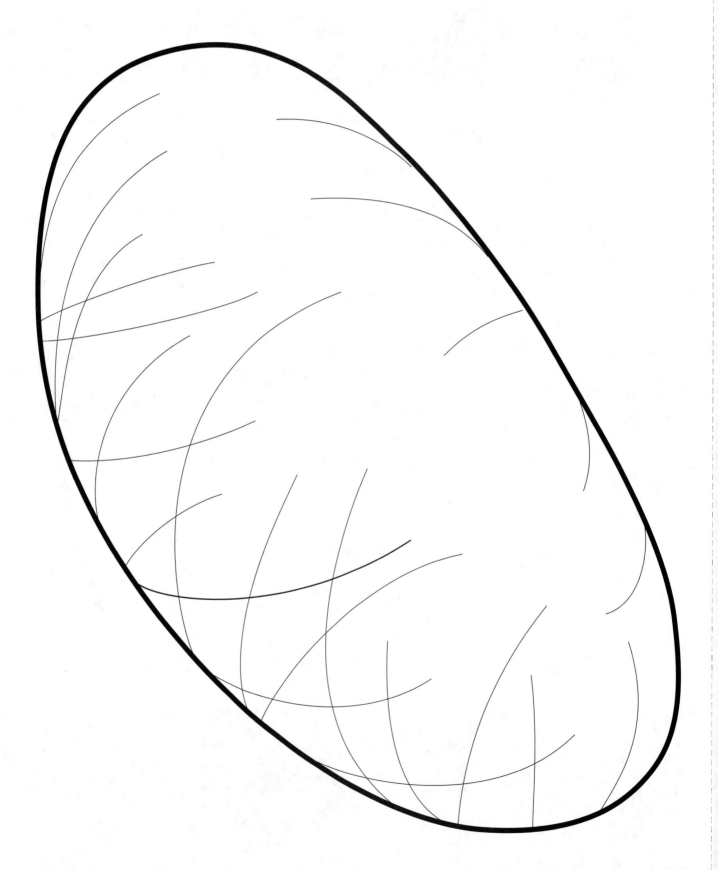

Light Designs Pattern

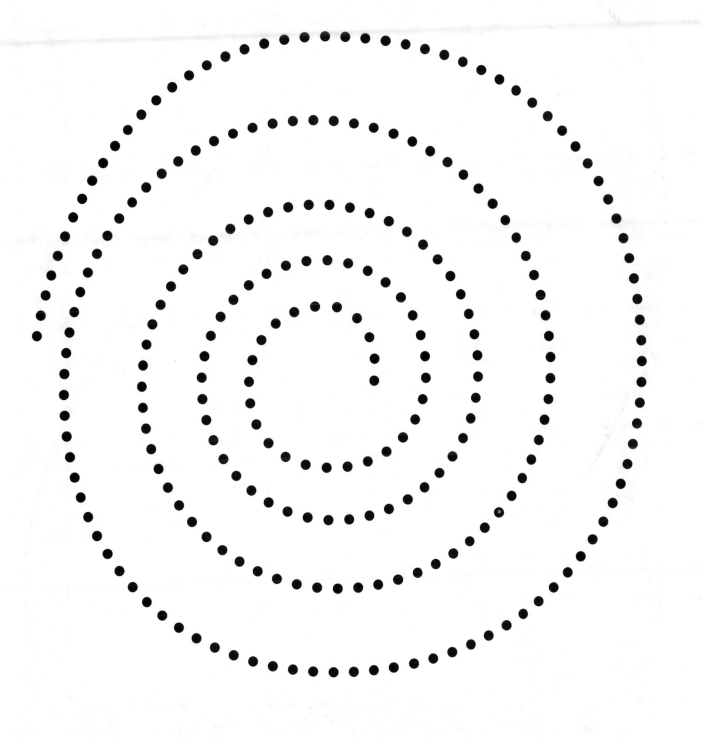

Parent Newsletter

_____

(Date)

Dear Parent/Guardian,

This month we are learning about _____

_____

Some upcoming events are _____

_____

_____

Below are some suggestions for fun-filled activities that you can do at home with your child to reinforce what we've been doing at school.

_____

_____

Here are some questions you can ask your child about what we're learning in school this month.

_____

_____

Items we will need for upcoming activities include the following:

_____

_____

Thank you for your help.

Sincerely,

_____

(Teacher)

_____

(School)

_____

(Phone)

Donation Request

_____
(Date)

Dear Parent/Guardian,

We would like to add to our classroom supplies. We can use practically anything old and serviceable. Please circle anything in the following list that you are willing to donate to our class. Then fill out the bottom of the form and send it back to school as soon as possible.

Thank you in advance for whatever you can donate.

Sincerely,

_____
(Teacher)

_____
(School)

_____
(Phone)

— 6" (15 cm) and 9" (23 cm) white paper plates
— adhesive bandages
— aluminum foil
— apple basket
— apple seeds
— appliances (blender, hot plate, snack maker, warming tray, iron)
— baby food jars
— baking soda
— balloons
— beaded garland
— beads
— berry baskets
— bingo markers
— blank index cards
— blanket
— bottle caps
— boxes
— brown or black shoe polish
— bubble wrap
— burlap
— buttons
— cake pan

— carpet samples
— cereal rings
— chalk
— cinnamon
— clay
— clean hosiery: socks, pantyhose
— clean, old clothes
— clean, Styrofoam meat trays
— clear dish detergent
— clothes hangers
— clothespins
— combs
— confetti
— contact paper
— cookie sheet
— cork
— cornmeal
— cotton balls and cotton batting
— cotton swabs
— coupons
— craft fur
— crayons
— curtain sheets
— cylinders

Donation Request *(cont.)*

- dental floss
- dish puffs
- dressmaker elastic
- dried beans
- dried coffee grounds
- drinking straws
- egg cartons
- egg shells (washed)
- electrical tape
- empty 35 mm film canisters
- empty roll-on deodorant bottles
- empty saline solution bottles
- empty toilet paper rolls
- empty toothpaste boxes
- fabric paint
- fabrics
- feathers
- felt
- felt-tip pens or markers
- flannel-backed vinyl tablecloth
- flat cardboard and cardboard tubes
- flavoring extracts
- floor or wall tiles: white or off white
- fly swatter
- foam rubber
- foil
- food coloring
- frying splatter screen
- funnel
- gift wrap
- glitter
- gloves

- golf balls
- hand, scrub, or vegetable brushes
- honey
- hot glue gun
- hot plate
- house paintbrushes
- hydrogen peroxide
- ice cube tray
- instant oatmeal
- instant pudding mix
- Koosh balls
- lace
- laundry basket
- leather
- lunch bags
- macramé cord
- magnets
- magnifying glass
- marbles
- margarine tubes
- mittens
- mouthwash
- netting
- newspaper
- packing and insulation Styrofoam sheets
- packing materials
- paint roller
- paper doilies
- paper grocery bags
- pellon
- pie tins
- pinking shears
- pizza pan
- plaster of Paris
- plastic bags
- plastic cups

- plastic darning needle
- plastic spoons
- pompoms
- ribbon
- rice
- roofing shingles
- rubber bands
- rubber hoses
- rubber or plastic horseshoes
- rubber tubing
- sandpaper
- scarves
- sequins
- shoeboxes
- shoelaces
- small, bathroom–size paper cups
- sponges
- spools
- spray bottles
- stamp pads
- sterile gauze
- streamers
- string
- tape
- tissue paper
- uncooked pasta
- upholstery foam or padding
- Velcro®
- vinegar
- wallpaper samples
- wax paper
- wood scraps
- zippers

Your Name: _____

Your Child's Name: _____

Work Phone Number: _____

Home Phone Number: _____

Planner Sheet

Theme: _____

Topics: _____

Big Book Topic: _____

Student Suggestions: _____

_____

_____

_____

Parental Involvement: _____

_____

_____

_____

Field Trips/Visitors	Date/Time

Notes/Reminders: _____

_____

_____

_____

What Worked: _____

_____

_____

_____

What Didn't Work: _____

_____

_____

_____

Suggested Improvements: _____

_____

_____

_____

Authors' Tea Invitation

_____

(Date)

Dear _____,

Once upon a time in Storyland, two groups joined forces to write, illustrate, and publish big books. As they close this chapter of the school year, they would like to celebrate the efforts that bound them together.

You are cordially invited to an Authors' Tea to share the children's stories and accomplishments.

Date: _____

Time: _____

Place: _____

We look forward to seeing you there.

Sincerely,

_____

(Teacher)

_____

(School)

_____

(Phone)

Thematic Web

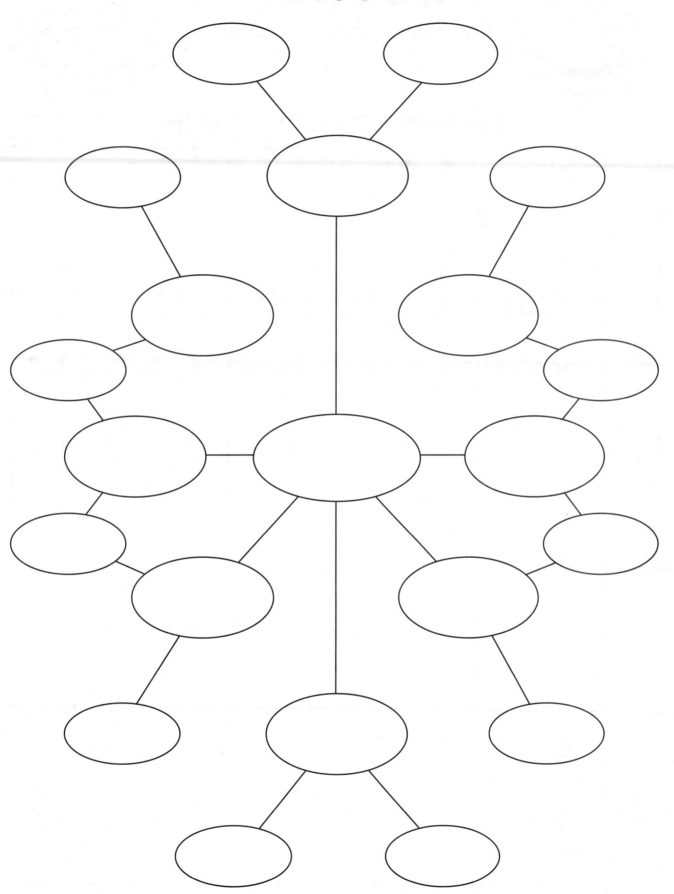

Bingo Card

THEME:		